Training and Developing
the Professional Salesman

Training and Developing the Professional Salesman

THOMAS F. STROH

A Division of American Management Associations

International standard book number: 0-8144-5337-6

Library of Congress catalog card number: 73-80185

First printing

Preface

THIS BOOK was written to answer many of the questions repeatedly asked by sales managers and trainers from all over the United States in seminars conducted by the author. Managers have little time or patience for academic theory and vague generalizations. They want to know how to motivate and train their men to become highly productive salesmen. They want to know exactly what to do when a training problem occurs.

Written primarily for the first-level sales manager who is out in the field with his salesmen every day, and whose training and guidance will determine their level of performance, this practical guide focuses on the initial training of new salesmen, the continuous training of experienced salesmen, and the career development of all the sales manager's personnel.

Modern sales training requires an understanding of the individual. This book provides guidelines for tailoring the contents and methods of sales training programs to the specific needs of the individual but does not lose sight of the fact that the trainer will frequently be dealing with salesmen in groups.

The scope of modern sales training has broadened to encompass such skills as probing, effective listening, sensitivity in communicating, psychologically oriented persuasion, creative thinking, and decision making, in addition to more traditional techniques such as approaching the prospect, presenting the sales proposition, and closing the sale. This work describes what can be taught in the areas of information, skills, and work habits and attitudes and suggests how the manager can select the appropriate level of sophistication for his unique program.

Just as training content has changed, training methods have been radically updated as a result of new technology. Many illustrations and practical suggestions are offered for the use of such techniques as computer games, video instant replay, and programmed instruction with audio cassettes.

Training and career development of both new and experienced salesmen should be continuous processes; thus, on-the-job coaching, improving salesmen's performance, adding new skills, and motivating mature salesmen are discussed in detail. Alternate career paths are also discussed and illustrated. Sales managers will find in these chapters ways to plan programs so as to reduce training time and costs, as well as ways to justify training costs to higher management. To enable managers to continually upgrade the quality of sales training, various techniques for measurement and evaluation are explained.

This pragmatic, realistic book is intended to serve the sales manager or trainer as both a guide to planning and an authoritative reference for dealing with training problems he may face today and in the future.

Thomas F. Stroh

Contents

CHAPTER 1

Identifying Training Needs and Justifying the Cost of Training

NORMAL HUMAN BEINGS are capable of learning until they become senile. Psychologists report that it is normal for a mature person to want to please important people in order to gain recognition and reward and to want to improve himself. Thus, a sales trainee who has the desire to learn, the mental and physical capacity to learn, and the necessary materials and instruction certainly can learn.

Too often, education is assumed to be the answer to most problems of human behavior. For example, when salesmen often come to meetings late or are absent, the top sales executive may suggest training the district sales managers to enforce the rules. They think that if the managers know how to enforce rules, they will automatically do so. Such simplistic thinking ignores the many variables that influence human behavior.

In some situations, it may not be worth the time, money, and effort to change certain people. You can teach an old salesman some new tricks, but he may have difficulty learning them because his life experiences have reinforced his current behavior. A young sales trainee may also be very rigid in his behavior and not readily willing to change. For example, if he enjoys winning an argument and alienating his antagonist to prove that his logic is superior, he is not apt to use the illogical appeals to the prospect's emotions which he may be taught. The time and cost of psychological help to change such a man may not be justifiable, and he may be better suited to another profession.

Experience has taught a few sales managers that survival of the fittest is the best form of sales training: Throw a salesman into the territory and very quickly he will sink or swim. Under such circumstances, marginal salesmen who could have been trained will give up. Even a number of good salesmen who could have been trained to become outstanding will struggle to be, at best, average producers.

However effective education and training are as a means for changing behavior, they cannot possibly be the sole answer to solving all human problems. A trainee's previous experiences and personality traits may hinder his development as a salesman, as may such factors as racial or ethnic prejudice either on his part or on the part of his supervisors, colleagues, and business associates. Anyone considering a sales training program should be aware of both the limitations of education and the ways in which training can be made a constructive part of the total developmental program.

PROBLEMS THAT TRAINING CAN CORRECT

Ignorance

Most newly hired sales trainees are not familiar with the products or services which they are to sell nor do they know the market. As a company develops additional new products, the entire sales force may need education. Ignorance in this sense is not shameful; instead, it is comparable to a blank slate. It is a common problem, and salesmen respond very positively to training to correct it. Many good potential sales recruits will choose a job on the basis of the offer of an outstanding sales training program.

Many factors govern the amount and complexity of the knowledge and skills a trainee will need to acquire from the training program. The most obvious of these is the trainee's previous experience and education. For example, if he has never sold before, he will be ignorant about the fundamentals of effective interpersonal communication and persuasion.

The nature of the product or service is another factor. A new, very complex, or highly sophisticated product may require greater ability to relate a convincing sales message than a product that is simple or already well accepted.

The type and extent of training also depends on the kind of customer the salesmen will be visiting. For example, if the customer is an expert buyer for a department store or a purchasing agent for an industrial company, the salesman may need to become a legitimate authority in his own industry and customers' businesses. In some fields, the salesman's job is more socially oriented, and he may need guidance and training in dealing with a new level of social or psychological sophistication.

Forgetting

A second problem that training can correct occurs when a salesman forgets part or all of what he once knew. If he does not implement his knowledge and skills, he will not readily recall them without some distortion. The longer the period of time between learning something and using the knowledge, the more difficult it will be for the salesman to remember and correctly apply the appropriate behavior.

Because sales training is often expensive, many programs attempt to teach a lot in a short time. Afterward, the salesman is sent off to a territory to apply his new knowledge and skills. Without any direct observation by his manager, he may gradually and unknowingly omit or distort part of what he has been taught. For this reason, older salesmen often require refresher courses. For some salesmen, forgetting is no more than a very minor problem. But for others, it may be a major area needing immediate correction.

The sales manager, supervisor, or trainer can make calls with each man to observe his strengths and weaknesses. But if the observer notes the same weakness in two or three salesmen, he should not jump to the conclusion that the entire sales force has this problem. Any training or refresher program for all salesmen based on such a faulty conclusion is bound to be a waste of time for some salesmen, and their resistance should be anticipated. By dividing the sales force into subgroups based on observed needs, the manager can tailor the training to the needs of the individual.

In some cases, the observer can simply remind the salesman to act or behave as he was taught. This is most applicable when the salesman knows the proper behavior but is not conscious of his deviation from it. For example, a salesman may be preoccupied with making many calls on a given day and rush up to a receptionist still wearing his hat and coat. A gentle reminder by the manager should get him to slow down, remove his hat and coat, and clearly signal his self-confident expectation of seeing the party on whom he is calling. In many such cases, the correction is of a minor nature, and the results are both immediate and long-lasting.

Lack of Specific Skills

A third problem that can be corrected by training occurs when a salesman knows what to do but is unsure of how to accomplish his objective. In other words, the salesman lacks the essential skill for handling the particular situation. For example, a salesman may wish to learn what his prospect thinks of his proposition, but every question he asks solicits little or no information. The salesman knows he should probe but does not have sufficient skill to elicit adequate responses. This problem can be easily corrected in a one-day seminar dealing with the theory and practice of probing skills.

The failure to close a sale is often due to the salesman's inability to ask for the order in a positive way. Once again, this lack of a particular skill can be corrected relatively easily by training and daily practice. If the sales manager berates the salesman for his failure to ask for the order, little will be accomplished. In fact, the salesman may become more confused and clumsy in attempting to close a sale in the future. On the other hand, if the salesman is shown several alternative ways to close a single sale and he practices using them in role-playing situations, he can readily develop this skill.

Lack of Self-Confidence

Another common problem that can be corrected by training occurs when the salesman lacks self-confidence. He may know what to do and how to do it, but he is afraid to try. For example, the simple technique of twisting a prospect's objection may be used to turn the objection into a positive close. If the salesman seems afraid to use this technique on the job, he can be shown how to use it with little or no risk of offending the prospect in the protective atmosphere of a training situation. The salesman can practice using the technique until it becomes natural and easy, thereby building his self-confidence. Afterward, when a customer objects to his company's higher price, for example, the salesman should feel comfortable in asking the prospect, "If I can prove to you that our product actually costs less in the long run, will you order it?"

Many techniques used by successful salesmen can be taught to inexperienced men to increase their self-confidence, and training and daily practice will help correct the problem. Sometimes the method a salesman has been taught is needlessly long or overly complicated. The sales trainer should look for a simpler or better way. Often the salesman himself can suggest an easier way which is just as effective. Given the endorsement and support of his manager, the salesman will develop confidence in his own solution and be more apt to use it in the future.

Improper Attitudes

One of the gray problem areas which training may be able to correct is the lack of proper attitudes. For example, a salesman may not use copies of national advertising in his sales presentation because he does not believe they are appropriate for his particular customers. He may not understand that the pictures and copy are aimed at a particular market segment. He may not know that the advertisements were pretested for ease of understanding and ability to persuade. The salesman may not be aware that the particular advertisement may make his oral presentation much more convincing because many prospects believe the printed word much more readily than the spoken word. In a training seminar the salesman can be taught these facts as they apply to his unique situation.

Improper attitudes often result from a lack of understanding, which breeds suspicion and distrust. If the salesman does not know what his company's advertising people are trying to do, he is most apt to think they are wasting a lot of money. If he is not familiar with the purpose of a sales promotion program, it will be difficult for him to use the promotional literature properly. After a few negative experiences, he will learn not to trust and not to use that literature on his sales calls.

Improper attitudes are in the gray area with respect to correction by training because they are sometimes caused by the salesman's correct judgment of a poor management practice. Clearly, if the advertising program in this example does not have specific measurable goals, if it is not aimed at a particular market segment, or if it has not been pretested, then a salesman may well be justified in forming a negative opinion of it. Under such conditions, sales training would be futile, whereas training of the advertising people would be mandatory.

PROBLEMS THAT TRAINING CANNOT CORRECT

Improperly Placed Positive Incentives

Perhaps the most common problem areas in which training has little or no effect are those concerned with incentives or motivational programs. A top sales executive who feels that the salesmen ought to want to get new accounts may suggest a sales training program which will emphasize the importance of new business. If he thinks that training is the only requirement of a program to encourage new business, then the odds are strong that his efforts will fail.

Improperly placed positive incentives will cause most salesmen to spend their energy in some selling activity other than that desired by management regardless of sales training. For example, if the vice-president of sales wants more new accounts but continues to pay salesmen a commission or bonus based on total dollar sales volume, he will probably become frustrated. The person in charge of sales training should not be blamed for any failure because the incentives are placed on the wrong aspect of the job. Salesmen most often find it is easier to sell to an old account than to lure a new prospect away from competition. Clearly, if total dollar sales is the only criterion for a bonus, then the salesmen will take the easier path and continue their efforts to sell more to old accounts. The positive incentive, a bonus in this instance, is wrongly placed, and sales training alone cannot correct this problem.

No Incentives

A second problem occurs when there are no incentives, at least as the salesmen perceive the situation. The salesmen feel that management doesn't care whether or not something is done. Since there are no positive consequences for doing something, why make an extra effort to do it?

For example, most salesmen are taught how to cover their territories efficiently and to make a specific number of calls per day on the average. Then they observe an older salesman gaining the manager's praise for going over his quota one month. This man may be the least efficient salesman with the lowest number of calls. They may then see a young salesman getting encouragement to keep trying harder to make his quota. But the other salesmen may know that this man just loafs every afternoon. Observing a few other salesmen making the required number of daily calls without any comment from the sales manager, the sales force quickly learns that it simply does not matter how many calls per day they make.

A more extreme case, but unfortunately just as common, is that of the sales manager who does not give his salesmen direction for their efforts or goals and targets at which they can aim. One salesman may seek more new accounts. Another may aim for higher dollar volume. A third salesman may try to lower his expenses-to-sales ratio. Too often the traditional sales manager will tell each salesman that he did all right in the one area he emphasized but poorly in other areas. The salesmen feel there is no way to please this type of manager and often they give up trying. Lacking specific direction, they cannot develop effective selling habits.

Negative Incentives

Perhaps more subtle is the problem of negative incentives; many sales managers and trainers are not even aware they exist in their organization. A negative incentive is an informal brake or resistance to management desires. For example, the salesmen may set a limit for themselves and not report more than four calls per day. Any new salesman who violates this unwritten agreement is needled by the others—perhaps jokingly at first, but more seriously as he continues to break their informal rule. A regular offender may be completely ostracized from the group. He will not be welcome when the men go for morning coffee or for lunch. Conversation will cease when he joins a group. Business messages for him will be delayed or lost completely. Thus, the offender quickly learns either to accept the informal group norms or to live alone.

A few senior salesmen who may be cynical because of past experiences with their company can very effectively negate sales management directives or training programs. If they are afraid that new salesmen will embarrass them through superior performance, they may take desperate steps to discredit any new salesman. They may spread half-true or totally fraudulent rumors about the new salesman's sex life, drinking habits, or methods of selling. They will quickly point out his errors and anything else negative while explaining away any degree of success as pure luck.

As long as such negative incentives exist and are tolerated by management, training and development programs are likely to fail. Negative attitudes can be changed and informal leaders can be manipulated to work with management rather than against it. The negative climate must be changed before any training program is begun; training, in and of itself, will do little to change it.

Inconsistent Directions

Another problem which training cannot correct is that of inconsistent directions by management. For example, a sales manager of an office furniture and supply company might begin the sales year with a contest to promote filing supplies. Seeing little improvement after ten weeks, he switches the contest to selling office safes. After three months, the salesmen are given extensive training in planning furniture layouts and directed to sell desks and chairs as a total system. The salesmen who have worked hard to develop business earlier in the year are faced with the dilemma of trying to close sales for filing supplies and safes while ignoring the new directions or dropping older prospects and developing new ones. Such on-again, off-again tactics confuse and frustrate salesmen.

The sales manager who continually searches for new incentives to motivate his sales force runs this risk. His directions or incentives are positive but they change so quickly that the salesmen may feel it is impossible to meet his demands. They do not have the time to develop effective selling habits for any one line of products before they are spurred on to another. This negative effect cancels out the positive incentives, and there is no behavior change. Any training program given under these conditions will have little chance to succeed.

Impossible Goals

The fifth problem which training cannot correct occurs when management inadvertently sets impossible goals or sales targets. It is obvious that salesmen cannot be held responsible for selling a poor product or any product at an unrealistically high price. It is much less obvious, but equally true, that salesmen cannot be held responsible for the economic conditions of their customers. For example, a salesman selling to the airline industry, which normally undergoes economic cycles, might receive many orders one year and very few orders the next year. If he is judged and rewarded on the basis of profitable orders, in effect, he is overpaid in good years and underpaid in poor years.

Many sales territories are affected by the general economy of the dominant industries in their locale. Weather, strikes, local government spending, competitive actions, and many other variables beyond the control or influence of the salesman can affect the sales in a territory. Clearly, the salesman should not be rewarded or punished for windfalls, obstacles, or other factors affecting his business which are beyond his control.

Specific guidelines for setting goals, quotas, sales targets, and so forth are beyond the scope of this book; however, anyone concerned with sales training and development should be aware of this pitfall. Education by itself cannot correct poor management practices and policies. Sales training should cause a specific change in the behavior of the salesmen; it cannot be expected to change management. Training under these conditions may very well boomerang, inducing some good salesmen to resign to seek better management elsewhere.

IDENTIFYING SPECIFIC TRAINING NEEDS

Once a problem has been identified which training has a reasonably good chance of correcting, specific training needs must be determined. This is a four-step process.

Define the Normal Behavior of Effective Salesmen

The first step is to analyze exactly the normal behavior exhibited by a salesman performing his job properly. Normal behavior may involve making a certain number of calls per day, selling up the line, making multiple sales to a single customer, selling to a certain number of new accounts, obtaining research information, or many other duties in various combinations.

The normal behavior of an effective salesman can be systematically recorded by a trained observer in a few days because the salesman's work habits and patterns will be readily apparent. For example, he may plan his day's work a week in advance, allowing enough flexibility to cover unforeseen or emergent events. He may use the telephone to line up appointments. He may prearrange coffee breaks and lunch meetings with certain influential people in the target companies. He will probably have a record system to ensure that he maintains the proper balance between selling to old customers and soliciting new prospects. On individual visits with prospects, he may probe intelligently and attempt to identify and solve problems. With established accounts, he may be more sociable yet persistent in his search for additional business. His behavior in his home sales office will also reflect a general pattern—of cooperation with supporting people, for example. Each sales organization should be able to put together a description of the normal behavior of its most effective salesmen. This description then becomes the basis of the desired norm for all salesmen in that company.

With this norm as a general foundation, management may desire to upgrade or otherwise modify certain specific standards. The sales manager may wish to put more emphasis on soliciting new accounts, for example. In any event, the final description of the normal behavior desired should encourage individual differences among effective salesman. For instance, one good salesman may solicit new accounts using a third party as reference. Another good salesman may solicit new accounts through leads from publications such as newspapers and trade journals. If the description of the normal behavior desired includes soliciting new accounts, the salesmen should be allowed to do so in their own way. The description should not be so narrow as to force all effective salesmen into a stereotype which may be unnatural and less effective for them.

Identify the Deviation from the Norm and Determine Its Causes

Once the normal behavior patterns have been developed, the sales manager should carefully and objectively identify the significant deviations from the norm which a less effective salesman exhibits. Do his long hair and flashy clothes really affect his sales record, or are they simply contrary to the personal bias of the manager? Clearly, what the customers want and are willing to accept is most important, not what the sales manager personally prefers.

Is the less effective salesman making fewer calls per day than the desired number? If this is so, is the problem that he doesn't know how to plan his work? Or does he lack the skill of communicating concisely? Or perhaps he gets bogged down in petty details. Once the deviation from the norm is identified, the sales manager should attempt to discover the cause of the deviation. For a new salesman the cause may be ignorance: He simply may not know how to meet the desired norm. A more experienced salesman may have forgotten what he was once taught, such as to keep his conversation on a business level.

Is the less effective salesman taking orders for a single item without attempting to add accessories or other products which might normally be purchased at the same time? If this is the case, was he ever taught to look for such associations, to suggest extra items, or to suggest that the value of one product may be enhanced by using another product along with it? Does the salesman know what he should be doing but lack the skill or confidence necessary to accomplish the task? By probing to identify the cause of the deviation from the desired norm, the sales manager or trainer can identify specific training needs.

The outstanding sales producers may show that they are adept at asking probing questions and that they listen effectively. Less effective salesmen may be more impatient and may interrupt the prospect's conversation, for example. Inexperienced salesmen may become uncomfortable when a prospect is silent. Rather than wait patiently while a prospect thinks through a point, the new salesman may continue to add information, confusing the prospect so much that the entire thrust of the proposition is negated. Such behavior is easily recognized, and specific training programs can be designed to correct it.

The use of probing questions might be extremely important for certain concerns or industries. For example, in selling insurance, stocks and bonds, or investment real estate, the salesman must find out the true financial status of the prospect and his investment purposes. Some people are highly sensitive to direct personal questions, and certain salesmen may not be effectively probing for useful information by means of indirect and projective questions. An alert sales manager or trainer can analyze the deviation from norm to determine its causes, identify the training need, and set up a program to correct the problem.

Determine the Extent of the Deviation

The third area to probe in identifying specific training needs is the extent of the deviation from the norm. Is the difference in behavior important enough to warrant attention? If observation indicates that many salesmen are not performing as desired, clearly, corrective action is warranted. However, if the performance of only one or two salesmen is deviant, there is no reason to subject the entire sales force to an extensive training program. The observer must make a value judgment by weighing the degree of deviation against the cost of training to modify the group behavior.

When many salesmen are not performing an important task, corrective training is required. A New England communications company asked 200 of its sales engineers what they felt were their most important duties and how much time they spent on each activity. Management was surprised to find that a comparatively small percentage of the engineers' time was spent selling. Most of it was taken up by detailed research to solve customer problems. This discovery caused management to restructure its training program.

If, on the other hand, the deviation from the norm is minor, it may be corrected during a regular sales meeting. The sales manager is in the best position to judge whether to ignore a deviation because it doesn't really affect the sales effort or to spend considerable time, money, and effort to correct it because it is seriously hindering the effectiveness of the salesmen.

Determine Whether the Deviation
Is in a High-Leverage Area

The final step in identifying specific training needs is to ask if the deviation is such that training will produce significant results. In many cases the sales manager will want to upgrade the salesmen in a number of different areas, such as prospecting, selling up, probing, and handling objections. He must decide in which area training is likely to produce the best and most visible results with the least effort —in other words, which area has the highest leverage. He may have to establish a priority system in order to concentrate attention and energy on one phase at a time, beginning with the area which has the greatest leverage.

The salesmen are most apt to cooperate with a program designed to modify their behavior when they can see immediate benefits to themselves. For example, if they are taught first a new technique which helps them close a higher percentage of their sales interviews successfully, then they will probably want to learn additional techniques and skills. For this reason, the sales manager should begin in an area which produces the most results for the least effort.

DEFINING TRAINING OBJECTIVES

Sales training earns the strongest support from higher management when the results can be seen and easily measured. The training objectives, therefore, should clearly state the behavioral change desired— that is, precisely what the salesman must do to meet the objective or achieve the norm. For example, before training, one group of industrial salesmen interrupted the prospect an average of five times in a ten-minute conversation. After training, they interrupted the prospect an average of only once in a ten-minute conversation. In this case the salesmen used tape recorders to measure changes in their behavior precisely.

Training objectives should also state the conditions under which the salesman will demonstrate his newly acquired behavior. For example, he may be expected to demonstrate an office machine in his own friendly showroom or in the hostile environment of a purchasing agent's office. He may be expected to give a persuasive sales talk on the telephone using notes or an outline. He may be required to give a two-hour formal presentation to a committee or to carry out a convincing one-minute door-opener. He may need to be able to conduct a sales interview under great stress in a prospect's office with competitors present or in the relaxed atmosphere of a cocktail lounge. By defining training objectives as visible action patterns under specified conditions, the manager can prepare the trainee to deal with the various situations likely to occur in the real world of his territory.

A training objective should also specify how soon the desired change in behavior can be reasonably expected to occur. For example, effective-listening skills can be acquired in two hours on two consecutive days. Speed-reading skills can be acquired in 30 days with an average of two hours of study per day. For both of these types of skills, comprehension can be demonstrated and measured, and a minimum level of performance can be stipulated as acceptable. Techniques for closing or handling objections can be taught, for example, in one week. The number of techniques that a salesman can demonstrate can be counted, and his learning progress can be measured over a period of time. Clearly, a lifelong habit of dominating conversations cannot be eradicated in one week in the protective atmosphere of a training classroom; however, a salesman with this habit can be taught to recognize signals of annoyance from prospects and to modify his behavior.

Development programs should have similar constraints and stated measurable objectives. For example, if an experienced territory salesman wants to become a national-account manager, he can be told the various skills and techniques which he will have to master in one year. Each phase of his development can be planned to cover a certain period of time, with the understanding that he will continue to demonstrate his accumulated knowledge and skills as he progresses. In this illustration, the salesman may be expected to attend several formal seminars on relevant topics throughout the year, as well as to complete a required reading list. Everyone concerned should know exactly what is expected, how it is to be measured, and what degree of competence should be achieved in a specified time period.

In defining training objectives, the sales manager or the director of training should be aware of the action needed to reinforce the new behavior patterns. Any new knowledge or skill that is not used regularly is likely to be forgotten. After formal training is completed, the incentive system should encourage the effective use of the newly acquired skills until they become habitual. The salesmen should know that their manager expects them to do certain things and cares enough to be measuring their performance in those areas. If reinforcement is preplanned at the time the training objectives are defined, differences between training and managing goals can be uncovered and resolved, and a complete accord can be reached. If these goals do not agree, an otherwise perfect training program is likely to fail.

JUSTIFYING THE COST OF TRAINING

Measurable Costs

What happens to the profit-and-loss statement if sales training accomplishes its stated objectives? While the training function is only one of the variables that can influence sales and profits, it should have a direct and measurable impact. Knowledgeable training directors and sales managers are aware of the costs of the various aspects of their operations and they can compute the contribution to profit for most categories. Sales managers, for instance, should know the cost of recruiting, hiring, and training their salesmen, as well as the rate of turnover of the sales force. They should be able to compute the positive value of an effective experienced salesman as well as the loss to the company if he leaves.

Annual surveys of sales managers show a repeating pattern in most industries. The top 20 percent of the sales force produces about 40 percent of the orders; the middle 60 percent of the salesmen produces nearly half the total sales; and the lower 20 percent of the sales force produces only 10 percent of the total sales. Typically, managers report that they would replace the lower 20 percent of the salesmen if better men could be attracted to their companies. Each of these poor producers costs his company an average of nearly $8,500 in direct salary plus $4,000 in expenses every year. If a firm has a sales force of one hundred men, the twenty poorest salesmen represent an expenditure of $250,000 annually in direct costs alone. Of course, these marginal salesmen can be replaced at a predetermined cost to recruit, screen, hire, and train. However, sales trainees may be no better, and newly hired experienced salesmen are likely to have been another company's marginal producers.

Since sales managers can identify these poor or marginal producers, they may also be able to create a training program to increase their productivity. The cost to upgrade twenty marginal salesmen could not possibly exceed their direct costs to their company. Moreover, any training program could also be designed to make many average producers into top salesmen. Every year the upgraded salesmen stay with the company after training, they yield a geometric return on the training dollars invested in them.

Conversely, if salesmen do not receive good training, they run the risk of losing their effectiveness, or of being outsold by their well-trained competitors. Men who were once top producers fall back to average, and many who were formerly average may become poor or marginal sales producers. In other words, failure to provide good training can have a direct negative impact on the P&L statement well in excess of the short-term positive effect of the money saved on training.

Top salesmen are continuously sought by most industries, and psychologists report that they rarely leave a company because of money. Salesmen switch companies for better opportunities to grow and develop themselves. Training and career development thus are positive attributes of a company which attract and keep top sales producers. Their contribution to the P&L statement can be readily measured, and good training programs should receive part of the credit.

Hidden Costs

Beyond these direct costs, which can be identified and measured in most companies, are the hidden costs. These hidden costs are often much larger than the visible, direct costs of training.

One hidden cost is the amount of time wasted by sales managers and supervisors in correcting errors made by untrained salesmen: making explanatory phone calls, writing letters of apology, checking records, or making personal visits to customers simply because the salesmen did not do their job properly. Often sales managers must make calls jointly with salesmen because the men have not been trained to handle a large proposition. These sales managers are so busy fighting fires that they do not have time to manage their people.

Without personal development, salesmen become bored or frustrated, and turnover increases. This sequence of events becomes a vicious cycle, and costs tend to get out of hand. Training can break this cycle if the sales manager is mature enough to admit that he cannot do everything himself and that his salesmen are capable of doing most of the work without his help.

Another unknown cost is the total sales loss due to the inexperience or poor training of salesmen. Consumers and companies are shopping more carefully today, and the salesperson can exercise a strong influence on their brand selection. Experienced buyers resent being misinformed or told half-truths, and they are suspicious of a salesman who cannot prove his claims. Many professional purchasing agents will not waste their time with a salesman who has shown himself to be ignorant or untrustworthy. If the item is rarely purchased, the lost sales opportunity may not come around again for years. When a salesman permits a buyer to order the wrong item for his need or application or to order in unduly large quantities, he risks losing the customer for many years in the future.

Once a company loses its goodwill or reputation with an account because of a poorly trained salesman, it may take years to regain the confidence of that account. In such a case, the loss of the current sales becomes insignificant when compared with the total loss of sales for many years. The account may learn that competitive suppliers can do a better job and may never do business with its former supplier again. Once a company considers an item standard, it rarely reviews subsequent brand selections. Its buying becomes habitual or automated, and the poorly trained salesman is not given a second chance.

The cost of order cancellations and returned merchandise can also be related to poor sales training in many cases. Rather than wait for these expenses to become so large as to be a problem, management can institute a good training program as a preventive measure.

Demonstrating the Contribution of Training

While much of the discussion above has a negative slant, sales training is one area of a business that can often show a dramatic positive contribution to the P&L statement. A controlled experiment can be designed to demonstrate and measure the contribution of sales training to the development of effective salesmen. For example, half the salesmen in one division or department can be given sales training, while the other half are told that they will be trained during the next quarter. Incentives remain constant for both groups, the advertising program is the same in all territories, and the other variables remain the same. If the training program achieved its objectives, then the final behavior of the experimental group should be significantly different from the behavior of the control group and considerably closer to the desired behavioral norm. Department stores have proved sales training to be effective in this way, and so have industrial manufacturing companies. In most cases, when appropriate training objectives have been set and proven methods and techniques are used, the results of training are such that the cost of the training program can be recovered in increased sales and contribution to profit in a matter of months.

SUMMARY

All normal people can learn, and sales training and development programs take advantage of this ability in two ways. First, they give trainees the knowledge and skills they need to become successful salesmen. Second, they provide salesmen with opportunities for personal growth and career development that will enable them to gain recognition and admiration for their accomplishments and add a sense of fulfillment to their lives.

Sales training goals are designed to achieve specific behavior changes that will increase the salesmen's ability to sell effectively. However, salesmen usually resist being forced to change their behavior. If the compensation policy is poor, for example, a sales training program cannot be expected to change basic negative attitudes of the salesmen. When sales territories are grossly unequal, the education of salesmen can hardly be considered as a remedy for the equality of opportunity to earn commissions. Sales managers must see to it that salesmen can be assured of management's desire to help each salesman to grow and develop before any training will have a chance of producing positive results. In some cases, management may have a fair system for compensation and rewards, but the sales force may not understand or appreciate its value. The burden remains on management to clear up any misunderstandings by both words and deeds.

When specific training needs are identified and a proper motivational climate has been established, then measurable training objectives can be defined in behavioral terms. Values can be placed on a series of training needs to determine the order in which these needs should be met. Some trivial deviations from the desired behavior norm will be ignored, while other deviations will be in areas of potentially high leverage. In this early planning stage, the manager should note the limits of sales training and the follow-up that will be needed to reinforce the new or modified behavior which is the specific training objective.

As a part of the training program, managers should plan clear-cut ways to measure the salesmen's progress in acquiring new knowledge and skills. When salesmen can see their improvement and they receive positive feedback from their accomplishment, they are apt to cooperate more fully. In addition, when training results can be quantified, higher management can be convinced to lend more support to the educational effort. Finally, the training objectives should include a description of the conditions under which the salesmen will be required to perform the new skills, as well as a schedule indicating the amount of time during which they will be expected to bring their performance up to the desired level.

A good training program requires careful planning, direct observation, and painstaking execution. Consequently, it may appear too expensive and time-consuming, and sales managers may be tempted to use shortcuts which seem to save time and money. But managers should bear in mind that good training and development programs are designed for the long-term improvement of the entire sales force, although they often show a dramatic return on investment in even a short period.

To justify the time and dollar costs of a training program, the manager can compute his direct costs of maintaining marginal salesmen. He can also compute the cost to recruit, screen, hire, and train replacements—although there can be no assurance that the new salesmen will be any better than the ones they replace.

The benefits of upgrading marginal producers so that they become average, self-supporting salesmen can be computed on an annual basis. The benefit of turning some average producers into outstanding salesmen with many future years of productivity can also be computed. These figures have a direct impact on the profit-and-loss statement of any organization.

Continuous or ongoing sales training and development programs may be thought of as preventive maintenance of the sales force. Education is essential if salesmen are to keep abreast of rapidly changing products, services, market segments, and individual customers so that the company can protect its share of the market. The intangible or hidden costs of withholding training include the waste of managerial and supervisory time and the loss of current and future sales.

A well-planned sales training program will state specifically and realistically what can be expected, after how long, and at what cost. In many cases, the return on the investment in training dollars is considerably higher than the return offered by functions in competition with sales training for a share of the annual budget. Of all corporate functions, the training and development of salesmen is one of the highest with respect to leverage because it can show good, tangible results for a minimum of investment.

SELECTED MATERIALS

Gardiner, Harold W., "The Purposes and Benefits of Sales Training" in *The New Handbook of Sales Training*, Robert F. Vizza, ed. Englewood Cliffs, N.J.: Prentice-Hall, 1967.

The superintendent of management development for agencies of Northwestern Mutual Life Insurance Co. provides an overview of what can be accomplished and expected from sales training.

Geriach, Vernon S., and Sullivan, Howard J., *Constructing Statements of Outcomes*. Inglewood, Cal.: Southwest Regional Laboratory for Educational Research and Development, 1967.

Two self-instructional programs teach the reader to set up behavioral objectives; the definitions of several behavioral terms are also included.

Krasner, Leonard, and Ullmann, Leonard P., eds., *Research in Behavior Modification*. New York: Holt, Rinehart and Winston, 1965.

Research, training, and social application of psychological training are discussed. Extensively documented.

Mager, Robert F., *Goofing Off with Objectives.* Los Altos Hills, Cal.: Mager Associates. 16 mm, B&W.

An amusing 14-minute film helpful in establishing instructional objectives.

————, *Preparing Instructional Objectives.* Palo Alto, Cal.: Fearon Publishers, 1962.

This self-instructional program teaches the identification of behavioral objectives in terms of measuring results.

Manager Wanted. Beverly Hills, Cal.: Roundtable Films. 16 mm, B&W.

An entertaining dramatization that helps emphasize the importance of both training subordinates in a climate of acceptance and growth and justifying the time and cost of training.

Michael, Gerald E., "Methods of Identifying Sales Training Needs," in *The New Handbook of Sales Training,* Robert F. Vizza, ed. Englewood Cliffs, N.J.: Prentice-Hall, 1967.

The manager of sales education for the data processing division of IBM describes ten methods to determine the needs of new and experienced salesmen.

Popham, W. James, *Educational Criterion Measures.* Inglewood, Cal.: Southwest Regional Laboratory for Educational Research and Development, 1968.

This self-instructional program shows procedures for constructing tests that measure behavioral objectives.

CHAPTER 2

Learning Theory and
Its Application

ACADEMIC THEORY and vague abstractions have little value to the sales manager who is facing a particular training problem. On the other hand, when adequate time is available to plan an effective training program, some guidelines are most appropriate.

To the cynic who would doubt the value of learning theory for improving a skill such as salesmanship, it can be said that it is not necessary for a student to repeat the same mistakes which we in marketing have made for 25 years in order for him to learn. Training authorities have recognized educational techniques and patterns which are consistently more successful than the older methods. The experience of others should be used profitably in the planning and development of an effective sales training program.

PRINCIPLES OF LEARNING

To manage the training function, a sales manager should become aware of and utilize the accepted principles of learning. Any skill is developed and perfected by actual practice, and the manager must put his knowledge of these principles to use so that the appropriate behavior becomes a habit. With the aid of these principles, the sales manager will be able to eliminate some of the frustrations and irritations of his attempts to modify the behavior of his salesmen.

The principles of learning theory are intended as guidelines which may be combined or modified to suit each unique training situation. The sales manager should make value judgments as to which methods are most likely to be effective with his salesmen. Finally, the sales manager probably will want to tailor the learning experience to fit his short-term marketing goals.

Three general principles of learning are especially applicable to sales training: reinforcement, generalization, and reappraisal.

Reinforcement

The child in school who is repeatedly praised by his teacher for handing in a neatly written assignment soon learns that to this teacher, neatness counts. A person who approaches a stray cat to pet it and receives an unsociable scratch will learn to be more cautious in trying to befriend unfamiliar cats. Someone who finds an unexpected windfall in the coin-return box of a public telephone may quickly develop the habit of checking the box of every public phone he has occasion to use. This principle of learning through reward or punishment is called reinforcement.

Educational authorities report that rewards, or positive reinforcement, are more effective in training people than punishment, or negative reinforcement. A reward for good sales performance can be tangible, such as a cash commission, or it can be intangible, for example, praise from the sales manager. Negative reinforcement in sales training might be a severe chewing-out by the manager or, for some trainees, destructive criticism of their performance. The difficulty with negative reinforcement is that the learner may worry so much about his possible failure and the resulting punishment that his concern may interfere with the learning process. He may concentrate on ways to explain his poor performance rather than build confidence by thinking positively.

Positive reinforcement in sales training is designed to encourage the student to try again and again to improve his performance. The manager generally compliments the trainee on his efforts, but he also offers some constructive suggestions to help the student on his next trial. In this manner the emphasis is placed on improvement, and the manager's praise must be earned honestly. During the learning process, the new behavior is conscious and highly tentative. With positive reinforcement, the desired behavior is encouraged until it becomes habitual and drops below the conscious level. As the new behavior pattern approaches the level of a habit, the trainee can gradually devote his attention to other things without giving it any further conscious thought.

Feedback from the manager or instructor to the sales trainee is essential if reinforcement is to work. The positive reinforcement should clearly relate to the desired behavior demonstrated by the salesman. It is usually advisable to concentrate on one area or skill at a time and to minimize criticism in other areas. During the learning session, the trainee is asked to focus his attention on one phase of his behavior. When he performs that task as desired, he is rewarded with direct positive praise. Other areas of inappropriate behavior are unimportant at that point in training.

As the trainee learns the first phase of the desired behavior, he can begin a second phase, which may build on the first. He is then expected to continue practicing the first skill, more and more automatically, while concentrating his attention on the second skill. The instructor continues to give positive reinforcement to the proper performance of the first skill in addition to reinforcement or constructive suggestions to improve the second skill. In this manner, quite a complicated sequence of skills may be taught.

Industrial sales trainees are taught through positive reinforcement to build a prospect's confidence in them. In role-playing sessions, for example, a trainee is given an opportunity to help the prospect in some way not directly related to a sale. Later, if he has missed the opportunity, the instructor or the other salesmen observing can offer suggestions to improve his performance. However, if he has done a good job in this area, the instructor should make a point of publicly praising the method illustrated.

Representatives selling stocks and bonds can be taught through positive reinforcement to maintain records of each investor's financial objectives, holdings, and areas of interest. They can be shown how to cross-reference such a file so that certain events or changes in the market will signal a group of investors who should be contacted. The sales manager can encourage such desirable behavior by rewarding salesmen who demonstrate it with recognition and praise.

Usually it does little or no good to ridicule salesmen who do not perform as desired because negative reinforcement is likely to boomerang in a learning situation. A nagging sales manager is turned off just as a nagging wife, and the intended message is blocked or distorted by the mind of the listener. In a training situation, this can become a serious problem because the salesmen, to defend themselves, are apt to discredit the instructor and not believe anything he says in the future on any subject. One young sales trainer made this mistake on a new job and within three months was asked to resign because he was totally ineffective.

Generalization

Generalization is the process by which a person makes certain assumptions about unknown things on the basis of their similarity to known things. For example, if a man drives a particular model of automobile for several years and is highly satisfied with its performance, when the time comes for him to buy a new car, he will be predisposed to choose one of the same make, even though the new model may be different from the one he now drives. If he is again satisfied, and if people he knows report similar experiences with this make of car, then he is likely to come to the conclusion that all cars made by this particular manufacturer are high-quality products. Thus, he will have generalized the notion of high quality to apply to any specific automobile produced by this manufacturer.

Once a generalization has been made, new information is easily accepted, understood, and retained when it seems to agree with the previously learned characteristics of the group or category. If the new information does not seem to fit in with previous learnings, it will seem confusing and may be forgotten quickly. For this reason, educators recommend that any sales training program should begin with the known and familiar and gradually work up to the unknown in a logical progression.

The relationship between previous generalizations and subsequent ease of learning new, related information was used to particularly good advantage in training salesmen for an office furniture and supply company that had over 5,000 different products. The products were divided into five major categories: desks, chairs, insulated products, files, and filing supplies. A general theme or rationale was developed and taught for selling each of the product lines. (Correct seating would diminish fatigue and thus reduce errors; point-of-use insulated cabinets would protect vital records where they were normally used rather than in a distant vault; and so on.) Each theme could be used in selling hundreds of different products within the general group. The salesmen were then taught to recognize appropriate applications of each individual product. Then, depending on the interior decoration of an office, the salesman had a range of colors, finishes, and fabrics from which he could offer each prospect a choice of two or more positive alternatives. This sales training program taught new men to sell the line of 5,000 products in three months rather than the year or more the previous program had taken. Without an understanding of the principle of generalization in the learning process, this undertaking would have been difficult, if not impossible.

In a similar manner, an automobile dealer in Kansas City constructed a training program which enabled new salesmen to sell as well as experienced salesmen by the end of their first year in the business. A theme was developed for each model in the manufacturer's line. Each of these themes was designed to appeal to a particular segment of the market. Finally, depending on the prospect's interest, there were hundreds of options for each group, such as engine size, transmission type, power steering, and power brakes. A new salesman could be taught to generalize the many combinations into a few groups with a common theme. For example, ease of handling might be the theme to use for the older prospect who could afford many expensive options. This theme could be used to justify all of the added options. Of course, the training program included many things beyond product knowledge; however, the application of the principle of generalization was one of the keys to its success.

Generalization can also work to the disadvantage of a sales trainer or a student. If a sales manager or trainer makes a few mistakes in a training session, his salesmen may make the generalization that the manager doesn't know anything about any subject.

Some sales trainees have a fear of failing. During the training period, such a trainee may perform comparatively poorly on one or more assigned tasks. If the manager berates him, his fear will be strongly reinforced by this punishment, and it may generalize to situations beyond the training program and seriously restrict the trainee. For example, he may subsequently shun all competitive activities or refuse to try any new sales technique if he is not sure that he will succeed.

As we all know, generalization does not always lead to correct conclusions. However, if a sales manager presents a valid generalization as the starting point for teaching a particular subject or skill, he can make good use of this principle of learning.

Reappraisal

The third principle of learning is reappraisal of past experiences. This process involves a few trials of the new behavior pattern, a period of deductive reasoning and, finally, the effective performance of the new behavior. The learner analyzes his past mistakes and, through the use of logic, decides what alterations or modifications are necessary to improve the results.

A salesman should be taught to analyze every sales interview every day to reappraise his experiences. With the call fresh in his mind, it is relatively easy for him to review what happened and determine how a different presentation might have avoided mistakes. Given a critique outline, the salesman can make a habit of reappraising his interviews and vastly improve his ability to correct errors before they are repeated on subsequent calls.

One paper company, for example, recommends that its salesmen use a questionnaire to help evaluate each phase of the call. It begins by asking what the precall objective was. This causes the salesman to plan ahead as well as follow up in his review after the call to see how well the objective was met. Next, it asks how the objectives might have been made more realistic. Perhaps fact finding would have been a better objective for an initial call than getting an order. What customer research would have been helpful? How did the salesman tailor his approach to fit the customer's needs? What additional information might the salesman have learned by asking questions? Clearly, each sales manager will want to stress the things that are especially important to his company; however a critique outline normally reviews precall planning, the approach, the opening, the presentation, handling objections, and the close. Self-analysis of sales calls encourages each salesman to learn by reappraising.

BEHAVIORAL CHANGES

Individuals react differently to the ideas presented by an instructor or manager. Whereas the same general principles of learning apply to all of them, sales trainees differ in personality, background, and the ability and willingness to learn.

It takes time for people to learn anything, and learning new behavioral patterns is not easy. The sales trainee must practice to acquire new skills, and some men may have to break old habits that interfere with their efficiency on the job. Not only does learning take time but different people take different amounts of time to learn the same skills.

The sales manager should not assume that a slow learner is stupid or that he has a poor attitude and is unwilling to learn. Very few people can be told once or twice what to do and then do it correctly. Many very intelligent salesmen find it difficult to be silent for a long time while listening to a prospect talk. Their past training and experience have developed in them a strong habit of attempting to dominate a conversation, and 40 hours of training may be needed to change this lifetime conversational habit.

Measurement

In general, people learn faster when they get regular feedback on their progress than when they merely practice without receiving criticism. If sales trainees can see evidence of their progress, they will feel a sense of accomplishment and increasing self-importance. For these reasons, it is often advisable to test the salesmen before the training is begun. Pretraining tests will establish a bench mark for each man and enable the instructor or sales manager to give him feedback based on objective data during training. The starting point may be established by an objective written test for knowledge of company policy, for example, or by observation of salesmen in the field making regular sales calls. In the latter case, objective measurements, such as the number of times salesmen use probing questions, should be used as the criteria.

In many training situations, it is advisable to measure the behavioral change about halfway through the training program. A few salesmen who learn quickly may have already achieved the desired level of performance or knowledge. Such men could be given more advanced training instead of being held back by the slow learners. Normally, most of the salesmen will have shown some improvement but not nearly as much as desired. These salesmen should be informed of their progress so as to encourage them to continue their efforts to learn the material or skill being taught. Testing at the midpoint in training will often indicate the slow learners and those few salesmen who may need some special help. These men can be given some tutorial assistance to bring them up to the group norm before they become so discouraged as to give up trying.

Finally, individual posttraining measurements should be made whenever possible and compared to the scores on the pretraining test. The behavioral change of each man can be considered in conjunction with the time he spent learning the different skill and the cost of the training program per salesman. In this way, the manager can evaluate whether the amount of change was worth the time and effort spent to achieve it. In addition, each individual can be compared to the entire group to see how he has improved relative to the rest. By compiling such data, the manager can compare one group with another objectively and evaluate the training program itself. If no measurement is made after the training, it is practically impossible to evaluate either the salesmen or the training on anything but a subjective basis. Such a use of opinions is entirely inappropriate to modern sales training.

Representing Progress Graphically

Learning curve. Training specialists frequently plot a learning curve to record a trainee's progress over a period of time. After one session, the trainee may be able to open his presentation with a strong initial-benefit statement. By the tenth session, he should be able to show a complex set of behavioral patterns which includes handling objections and closing the sale. Typically, the early learning is relatively simple, and the trainee appears to catch on fast. As the lessons become more complicated, the rate of learning may decrease. Finally, when the newly acquired behavior pattern becomes habitual, the trainee reaches the plateau of the learning curve (see Figure 1).

After a number of sales trainees are tested, their average can be computed and a curve plotted for the average learning rate. This rate can then be considered the norm or standard that new men are expected to achieve or surpass. In this manner, the rate of learning for future training programs that use differing contents or methods can be compared to the original rate. If the same program is continued, each new group of trainees can be compared to previous groups. With a bench mark, the manager can see if varying the time spent on important parts of the training will raise the men's achievement above the norm. Using this system, one large industrial manufacturer was able to reduce its sales training program from two years to six months while actually improving the skills of its trainees.

Bar graph. Individual trainees get lost in group averages, however, because a few slow learners are offset by an equal number of fast learners. For some purposes it may be desirable to show a group's behavior modification in another manner. A bar graph with lettered blocks can be used to indicate the performance level of each trainee before and after training (see Figure 2). This format permits both the group's behavior modification and the individual progress of each trainee to be seen at a glance.

The disadvantage of the bar-graph format is its inability to indicate where the sales trainees are on the learning curve. For example, if the program continued another week, would the slower learners

Figure 1.   A typical learning curve.

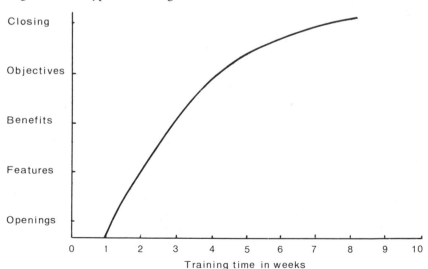

Figure 2. Typical behavior modification.

achieve their highest scores? The advantage of a learning curve is that it clearly shows when the amount of learning reaches a plateau (levels out). After this point, there is little or nothing to be gained in prolonging the training program. Conversely, if the group has not reached its peak of learning, then additional time spent in training will probably be justified.

THE FOUR-STEP TRAINING FORMAT

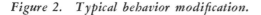

While every training program will be different in some respect, a successful sales training program will probably follow a proven pattern. One time-tested pattern is the four-step format:

- Preparing the learner
- Presenting the lesson
- Student action
- Testing performance

Preparing the Learner

Very often, salesmen are simply told to report for sales training at a certain time and place. Since they have been given no reason for their compulsory attendance, they may infer many things. Perhaps the manager thinks they are stupid. Perhaps he feels they are too rough or too aggressive. Perhaps he thinks they are careless in territory management. Whatever a salesman reads into the directive, his attitude will probably be negative. He may enter the first training session with a chip on his shoulder, defying anyone to teach him anything. Even students who voluntarily enroll in a sales training course are often skeptical of its value or of the instructor's ability to teach them. They enter the first class with a wait-and-see attitude.

Whenever a salesman has a hostile or negative attitude, it is difficult for anyone to teach him a skill or modify his behavior. He is mentally set to resist, although outwardly he may act friendly and cooperative. Secretly he is looking for ways to discredit the instructor or the program. This is normal behavior; it protects the salesman's self-image as a competent person who has achieved a degree of success and reassures him that the sales manager or instructor's judgment of him must be wrong.

For these reasons, the sales trainer should open his program with strong, positive motivational ideas. What can the average salesman hope to gain by participating in this training session? Why is this particular program the best of its kind for the salesmen at this time? In other words, he should tell the salesmen what's in it for them.

Preparing the learner means neutralizing any hostile or negative feelings by showing the value of sales training to every man in the program. Perhaps the training will enable him to sell national accounts, which he was not able to do previously. Perhaps it will enable him to locate more good prospects and reduce his discouraging number of nonproductive sales calls. The salesman should understand and accept the objectives of the training program and realize how he can benefit by participating.

An interesting method of preparing the learner can be used when the salesmen are very experienced or very intelligent. When they feel that they already know how to do something or that they can easily figure out a solution to any problem, the case-history method can change their attitude. The salesmen are confronted with a sales problem, and their proposed solutions are rejected as inappropriate. After being thoroughly frustrated, they are ready to hear and accept the "correct solution." The technique of motivating the salesman by means of frustration should be used only with superior salesmen who are mature enough to maintain their desire to learn after being put down by the instructor.

Preparing the learner also means providing a common entry level of knowledge or performance. Before a student pilot gets into an airplane, he is expected to master certain theories and facts. Before a scuba diver leaves the boat, he is expected to know many safety rules and procedures. In the same way, before a sound sales training program can proceed, the trainees should be brought up to a minimum level of competence. This may require several training meetings and some individual help; it may require the setting of certain standards for entry, such as a minimum of six months' selling in the field. Whatever the prerequisites, the trainer should attempt to create a common base for the trainees so that they will be able to discuss problems and skills on the same level.

Presenting the Lesson

Presentation may take a simple form, such as a lecture, or a very sophisticated form, such as the modeling of the ideal behavior by the instructor. In training pilots, the instructor would fly the plane while the student passively observed. In training salesmen, the sales manager might make a sale while the trainee silently observed. A training film might be shown in which actors dramatize the real event. In any case, the students are told the aim of the lesson and the key things they should look for before the event. After the event, the instructor should explain to the trainee what was done and why certain words or actions were most appropriate.

In a simulated sales situation, it is often wise to stop the action and ask questions of the trainees. Did they notice the key words or actions? What would they recommend doing next? This sort of questioning helps to involve the trainees, who might otherwise be very passive. Since they do not know when the action will be stopped or when they will be called on to answer a question, they are inclined to participate mentally, as if they were performing the action themselves.

By focusing the students' attention on certain areas, the instructor is training them to think according to established patterns. With practice, the trainees will continue to look for these key areas when they are in a simulated or real situation themselves. Consequently, the instructor or sales manager should be sure not to ask trivial questions simply to maintain attention. He can inadvertently teach his sales trainees to focus on trivia.

The lesson may be presented in a single meeting or it may require many sessions over a period of weeks or months. In this way, very complicated and sophisticated behavior patterns can be broken down into small, easily accepted sequences which can be logically connected. The skill of the instructor and the learning ability of the sales trainees often predetermine the rate at which the lessons may proceed.

Student Action

The third step in the training format is the student's demonstration, under protective conditions, that he can do what he observed the instructor doing. In this step in pilot training, the student actually controls the aircraft while the flight instructor observes and insures their safety. In sales training, the trainee may role-play in the protective atmosphere of the classroom. He may also demonstrate his skill in the prospect's office or home, but with the protection and assistance of his sales manager.

After each practice session, the instructor critiques the performance and offers advice on how it may be improved the next time. The emphasis is on constructive criticism and on building the sales trainee's confidence in himself to accomplish the task unaided. By occasionally asking the trainee to critique his own performance, the instructor can see how well he understands himself and the situation. If he is too severe in his self-criticism, the instructor can reinforce the trainee's good points to bolster his self-confidence. If the trainee is too forgiving of mistakes, the instructor can point out the dangerous consequences of taking mistakes too lightly. In this way, the trainee will have a high degree of self-confidence when he is ready to take the next training step.

Testing Performance

The final step in the four-step training format is to test the trainee's performance under the real conditions of his job. In pilot training, this is the crucial moment in which the student pilot first solos, flying the plane alone and taking sole responsibility for his own safety and for the safety of the aircraft. If he is well trained, he will fly safely—perhaps not as well as his instructor, but safely. In the same manner, a well-trained sales trainee on his first solo sales call will do an adequate job—perhaps not as good a job as his instructor would do, but an adequate job. Afterward, he should review the sales call and discuss it with his manager or instructor. When he makes his first sale, he will be exhilarated and abound with self-confidence, much as the student pilot who passes his final flight test and receives his pilot's license. This sale will be a milestone in the career of the young salesman.

Positive reinforcement is very effective at this stage because it builds the sales trainee's self-confidence, which is essential to his success. He should continue practicing what he has been taught until the proper new behavior becomes habitual. In the beginning, the praise of the instructor or sales manager is the reward he seeks. Later, as he succeeds in selling, the orders become the reward, and the young salesman will be pleased when he has done a good day's work even though no one directly observed his behavior.

SUMMARY

Human behavior is very complex; thus, when a sales manager attempts to modify the behavior of his salesmen, he should have some understanding of learning principles. One of the most important principles is reinforcement. The experience of educators and modern sales training executives has shown that positive reinforcement, or praise for a behavior change in the desired direction, tends to increase the learning process, while negative reinforcement, or punishment for incorrect behavior, is likely to interfere with it. Where discipline is not a problem, the trainer should concentrate on the positive and focus the trainee's attention on the desired behavior.

Another learning principle particularly appropriate to sales training is generalization. Rather than attempting to teach hundreds, or even thousands of isolated facts, the instructor creates common groups or categories of facts. The sales trainee is taught a rationale or selling theme for each general classification which he can apply to all the items in that group. If new products or new systems, for example, are later added to a general classification, the salesmen will be able to learn to sell them quickly because the old rationale can be logically extended to the new items. By relating new and perhaps more complicated concepts to those which the trainees already know, the sales trainer is making good use of the principle of generalization.

Through trial and error, animals can be taught to perform a few simple tricks. Human beings are capable of much more complicated learning because they can reevaluate their past experiences and use deductive reasoning to project future behavior. This learning by reappraisal is appropriate for the salesman's self-evaluation of his work in the field. The training director or sales manager can help the salesman by providing him with an outline for self-criticism which focuses his attention on key areas rather than on trivia.

A training director can gauge the initial level of competence of the sales trainees by administering pretraining tests. He can test them again at one or more points during the program and again after the training is completed. Such measurements provide objective data for evaluating many parts of the training program. By plotting learning curves for past training groups, a sales trainer can establish bench marks to aid him in setting both specific behavioral goals and time limits in which these goals are expected to be achieved. He can also use the curves to test the effectiveness of different teaching methods and various program contents by comparing the learning time required and the degree of skill attained by several groups of sales trainees. Variations of bar graphs can be used in a similar manner when an individual trainee's performance is the point of interest.

The four-step training format—preparing the learner, presenting the lesson, student action, and testing performance—is a proven method for increasing the efficiency of the learning process. These separate areas require considerable attention in the planning stages of any sales training program. Many members of the National Society of Sales Training Executives use this format in very sophisticated training programs and are teaching it to trainers in many foreign countries.

A word of caution is appropriate at this point. Sales training should not be thought of in isolation from the rest of the sales job. When a formal sales training program ends, its message can either be ignored or forgotten back on the job or be reinforced by the local sales manager. Training by a staff specialist should be planned and conducted with the full understanding and cooperation of the line managers, who are ultimately responsible for the performance of their salesmen. It is to the advantage of the sales training executive to inform these managers regularly and without ambiguity of the behavior changes he is striving for and the ways in which they can reinforce his efforts when the salesmen are back on the job.

SELECTED MATERIALS

Bandura, Albert, and Walters, Richard H., *Social Learning and Personality Development*. New York: Holt, Rinehart and Winston, 1967.

Cronbach, Lee J., *Educational Psychology*, 2d ed. New York: Harcourt Brace Jovanovich, 1971.

Fryer, Douglas H., Feinberg, Mortimer R., and Zalkind, Sheldon S., *Developing People in Industry*. New York: Harper & Brothers, 1956.

Halsey, George D., *Training Employees*. New York: Harper & Brothers, 1949.

Kanfer, F. H., and Marston, A. R., "Conditioning of Self-Reinforcing Responses: An Analogue to Self-Confidence Training," *Psychology Report*, Vol. 13 (1963), pp. 63–70.

————, "Human Reinforcement: Vicarious and Direct," *Journal of Experimental Psychology*, Vol. 65 (1963), pp. 292–296.

————, "Determinants of Self-Reinforcement in Human Learning," *Journal of Experimental Psychology*, Vol. 66 (1963), pp. 245–254.

Lauwerys, Joseph A., and Scanlon, David G., eds., *The World Year Book of Education, 1971–1972: Higher Education in a Changing World.* New York: Harcourt Brace Jovanovich, 1972. Published annually.

Lynton, Rolf P., *Training for Development.* Homewood, Ill.: Richard D. Irwin, 1967.

Shaffer, Laurance Frederic, and Shoben, Edward Joseph, Jr., *The Psychology of Adjustment,* 2d ed. Boston: Houghton Mifflin, 1956.

Skinner, B. F., *Cumulative Record.* New York: Appleton, 1957.

Staats, A. W., *Human Learning.* New York: Holt, Rinehart and Winston, 1964.

CHAPTER 3

Five Levels
of Sophistication in Selling

THE SALES STRATEGY which a company chooses to employ often dictates the minimum level of competence which a trainee must achieve before he is assigned to a territory. If the manufacturer's marketing executive decides to sell to wholesalers, for example, his sales force will have certain duties and goals. These duties might include the training of the wholesaler's salesmen. On the other hand, the same marketing executive may decide to sell directly to the consumer, in which case his sales force will have very different duties and goals. However, once the broad marketing strategy has been formulated, the sales manager usually has considerable discretion in determining how sophisticated his sales training may be.

If one observes many salesmen in a range of industries, he may correctly conclude that there are thousands of ways to sell products and services. Further analysis and logic will indicate many similarities among the methods, and general categories will emerge into which most will fall:

- Stimulus-response selling
- Formula selling
- Want-satisfaction selling
- Problem-solving selling
- Depth selling

Experienced and highly successful salesmen can be found using each of these methods, and one level is not necessarily better than another level. Success depends on matching the sales strategy to the target market segment and the competence or qualifications of the sales force. In general, the sales manager tries to sharpen his salesmen to a minimum level of sophistication for his market.

Several different divisions of the same company may teach their salesmen to sell on different levels because their markets are unique. In addition, within one group of salesmen, the manager may correctly train different men to sell using different levels of sales strategy because the men themselves have reached varying levels of achievement in selling ability.

Obviously there are financial or budgetary constraints under which the sales manager must operate. The profit margin on many products and services will not permit hiring college graduates only and a full-time sales trainer in a staff capacity. When the money is budgeted, often the manpower is not available. The sales manager must start with his existing sales force and budget limitations and build from there.

Training and development help salesmen to grow and become more productive, and it is the sales manager's responsibility to upgrade his salesmen to the limit of their potential ability. He may call for weekly or monthly sales meetings and he has the choice of various alternative strategies to teach his salesmen. Rather than teach one strategy after another in trial-and-error fashion, the sales manager should analyze the needs of the job and the capabilities of his salesmen before launching any training program. He should then be able to predict, with reasonable confidence, which strategy is most appropriate.

STIMULUS-RESPONSE SELLING

A sales plan that is written out and memorized word for word by the salesman is called a canned talk. When the salesman uses only selected parts of such a presentation and substitutes his own varied talks for other parts but still follows the preplanned outline, the presentation is called a planned talk. If the prospect says one thing, the salesman plans to answer with a particular memorized paragraph. In either form, canned or planned, the talk is a fairly standardized presentation and is given by the salesman to all prospects. It becomes a habit that the salesman may not even be conscious of.

Whatever form it takes, the planned talk is designed to communicate rapidly to the prospect as many buying benefits as possible in an attempt to elicit a favorable buying response. The salesman is trained to say many emotionally appealing words and to raise certain issues which will trigger a favorable response in most buyers. All the facts and emotional appeals are assembled in a logical sequence to tell a complete and persuasive story. A good planned talk has an engaging beginning, a logical and effective presentation, often a demonstration, and, finally, as many as ten standard phrases to use in closing the sale. Common objectives are answered only when raised by the prospect, and these answers are also relatively standardized.

There is nothing wrong with using such a well-organized presentation on the proper occasion.

Despite its obvious pitfalls, this sales strategy is prevalent today in many industries, and generally with management's encouragement, because of the mass markets which have yet to be contacted. When selling a single product to a broad market, one is working on the law of averages. The salesman who gets the greatest exposure to prospects and effectively presents his stimulus-response sales plan will get the most orders. Many life insurance companies use this sales strategy because practically everyone is a prospect. Large mutual fund sales organizations require their salesmen to learn a two-hour canned speech before they are permitted to make their first call. The speech includes those ideas that sales management has found useful for selling mutual funds in a mass market and also insures that new salesmen will not misrepresent possible profits and that they will caution the prospect about possible losses. The result? New men can sell almost as effectively as old men.

The canned sales presentation is widely used—intentionally and knowledgeably—by marketing management in a number of industries. It is appropriate in training retail sales clerks as well as in training house-to-house outside salesmen. Mutual fund salesmen, stockbrokers' sales representatives, and real estate salesmen can all use this strategy to good advantage. These are generally consumer markets, but stimulus-response selling is also used extensively by wholesale salesmen calling, for example, on supermarket operators or appliance store owners; by medical detail men doing missionary sales work with doctors and dentists; and by salesmen expected to call on time-conscious architects. It is most common in attempting to sell textbook adoptions to college professors, and it is often used in selling industrial equipment directly for the manufacturer.

The advantages of a standard presentation to the salesman are that it saves his and the prospect's time, which enables him to see more people on a given day. It provides a logical order to his sales story and thus is easier for the prospect to understand and follow. It enables new salesmen to speak confidently without fumbling for words, which usually earns the prospect's respect, and it also assures a smooth and complete presentation and prevents wandering off the subject or the absent-minded omission of any important points. Finally, it leaves the salesman free to devote his attention to showmanship and to observe the prospect's reactions.

The advantages to the selling company and to the sales manager include easier recruiting of job applicants, selection of the men to hire, and training of new salesmen. These functions are simplified because lower manpower specifications can be set. The men do not have to understand the intricacies of their product, the persuasion process, the various selling techniques that could be available to them, or anything of the psychology of personality. Since standards are lower, the hiring, training, and compensation of the sales force presumably will be less expensive. The company and the sales manager can also be more reasonably assured that the desired message is being delivered to prospects. This, in turn, will eliminate or reduce salesmen's exaggerated claims for the product and other misinformation which causes poor public relations and subsequent service complaints.

The burden of preparing an effective stimulus-response sales program is, of course, on the sales manager. He should analyze his desired market and the product benefits to the individual buyers. Using techniques similar to those of mass communications and advertising, the sales manager should create a sales presentation that is as interesting as possible to the broadest potential market and yet is explicit enough to be understood by the individual prospect. A good presentation, particularly if it is designed for new salesmen, will contain a number of words or expressions to stimulate some prospects into buying immediately. The presentation should be complete and automatic, requiring a minimum of thought on the part of the salesman. When told to enough people, it should assure some degree of success. In addition, the presentation should be designed to encourage the buyer's confidence in the salesman as a likeable, trustworthy, sincere, and knowledgeable source of information—the perfect image of the clean-cut boy next door.

If the sales organization has many diverse products, the sales manager using this strategy should build presentations for each of the products. Also, when salesmen are expected to make repetitive calls on the same prospects, new presentations should be organized for each subsequent visit. This repetition with variation should have a cumulative effect.

It is relatively simple to train a salesman to use a planned talk. He is asked to memorize words and phrases from a written script and to show or demonstrate certain things. By listening to records or audio tapes he can learn the proper pitch and vocal inflections for the key words. By watching sound films or video tapes he can easily learn to mimic the actors. A trainee must practice until he knows every word by rote and has an actor's feeling for each line.

In addition, the new salesman should develop sustaining enthusiasm. Even though he may give his sales presentation hundreds of times, he should always bear in mind that it will be a new message to each audience that has never heard it before.

One final word of caution in training salesmen to use the stimulus-response strategy: If trial closes are built into the presentation, do *not* assume that trainees will know how to handle them. Many new salesmen will not recognize when the prospect is signaling his readiness to buy. The novice is too often concerned with giving a complete sales presentation and is likely to talk himself out of an easy sale. When a trial close elicits a favorable response, the salesman should learn to recognize it, skip most of the remaining talk, and write up the order.

FORMULA SELLING

Probably the most popular strategy taught to salesmen is a formula of mental steps encompassing such things as attention, interest, desire, conviction, and action. The formula method requires the salesman to dominate the interview and to maintain the prospect's attention on a desired phase of the product. The pace of the presentation is triggered by the prospect's responses. The salesman is taught not to go methodically through a planned presentation but to build interest before moving to the next stage. This enables the salesman to tailor his presentation to a specific prospect and to use some degree of creativity and imagination.

Formula selling is predominant in industrial sales and is more applicable to business sales than to retail or consumer markets because it normally takes the form of a lengthy two-way conversation. Whenever the product or service is complicated and difficult to understand, or when a salesman calls repeatedly on the same accounts throughout the years, formula selling predominates. If the salesman has a number of products in his line, this method enables him to vary his talk on each visit while still maintaining a set selling pattern or organization as a guide. Industrial goods, office supplies and equipment, and petroleum and chemical products, as well as goods sold by the manufacturer to a wholesaler or by the wholesaler to a retailer, are typically sold through a formula method of presentation.

A salesman may speak to a prospect and not be heard or understood because the prospect is thinking about another topic or is still considering a previous statement. The salesman should be taught to get acceptance on one point at a time and to focus the prospect's attention on one idea at a time. He should be taught to show pictures or illustrations without printed copy so that he can continue talking and directing the prospect's attention. If printed copy is shown to the prospect, the salesman must learn to remain quiet, or both his picture message and his verbal message will be lost. To pace his presentation, the salesman learns to pause after each point and frequently to ask a question to reveal the prospect's understanding and acceptance of the point being made. He should also be taught to observe the prospect's actions carefully and to be alert to what he doesn't say, which is often more important than what he does say.

When using the formula method of presentation, the salesman has a greater choice of sales material, sequence, and emphasis to be employed in a given situation. Because of this large degree of personal choice, the salesman should be more intelligent, more imaginative, and certainly better trained. His training should include detailed knowledge of the product and its applications and limitations, the sales formula his company uses, some aspects of the psychology of persuasion, and a certain amount of skill in analyzing a buyer's responses. He should be able to think on his feet and employ the appropriate part of his plan for every variation in the prospect's response. By knowing the prospect, the salesman can anticipate which benefits will be most likely to be appealing and which phases of his sales talk to play down or omit entirely. The salesman should be taught to become sensitive to the buyer's unspoken feelings and not to miss what is really on the prospect's mind.

Training for formula selling includes a detailed analysis of each product handled, and each technical detail, such as the gauge of steel used or its particular shape and form, should be directly related to a user benefit. Why is the product made this way instead of another way? What resulting benefits are exclusive with this product and will not be found in the competitive products on the market? Once the salesman is taught this kind of information, he can confidently answer any question on product technicalities and can develop a philosophy of company purposes and goals, which is so basic to imaginative, creative selling.

Training salesmen in product knowledge and formula application clearly takes much longer than simply having them memorize a sales talk. Preparation on the sales manager's part involves a new and detailed analysis of the sales job to provide specifications for hiring. Recruiting will probably be on a higher level, and selection should be extremely discriminating. Because of the higher-quality man desired, starting salaries are likely to be higher and competitive with other vocations. Training should be complete to be economical in the long run, and the trainers should be education-minded as well as sales-oriented, so that what is taught is of long-range value to the salesman and his company. Finally, a great deal of patience is required to supervise and motivate the trainee over an extended period of nonproductive activity in classes and during the early months out in the field.

WANT-SATISFACTION SELLING

The want-satisfaction sales strategy requires the salesman to discover a want or need within the buyer's mind and then bring it to his awareness. The salesman simply acts as the prospect's agent to show him how to satisfy this need through the purchase of the salesman's goods or services. The sales presentation is based on the prospect's self-interest or the emotional motive that carries the strongest appeal for him at that instant. Product considerations are secondary. The salesman's job is to determine which emotional wants are likely to exist and which are the dominant ones.

This technique is used most effectively by experienced salesmen who have enough self-confidence to permit the sales interview to wander in many directions as a true two-way conversation. In fact, the prospect is encouraged to do most of the talking and the salesman becomes a good listener, looking for the keys to unlock the hidden want from the buyer's mind. While this method is most widely used by experienced salesmen of life insurance, autos, and other consumer goods, it is growing in popularity in industrial selling, where it is used primarily on large prospects because of the length of time it takes to develop any one sale and to develop a substantial total sales volume.

The question-and-answer technique of drawing a prospect out of his protective shell is characteristic of want-satisfaction selling. The salesman is primarily concerned with getting the prospect to talk so he can discover the prospect's wants. The salesman is taught to use questions to direct the prospect's attention to broad areas of information in which the salesman is interested—to get information about specific facts as well as to see how the prospect habitually solves various problems. His primary purpose in asking questions is to communicate interest and stimulate a free flow of talk.

When the prospect begins talking he may be general and hesitating, deciding whether or not to say what he really has on his mind. He may make some light remark or be thinking out loud in an attempt to clarify his own ideas. Some people may even say the opposite of what they mean in an attempt to conceal their true feelings. Some people, negative in nature, do this habitually even when there is nothing to be gained. The salesman, therefore, should be taught to draw the prospect out patiently without jumping to conclusions.

The salesman should also be trained not to interrupt the prospect because interruption irritates and frustrates him in his effort to communicate, and he may stop trying. Interruption also implies that the salesman is more interested in his own thoughts than in the prospect's thoughts and that he can't wait for his turn to speak. The prospect may not feel like competing for the salesman's attention. In fact, the best way to drive a prospect's wants into hiding is to resort to a cross-examining approach. To draw the prospect out, the salesman should be taught to conduct the sales interview in an easy, give-and-take discussion: The salesman's willingness to reveal his own attitudes often encourages the prospect to reveal his.

Once the prospect's problems are revealed, the salesman attempts to make the buyer aware that he understands and sympathizes with the prospect's point of view. To do this the salesman should have so much confidence that he doesn't talk about the product or service that he is selling. Once the need is reinforced in the prospect's mind, the salesman can present a solution to satisfy the wants. The salesman will by then be considered a friendly source of authority, if not unbiased, at least primarily concerned with the buyer's interest. The prospect can now be more easily persuaded to do what he wants to do. Normally the prospect will also require a logical presentation to justify his action, and a well-prepared sales plan will quickly and efficiently justify his acting now.

Want-satisfaction selling is an application of the psychiatric technique of directive counseling: The patient is encouraged to volunteer information about himself, and the psychiatrist interprets the information and helps the patient see it in a new light and understand what is bothering him, what he needs to feel better, and what will give him greater satisfaction or make his life more pleasant and fulfilling again. To use this strategy, a salesman typically would need to learn the psychology of motivation and some techniques for discovering motives. In order to discover what will motivate a prospect at a given time, the salesman needs to know techniques for getting a prospect to talk, drawing him out of his protective shell, and learning the attitudes, ideas, and beliefs to which he is predisposed. In addition, he would need training in interpreting the prospect's expressed needs in a manner and form that will be acceptable to the prospect. Clearly this kind of selling is a job for an educated and trained listener, not for a compulsive talker. (These psychological skills are discussed in the next chapter.)

In addition, the salesman using this strategy should be taught in detail about his products and their applications and limitations. Although the emphasis in the sales interview is on the buyer's wants and needs, whatever questions do arise about the product must be answered clearly and correctly to maintain the atmosphere of sincerity and confidence.

In a market where product and service differentiation is difficult or impossible to obtain, competitive salesmen are most often judged on a personal basis. The buyer looks for the man with whom he can get along easily. The appeals may be based on the personal wants of the buyer or on his organizational role, that is, what he wants for himself within his company.

Fundamental to this strategy is a customer-oriented presentation rather than a product- or salesman-oriented prepared talk. Thus, the sales manager or trainer does not build a planned talk; instead, he teaches the salesman to probe, to recognize areas where the product will help satisfy needs, and to build his own customer-oriented presentation on the spot. These are skills of a much higher order than memorizing a talk or following a pattern or formula.

PROBLEM-SOLVING SELLING

Problem solving as a sales strategy is based on building a prospect's confidence in the honest service which the sincere salesman can provide. The salesman dedicates his efforts to the primary benefit of the prospect by developing the prospect's true needs, thoroughly investigating all feasible solutions, projecting their applications, and selecting the most appropriate solution. He lets the chips fall where they may, recommending the most appropriate solution even if it does not include the immediate purchase of his own product.

While this method of persuasion is used by some experienced salesmen in almost every field, it is relatively rare in general sales. On the other hand, it is fundamentally applicable in technical fields, where production standards or engineering services are important, particularly when the size of the potential sale justifies the investment of a great deal of time and effort. When a product has an easily demonstrated superiority over all competitors, a completely honest two-sided presentation is an effective technique. As competitive products become more nearly equal, with few demonstrable advantages, this method is less effective. The foundation of problem solving as a technique of persuasion is true sincerity without equivocation or mental reservation.

Most experienced salesmen become experts in their narrow field and are very often experts in related problems. Calling on their technical knowledge and experience, they can suggest alternate courses of action of which the prospect is not aware and provide him with honest appraisals. Thus, problem solving can be an effective sales presentation in many nontechnical fields as well, simply because the salesman is more knowledgeable in his field than the buyer. Many sales of accounting machines, office duplicating machines, and printing machines are due to a problem-solving technique honestly applied. When a salesman is selling simple products, often nothing astonishes prospects more than his common sense and plain, honest dealings.

Frequently a higher executive than a purchasing agent makes the ultimate buying decision, and dealing with a corporate vice-president, for example, calls for a sophisticated salesman. In terms of persuasion, the salesman who conveys a mood of sincerity in problem solving builds confidence in himself as the source of authority. After repeated exposure, the executive will know with the certainty of personal experience that this salesman operates entirely in the best interests of the prospect. He will learn to trust the salesman completely.

Clearly the training and development of salesmen to use this strategy is very different from the sales training required for the strategies discussed previously. The salesman is taught how to analyze an industry and a particular target company before he makes any direct contact. When he makes his first call, he should be prepared to offer a genuine and specific service to the prospect. He learns to be open and direct, making his first impression one of complete understanding of the prospect's company and not attempting to sell anything at that point. Initially, he may offer to make a survey or an audit of various processes to determine where costs may be reduced, service increased, duplication removed, and so forth. He uses questions to probe for areas of business interest and needs but does not yet give a sales presentation.

After he has conducted a legitimate study of the problem area, the salesman is taught to examine all the feasible solutions, not just those involving the purchase of his products. With the prospect, he projects the consequences of the likely alternatives and recommends the one best serving the prospect's objectives. The entire sales presentation is then clearly customer-oriented.

The emphasis in training a salesman to use the problem-solving strategy obviously is on technical knowledge of the product and how it relates to user benefits or can substantiate any claims made. The salesman should be taught where he can request minor changes to better suit a customer's needs and where basic costs will mount radically. In other words, he should be taught his production limitations, both physically and financially, and how they will apply to likely customer requests.

The salesman's training should include knowledge of the strengths and appropriate applications of both his own company's and its competitors' products. Knowing why one product is best for a given situation is more important than knowing how to woo a prospect. Each step in the presentation process, including the suggestion of alternatives which are feasible from the customer's point of view, should be related to facts and justified objectively. In this process, the salesman who is gruff but technically correct is usually more persuasive than the smooth-talking salesman who is too general or loose with the facts.

Second only to technical product knowledge in this method of presentation is the ability to educate the prospect. The salesman is supposed to be more of an expert in his limited field than the prospect, but he should be able to make his ideas simple and understandable to the customer, who may not be familiar with the technical terms involved. The salesman can be trained to make technical data clear and easy for the novice to understand. This skill should not be treated lightly in preparing technically educated people for their field sales experience. The technical salesman should be able to state his idea, illustrate it, and then restate it in different terms if necessary. Unless the prospect understands the suggestion and appreciates the minute technical point on which the idea swings, all the clear, scientific thinking involved may be lost.

The advantages of teaching the problem-solving sales strategy include complete customer orientation in serving the individual prospect, complete honesty in using an unbiased, two-sided argument, and an acceptable utilization of technically trained personnel in sales work. The problem-solving strategy builds long-range confidence in the source of authority, and this is essential in most repeat sales situations, where customer loyalty is cultivated.

DEPTH SELLING

At this point the reader should see the continuum of sales strategies ranging from the completely salesman-oriented canned talk to the completely customer-oriented problem-solving approach. Each of the four strategies was discussed in its pure form. In practice, they overlap, blend, and intermingle, but generally at random and without premeditated design or purpose.

Depth selling combines the best features of all the strategies but does so with forethought and intention. It is appropriately taught to senior salesmen and salesmen responsible for national accounts, who are experienced in analyzing individual prospects and problem situations. These men can be taught to think creatively of the many possible combinations of selling methods and to project the applications into the future. From the numerous strategies in their repertory, the salesmen decide which method is most appropriate to each stage of their sales plan.

The depth salesman is taught how diplomatically to get others inside his company to work with him to accomplish his objectives. He is encouraged to assume leadership of a team of experts, calling for help or support when and where he needs it. Many of these experts, such as research, engineering, and production personnel, will have little or no direct responsibility to the salesman. Their respect and voluntary cooperation must be earned and a proud team spirit cultivated. When visiting a key target account, the salesman may bring along a technical man to probe for information from, or to present information to, his counterpart in the prospect's company. On occasion, the salesman, as team captain, may request the presence of people from the accounting or credit department on a direct sales call.

Since depth selling is a combination of the various strategies, it can have the advantages of each without the disadvantages. This selling strategy is based on a thorough knowledge of the psychology of communication and persuasion and a well-researched investigation of the various people who may influence the buying decision in a particular target account. Each aspect of persuading any one person is given adequate thought before the person is approached. Also characteristic of this strategy is a customer-oriented attitude which causes problem-solving and want-satisfaction techniques to be interwoven into the sales presentation wherever applicable.

The depth salesman is highly sensitive to the changing moods of the prospect and can employ whatever technique best serves his purpose at any given moment. For example, when a prospect indicates an emotional inclination toward a favorable decision, the salesman may reinforce that attitude by using a stimulus-response talk which provides the essential logic concisely. When a prospect is in an impulsive mood, the depth salesman may use pure suggestion without a lot of facts to activate a decision. He may quote a single firm price and never vary from it or he may quote a price intentionally high, knowing that the buyer wants to bargain.

Being flexible, the depth salesman's presentation can vary continuously to suit the interruptions and changing elements in a selling situation. He is not bound by a memorized talk or the arbitrary rules of a formula; thus he can custom-tailor his presentation to the individual prospect or group of buying influentials according to the given time, place, condition, and mood. The legitimate services of many experts in the selling company can be offered as the salesman deems appropriate.

Since building confidence is also characteristic of this type of sales strategy, the prospect learns to recognize the salesman as a trustworthy and believable authority in his field. The depth salesman also typically builds personal friendships with his customers so he can gain leads and recommendations as well as repeat orders.

To be properly trained in depth selling, a man should be educated, responsible, and mature. His formal sales training will include knowledge of the technical qualities of his product to enable him to substantiate the customer benefits claimed, as well as knowledge of the policies and procedures of the selling company so that he understands why things are done as they are and can cooperate to achieve the company's stated purposes. His training and experience will also include a familiarity with his company's history, reputation, and objectives, which will enable the salesman to relate his own selfish goals to his responsibility to others in the company. Finally, his training will provide knowledge of the market, including both competition and customers, so that he can recognize good sales opportunities and develop friendships with the many people who may influence a sale.

Beyond knowledge, his training should include the development of skills such as probing for information, analyzing customer problems, and using the psychology of persuasion. The successful depth salesman will also be skillful in servicing the account after the sale and making fair adjustments when necessary. Obviously his skills would include operating equipment, giving demonstrations, and teaching his customer's personnel how to use and care for his products to obtain the maximum benefit from their purchase.

Work habits are normally developed as a part of the formal training process because depth selling is the most varied, flexible, and time-consuming strategy. The salesman should become an adept analyst of each individual prospect, his potential, and the proper time and effort to devote to each challenge. The depth salesman should be mature enough to be a self-starter, an independent and industrious worker, a problem solver with imagination, and a continuous student of people and persuasion. Such things as routing and frequency of visiting customers should be taught so that optimum use of time becomes habitual.

The final element in preparing a man to use depth selling is the reinforcement of proper attitudes. This can be woven through the entire training program and can serve to motivate the salesman to become truly outstanding. Knowing what purposes he serves, why such purposes, goals, policies, and procedures are of value to him and to society, and how to accomplish those purposes effectively can often motivate a salesman more than monetary rewards. Personal recognition, friendships with fellow workers and with customers, and the personal pride in a job well done are equally important in establishing proper sales attitudes and reinforcing motivation.

The preparation of salesmen to use the depth-selling strategy should be a continuous program covering knowledge, skills, work habits, and attitudes. It is a large job in both time and management effort. Successful salesmen in many fields have been self-educated in this method through years of trial and error. However, as management's knowledge increases and its attention is directed toward these training considerations, much training time can be saved.

TEACHING AT DIFFERENT LEVELS SIMULTANEOUSLY

Regardless of the entry level of a new salesman and the initial training which he receives, the first few months out in the field will probably be exciting and full of challenge. In time the salesman will become comfortable and more at ease with himself and with his customers. Some salesmen will be content to stay at this level for their entire career, but many will become bored or frustrated. When this occurs, the salesmen operate more and more automatically, with as little thought as possible. Selling becomes a tedious task, with success based on the law of averages or lucky windfalls. The fun and satisfactions in life are sought away from the job. When a salesman cannot grow, he is apt to wither and become cynical.

The modern sales manager is sensitive to the emotional needs of each of his salesmen and attempts to anticipate their changing attitudes. For example, after a salesman has been around his territory a number of times, he will have some degree of success. But he will have tried and failed to sell many prospects. If he must go back to these same accounts again and again, using the same knowledge and skills, one can anticipate that his frustration will build. If he is taught new knowledge, new skills, or new strategies, however, he will again feel the excitement of challenge. He will be interested in improving himself, growing, and he will realize the pride of accomplishment.

For a sales manager to achieve good performance with high motivation and productivity from every salesman, he should consider the various levels of training for each individual. As a salesman becomes less and less dependent on his manager, there is a danger of his behavior becoming habitual. One man may become complacent with a fair amount of success. Another man may work harder and harder but realize little or no progress. These signals should trigger in the sales manager a series of questions about additional training that might be appropriate.

One salesman may need encouragement to perfect his skills to become more successful. Another man may need to learn new techniques to increase his batting average. It would be unusual if every salesman needed the same training. Often the sales force can be divided into several groups according to common training needs. The least experienced group might practice planned talks to answer common objections, for example. Another group might exchange successful applications of formula-selling techniques. The skill of probing for information could be the training objective of a third group.

The training needs of salesmen do not necessarily relate to their ages or years on the job. Some young men are quite mature and some older salesmen will be very dependent on their manager. The effective sales manager will observe the individual salesman in the field and listen for clues which may indicate the appropriate level of sales training for that man at that point in his career. By matching the training to the needs of the individual, the modern sales manager can achieve better results than his predecessors, who attempted to teach all salesmen exactly the same thing.

But meeting the needs of the individual does not preclude training sessions of the entire sales force. Many topics are of interest and importance to all salesmen. For example, product modifications, new applications, company procedures, and the like should be reviewed with all the men. In addition, certain training methods enable the manager to run a large meeting with subgroups working on different but related problems. The level of training refers to content or subject matter, and this should be related to the needs of the individual, the subgroup, and the entire sales force.

SELECTED MATERIALS

Baer, Earl E., *Salesmanship.* New York: McGraw-Hill Book Company, 1972.

Baker, Richard M., Jr., and Phifer, Gregg, *Salesmanship Communication, Persuasion, Perception.* Boston: Allyn and Bacon, 1966.

Boyd, Harper W., and Davis, Robert T., *Readings in Sales Management.* Homewood, Ill.: Richard D. Irwin, 1970.

Particularly useful is Section II, "Developing Sales Strategies," pp. 55–142.

The Dartnell-Anderson 20 Point Sales System. Chicago: The Dartnell Corporation, 1972.

The seven audio tape cassettes and 13 booklets, quizzes, and exercises are particularly appropriate for new salesmen.

Hampton, Robert E., and Zabin, James Barton, *College Salesmanship.* New York: McGraw-Hill Book Company, 1970.

Harrison, Jared F., *Profitable Self-Management for Salesmen,* Englewood Cliffs, N.J.: Prentice-Hall, 1972.

Stanton, William J., and Buskirk, Richard, *Management of the Sales Force.* Homewood, Ill.: Richard D. Irwin, 1969.

Still, Richard R., and Cundiff, Edward W., *Sales Management,* 2d ed. Englewood Cliffs, N.J.: Prentice-Hall, 1969.

Stroh, Thomas F., *Salesmanship: Personal Communications and Persuasion in Marketing.* Homewood, Ill.: Richard D. Irwin, 1966.

Thompson, Joseph W., *Selling: A Behavioral Science Approach.* New York: McGraw-Hill Book Company, 1968.

Tritt, Robert E., and Harris, Clyde E., Jr., *Sales Management Organization Games.* Homewood, Ill.: Richard D. Irwin, 1967.

Two paperbound volumes of computer games.

CHAPTER 4

Essential Skills
for Successful Selling

THE SELLING JOB is basically a combination of industry and human relations skills. While each sales manager may wish to emphasize certain parts of the job, some skills are applicable to almost every sales job. In sales training it is wise to identify the skills which enable a salesman to become more effective in a short time. Teaching these key skills frequently produces the best results, which in turn builds confidence in the training function.

Communication is a fundamental skill essential to every sales job; however, the psychology of communication and persuasion is rarely considered basic knowledge for salesmen. After a salesman acquires the knowledge of this subject, he should be encouraged to apply it in his daily activities until it becomes so habitual that he need not consciously think about it. With regular use, the applied knowledge becomes a professional skill.

In many sales situations, the salesman is requested to obtain certain information before he attempts to build his presentation. Sometimes the salesman would like to know more about his prospect's attitudes and moods before describing selected benefits of his product. In such cases, direct questions may yield insufficient information or misleading half-truths. The salesman can be taught fairly sophisticated probing techniques to gain the sincere cooperation of most prospects and produce more effective sales interviews very quickly.

When the salesman uses these techniques successfully, they will become a professional skill.

For some sales jobs, if not for all, skill in effective listening is essential to success. The habitual conversational pattern of many salesmen is to dominate and direct the prospect rather than to exchange views and communicate. However, just as the ability to speak convincingly in public and to write effective sales letters can be developed, so can the ability to listen effectively. Sensitivity to other people's emotions, the ability to identify the key decision makers in a large organization, creative thinking, and cybernetic decision making are also at least useful, if not essential, skills for many sales jobs.

Sales training which includes the development of essential skills not only produces immediate short-term results, it also upgrades the salesman for life. The skills noted above are transferable to other occupations, such as sales management and general management, and they will give the salesman greater control in social situations and aid him in carrying out his civic responsibilities. Such a contribution to the personal development of others is one of the true rewards for the trainer.

APPLYING THE PSYCHOLOGY OF COMMUNICATION AND PERSUASION

In order to prepare a marketing program, a salesman should learn why and how people buy his products. Once the market target is identified and understood, then appeals can be designed which will interest the intended prospects.

Many factors influence people to buy: conditions that they may perceive relatively objectively, such as their immediate need for an item and their current economic situation; external pressures of their social group—for example, to wear a jacket and tie and to drive a clean, fairly new automobile; and personality traits such as their general willingness to spend money and the degree to which they trust other people. Most of these factors are beyond the control of the salesman. Nevertheless, understanding the various psychological influences on his prospect can help the salesman to persuade him to buy.

It would probably be futile to attempt to teach the language and the various schools of psychology in the normal sales training period. In the sales situation, the salesman is dealing with one person at a time and he should be concerned with that one personality.

The predictability of personality. Personality may be defined as the persistent tendencies of an individual to make certain kinds of judgments or appraisals and to make certain kinds of adjustments to stimuli. Although personality is formed partially by physiological and hereditary factors, basically it is developed through the social process of learning. A person acts in a certain way because his experience up to that point in his life has reinforced that kind of response.

In the sales situation, the salesman is most often concerned with the immediate thoughts and feelings of the prospect, as well as with his predispositions, the collection of attitudes, opinions, beliefs, interests, and psychological needs—the mental set of the prospect—before he is exposed to any stimuli or persuasive sales message. The prospect will react to certain ideas, people, words, and things according to what his individual experience has taught him. His behavior patterns may be conscious or unconscious, but whether his reactions are rational or irrational, premeditated or impulsive, they are predictable. The salesman will benefit if he investigates his prospect's predispositions as much as is consistent with the size of the potential sale.

The prospect's defenses. Every week people are bombarded with tens of thousands of persuasive commercial and political messages designed to change their behavior. It is normal and healthy for a person to attempt to maintain his balance and peace of mind by defending his predispositions. Just as the body seeks to maintain a constant internal temperature, the mind also seeks a constant state for its preservation. People defend their predispositions in predictable ways, and a knowledge of these defenses will help the salesman to communicate and persuade.

The prospect will read certain advertisements and listen to certain salesmen, while ignoring others, according to what he thinks their message may contain. This defense is *selective exposure.* For example, if the prospect is predisposed to prefer name brands, he may be willing to see only the salesman from a well-known company. Selective exposure thus screens out whatever seems to conflict with the prospect's predisposition. Knowing this, a salesman from a little-known company can design his approach to appeal to this particular prospect. For instance, he may gain an interview with this prospect if he states that he wishes to talk about how a large, well-known customer benefited by using his products.

The second line of mental defense of predispositions is *selective perception*. The prospect can easily see or understand those parts of a persuasive message which are in agreement with his predetermined ideas. Conversely, the prospect will not understand or will distort those parts of the message which conflict with his predispositions. For example, one man may think of economy as reducing the purchase price or cost of acquisition. Another man in the same company may think of economy as making some operation more efficient, even if it costs more to buy certain equipment. Each man will selectively hear or perceive that part of the sales message which relates to his own preconceived attitudes. Knowing this, the effective salesman will tailor his presentation to assist, rather than block, communication with each individual.

One week after the salesman has made his presentation, the prospect might forget key portions of the message. He is apt to remember the points which he liked and be confused about or completely forget those parts with which he disagreed. This so-called convenient memory is normal and honest because it is a further defense of his predispositions. *Selective retention* or *selective recall* will be anticipated by the knowledgeable salesman through the maintenance of open lines of communication. Rather than being angered or upset and getting involved in heated arguments and denials when confronted with this situation, the salesman will openly discuss the points of confusion and reassure the prospect that his doubts or fears are without cause. This action will help to reduce or eliminate complaints after the sale is made.

Selective action or attitude conversion is the objective of a sales communication. This is the process which builds a minor idea or opinion gradually, so as not to alert the prospect's mental defenses, until it dominates the matrix of other ideas or opinions. When this occurs, the prospect will treat additional information (such as testimonials or a new personal experience with the product) favorably, for he will be predisposed to be persuaded.

Training methods. Sales training for most organizations can benefit by the inclusion of these principles of communication and persuasion. Through discussion, role playing, and other methods, salesmen can readily understand the concepts and begin to utilize them in building their personal communication skills. In some organizations it may be worthwhile to expand training to include such concepts as one-sided and two-sided arguments or messages, side attacks, cross-pressures, primary groups, and the like. Several excellent studies of these concepts are available; however, the concepts are not nearly as universally applicable as basic communication psychology.

In training salesmen to develop their skills of communication and persuasion, the sales manager or trainer should emphasize the need for sincerity. When a sale is made, the buyer is not a customer until he realizes the benefits which the salesman promised. No matter what his personal ethics may be, the salesman should govern his persuasive tactics by the realization that he must live with the buyer after the sale.

A prospect usually needs to feel a proposition is in his own best interest before he will agree to it. Sincerity is paramount in any persuasion attempt. The soft sell without undue pressure and without underhanded, subconscious manipulation is the effective theme in sales training today. By sincere and honest means the salesman attempts to reeducate the prospect in ways to look at a problem and get around obstacles to achieve greater satisfaction of his needs or goals in life.

PROBING TECHNIQUES

Whether a salesman is using a planned sales talk or an in-depth approach to a national account, his chances of succeeding are often in direct proportion to his knowledge of the prospect. A market research group may provide the salesman with general information about a target industry. The salesman himself may obtain the annual report of a target company and from other customers he may discover the names of some of the key people in the account. Most of this data for preapproach planning is fragmented or less than complete, as well as nonpersonal. Before the account is sold, the salesman will learn much more about the company and about the people who manage it.

In the natural course of a series of sales interviews the salesman will get some clues about the prospect's personal experiences, his interests, and his desires in life. Of course, most of this information will relate to the prospect's role in his organization rather than his personal life. This kind of information is highly desirable, but it often takes a long-term association to acquire if the approach is casual, random, and conversational.

One buying influential, a purchasing agent, for example, may think in terms of pure economics. He prefers to do an exhaustive search of alternate products and services. A second buying influential, a manager of a department, for example, may think in terms of solving problems with set priorities and may seek only a workable solution rather than investigating many alternatives. Other buying influentials, such as higher executives, for example, may pride themselves on being quick decision makers, almost impulsive buyers. While the range of possibilities is quite broad, it is important for the salesman to become aware of the individual's preconceived ideas and adapt his communication to suit that person.

The salesman using probing techniques is primarily concerned with getting the prospect to talk so he can learn the appropriate language with which to communicate and so he can discover more about the prospect's predispositions. The salesman uses questions to direct the prospect's attention to broad areas of information in which the salesman is interested, to get information about specific facts, and to see how the prospect habitually solves various problems. By asking broad questions, the salesman communicates his interest and his desire to stimulate a free flow of talk.

When the prospect begins talking he may be general or hesitating, deciding whether or not to say what he really has on his mind. He may make some light remark to see if the salesman is just making small talk or if he is genuinely interested in the topic. The prospect may ramble with his answer or think out loud in an attempt to clarify his own ideas. He may even say the opposite of what he means in an attempt to conceal his true feelings. Some people, negative in nature, do this habitually even when there is nothing to be gained. The salesman should be taught, therefore, to draw the prospect out of his protective shell without jumping to conclusions.

Drawing-out techniques include asking questions that require an explanation for an answer rather than a simple yes or no. The asking of specific detailed questions may cause the prospect to feel that if the salesman wants to know something he will ask it. Thus, he tends not to give additional information which would be useful. Since a salesman cannot think of everything to ask, and since his purpose is to get the prospect to talk rather freely, he should use broad rather than specific questions.

Open-ended questions. One kind of broad question is called open-ended. An example would be, "Tell me how you got into this industry, Mr. Jones." Although such a question directs the prospect's attention to the beginning of his career, it gives him complete freedom to pick out whatever he wishes to discuss. One man may begin by talking of the "fickle finger of fate." Another may choose to emphasize the social contacts which influenced his career. The advantage of this procedure is that it lets the salesman see the kinds of things that the prospect feels are important enough to bring to the salesman's attention. This gives the latter a glimpse of the prospect's values and of the things he thinks will impress the salesman.

Questions that begin with "Why" and refer to the feelings and desires of the prospect are usually not very satisfactory. A question such as "Why did you choose this particular company for your career?" often brings superficial answers. Such questions can usually be rephrased into ones that begin with "What"—for example, "What led you to join this company rather than some other?" This puts the emphasis on what the prospect sees as advantages rather than upon his hidden feelings or desires. As a general guideline, open-ended questions should not lend themselves to yes or no answers or to very short answers because they produce little useful information. Leading questions should also be avoided because they tend to influence a prospect to answer with information that will please the salesman instead of revealing something about himself. A good open-ended question gives no clues about the desired answer.

Elaborative questions. Once the prospect opens up and begins talking freely, elaborative questions—for example, "Could you tell me more about that?"—make it easy for him to continue. Sometimes the simple phrase "Then what?" is enough to encourage the prospect to continue. Other variations are "That's very interesting, please go on," or "Yes, I understand that part, but how did the other thing occur?"

Reflective questions. By interpreting or restating in different words what he thinks the prospect meant, the salesman can strip away ambiguities, too-broad generalizations, or other camouflages. In this technique, reflective questions are used to uncover what is really on the mind of the prospect. For example, the prospect may say, "I just didn't seem to be making the progress I should, so we decided it would be best if I tried another industry." The salesman replies, "We decided?" The prospect answers, "Well, I mean my wife and I talked it over and she thought . . . ."

A useful reflective question is formed around some unclear word or phrase used by the prospect—for example, "What do you mean by 'pretty good progress'?" A variation is to repeat his last few words and remain silent; this is an unspoken request for him to continue or to explain in different terms. Such questions often turn up unexpected bits of information. Salesmen should also be taught that the specific meanings they attach to words are not necessarily the same as those understood by the prospect.

Salesmen should learn not to interrupt the prospect. Interruption implies that the salesman is more interested in his own thoughts than in the prospect's and can't wait for his turn to speak. This blocking of the prospect's self-expression may easily frustrate and irritate him, and he may stop trying to communicate. To draw the prospect out, the sales interview should be a friendly give-and-take discussion in which the salesman's willingness to reveal his own attitudes often encourages the prospect to reveal his.

Projective questions. Some areas of information are difficult to probe because the prospect feels particularly sensitive about them or because he has no strong conscious opinion about the subject. In such cases, the use of a projective question may solicit a wealth of information. For example, if a salesman wants to know how the prospect feels about drinking alcoholic beverages during the working day, a direct question might produce an evasive answer. However, if the salesman asks, "How much alcohol does the average businessman drink during the working day?" the prospect has no way of knowing the true answer. In this case, he is most likely to project his own habits as the norm for the group, replying, "Oh, I don't know, but I suppose the average would be a couple of cocktails before lunch."

If the prospect is not aware of any hostility between himself and other executives in the company, he certainly could not tell the salesman about such pitfalls. But by asking a projective question the salesman may learn more than by asking a direct one. For example, the salesman may ask, "Do you think most comptrollers and most purchasing agents cooperate with the line department managers in getting them the products and services they request?" Since the prospect doesn't know what most comptrollers and most purchasing agents think, he is apt to project his own experience as the group norm. For example, he may reply, "Well, I think most of them really try to cooperate, but after all, a purchasing agent makes his reputation by saving money for the company, so I guess we shouldn't be surprised when he recommends a cheaper substitute product." This kind of information can be important to the salesman because it alerts him to a possible future problem as well as to the need to reinforce certain sales points with the prospect.

In teaching the skill of probing for information, the sales manager or trainer can provide a series of examples of each type of question as they might be related to his own company. However, there is no way to predict how a future conversation will go; hence, one cannot tell a salesman exactly what to say for all situations. He should understand why and how the techniques are useful and then practice using them until they become habitual and a professional skill.

EFFECTIVE LISTENING SKILLS

Traditional sales training has taught salesmen to dominate and lead a conversation. Experienced salesmen have operated this way for years and reinforced their learning to the point where it is now a conversational habit. Modern sales training is based on the new marketing concept and stresses customer orientation. The salesman is taught to investigate his prospect's needs before he makes his first sales call and to ask questions to learn of the customer's wants and attitudes. Clearly he should listen when the prospect attempts to communicate. Nevertheless, most salesmen are in fact poor listeners.

Real listening. The author tested a random group of 25 highly successful salesmen, each selling over one million dollars per year, and found they could not remember more than 30 percent of a 10-minute talk immediately after listening to it. Studies done elsewhere report similarly poor results. Two major factors tend to block true two-way conversation. First, the salesman typically does most of the talking, thus preventing the prospect from communicating. Second, in the limited time the prospect is permitted to talk, the salesman is quiet, but he is planning his next statements rather than truly listening. He literally does not know most of what the prospect says.

In a normal sales interview there is a considerable difference between the rate of the prospect's talk, which might be near 100 words per minute, and the salesman's rate of comprehension, which is normally in excess of 400 words per minute. The unskilled listener rarely operates at more than 25 percent efficiency because his mind wanders from the topic at hand during this spare time. On the other hand, the trained listener will use this time to think about the meaning of the message to which he is listening, to review the main points periodically. This mental exercise takes only a few seconds but it helps the salesman to organize and retain the main points of the prospect's message for a longer period of time.

A salesman's communication ability is greatly hindered when he is overly concerned with the reactions of prospects, with the impression he is trying to make, and with the fear of making a mistake. Salesmen should be taught to overcome their self-preoccupation. Listening is an active process, and salesmen should be taught to work at concentrating their attention on what the prospect is attempting to communicate. They should become emotionally involved with the prospect rather than remaining aloof from his message.

Empathy. Empathy is another prerequisite to effective listening. Salesmen are often reluctant to become sympathetic with a prospect for fear of being persuaded themselves, for example, that he really can't afford their products. Being empathetic, however, enables the salesman to understand a problem from the prospect's point of view. Salesmen can be taught to put themselves in the prospect's shoes, to feel his responsibilities, and to evaluate a proposition using his criteria without necessarily agreeing with him. For example, if the salesman learns by listening that the prospect has had a bad experience with a similar product, he can then reduce the prospect's natural fears. He may point out how the product is different or the application and situation are not the same as before. By listening with empathy the salesman gains a much clearer understanding of the prospect's communication. He can effectively reply to the underlying fear while the two-way communication channel is open.

Patience. Another technique particularly appropriate for salesmen is to be patient until the prospect has fully explained himself. Too often, salesmen are impatient to ask a question or rebut an argument or error in a prospect's conversation. The good listener is one who does not interrupt a prospect, even though he may disagree with what the man is saying. The prospect may answer a question in his next sentence or qualify a statement with phrases such as "generally speaking," "sometimes," or "as a rule." He may state something negative about a minor feature of a product and still be ready to place an order. If the salesman interrupts at this point, he may focus attention on a negative point and lose the order. Salesmen should be taught to listen patiently and politely—for their own good.

Concentration on ideas. One technique taught in most effective-listening courses is to concentrate on ideas rather than to try to remember all the facts. The salesman who has been taught to listen well will identify the theme of a message and regularly review the main points as they unfold. Statistics, facts, incidents, and so forth are usually unimportant, used only to illustrate the main points. A trained listener generally remembers more facts more accurately than a fact-picker does because while he concentrates on the prospect's logic in building a chain of important points, he will have ample time to review and to note interesting illustrations, as well as to get a feel for the level of language which the prospect prefers.

Finding a common language. The prospect is predisposed to certain ideas, attitudes, and beliefs, and the salesman must learn what they are before he can use language the buyer will understand. The salesman should become sympathetic in his listening and neutralize any feelings of hostility the buyer may have for yielding some of his precious time. By listening with interest and repeating back to the buyer to demonstrate uncritical understanding (giving supportive feedback, in psychological terms), the salesman proves he is listening attentively to the buyer and is a nice guy who seems to understand him. This helps to establish a close and sympathetic relationship, which is desirable in any two-way sales interview. By producing examples that support the buyer's point of view, the salesman can create a feeling of togetherness. The buyer will then be favorably disposed toward the salesman and be more apt to listen when the salesman talks because he will feel that the salesman must be a better, finer person to appreciate the buyer's viewpoints. When the prospect feels satisfied that he communicated, he will also feel obligated to return the salesman's compliment and at least listen to his story.

Nonverbal communication. The salesman should be taught to understand and use nonverbal communication. The truly interested salesman's heartbeat, blood pressure, and body temperature increase as he leans forward, physically straining to understand what the prospect is saying. He works at establishing and maintaining eye contact for reasonable periods. He indicates interest by posture, facial expressions, or a nod of his head. He knows that changes in the prospect's tone, volume, and pitch may have special meaning or emphasis, as may his facial expressions, gestures, and body movements. Therefore, a salesman who is seriously interested in becoming an effective listener will continually search for speech patterns and the ways in which each prospect habitually converses. In fact, he pays attention to everything the prospect says and does.

Remembering the customer's interests. While the buyer is talking, the salesman should try to identify problems which his products and services will solve. He should search for discrepancies between what is and what might be. Initially the salesman should search for areas in which the buyer wants to do better. Second, he should look for problem areas in which the buyer's present performance is unsatisfactory or areas in which his products will give the buyer greater satisfaction. The most efficient way to learn of these areas is not to talk but to listen. The salesman should be taught to become fully aware of what is actually said, what is unspoken but intended, and the direction of the buyer's thoughts. He should stay with the buyer's interests.

Sales managers can help the salesmen by sharing their experiences in effective-listening techniques. In addition, a number of good packages are available—including tape recordings and programmed workbooks—which will greatly improve recall of the spoken word. These programs require only three or four hours and can be given individually or to a large group. However, to develop the skill of effective listening takes a considerable amount of steady practice and a genuine desire to understand what message is being sent out by a prospect.

SENSITIVITY AND HUMAN RELATIONS

Vanity or self-conceit plays fantastic tricks with a salesman's memory. A private and objective self-appraisal can be both awakening and educational. Every salesman holds a mental picture of what he is like as a person with respect to such traits as honesty, industry, intelligence, and good humor. At the same time his prospects also hold a mental picture of what he is really like, and their image may include such traits as greed, avarice, laziness, and baseness. In fact, the salesman may have a small part of each of these traits at any given moment. As events occur to make the salesman and the observing prospect more friendly, both mental pictures may become modified, but rarely will they approach the cold truth. This elusive truth is what one seeks in attempting to learn of his own strengths and weaknesses so he may improve and become more nearly the ideal person he desires to be. Building honest self-esteem is a difficult but necessary process if one is to become an effective salesman.

Congruence. Congruence is a term used to indicate conformity between the experience of an emotion and the awareness that the emotion has been experienced. For the salesman, it should be extended to cover the communication of the emotion. For example, take the salesman who becomes so involved in a group discussion that his face flushes, his tone communicates anger, and he shakes his finger at his opponent. When a friendly salesman says, "Well, let's not get angry about this," the offending salesman replies, "I'm not angry! I don't care about this one way or the other. I was just pointing out the logical facts." Although he was clearly sincere, the other salesmen break out into laughter at this statement.

At a physiological level, the salesman is experiencing anger, but he is not consciously aware of this experience. In addition, his verbal communication, "I'm not angry!" is contrary to the nonverbal communication of his tone, flushed face, and shaking finger. There is a real incongruence between experience and awareness and between experience and communication. The salesman's communication is actually ambiguous. When a salesman is not aware of his feelings in a stress situation, it is very difficult, if not impossible, for him to communicate clearly.

Any verbal interaction between the salesman and the prospect is marked by some degree of congruence in the salesman. The greater the congruence of experience, awareness, and communication in the salesman, the more likely it is that the prospect will receive the salesman's message clearly. If all the cues from speech, tone, and gesture agree because they spring from a congruence in the salesman, then there is little likelihood that these cues will be misinterpreted by the prospect.

The salesman's predispositions. From his total life experience every salesman learns to expect certain treatment from people in certain situations and to behave in a certain manner. His attitudes, ideas, opinions, and beliefs combine to predispose him to like certain people and certain phases of his job and to dislike and possibly ignore other people and other job responsibilities. To become more effective, the salesman should study his own attitudes as they relate to people and to the various duties of the sales job.

The salesman will tend to visit the people he likes regularly. Because he will more easily perceive what they are trying to do, he is more apt to remember from call to call what was really said and will act accordingly. On the other hand, people who do not treat the salesman according to his self-image will tend to confuse him. He will not understand their motives and will have difficulty in remembering what was said or how the prospect reacted during the last interview.

A common responsibility of a salesman is to help customers solve problems. The salesman's attitude should favor helping others above or at least before helping himself. While there should be no conflict with such a noble attitude, many prospects and customers do not want the salesman's help in solving their problems. Attempting to help people under these conditions may be difficult and may cause a salesman with weak convictions to withdraw from the particular sale or even to leave the field. To be more effective, the salesman should learn to help his customers in ways which are acceptable to them. For example, in the highly competitive corrugated box industry, salesmen are taught to swallow their pride and go into a customer's warehouse or dirty plant and count the box inventory as a reorder service.

Arguing and bargaining are often part of the selling job, and both salesmen and buyers may consider this phase an enjoyable exercise in the ancient game of rhetoric or an annoying problem. Some customers will easily perceive a salesman's negative attitude toward bargaining, and they may react unfavorably. It is essential for the salesman to understand his customers' psychological needs in this area if he is to be effective with those who enjoy bargaining as well as with those who prefer a single, firm price quotation without further negotiating. Catering to a customer in this context is simply being sensitive to his needs and then exercising good human-relations skills.

Emotional maturity. To the customer, the salesman is the entire supplying company. Any errors or problems—for example, in product quality, shipping, or invoicing—are his direct responsibility, and he must take the blame. The salesman normally has little or no voice in such matters and is aware of errors only after they have led to problems which irritate his customers. An immature salesman may argue with his customer or avoid calling on him until the anger dies down. A mature salesman, on the other hand, willingly accepts full responsibility for every action of his company. He makes it his business to know every operation and policy in order to enlighten customers and to reduce or eliminate future errors.

On many occasions regular customers will tell the friendly salesman of their personal troubles involving an errant son or daughter or some serious health problem in the family, for example. While listening sympathetically, the salesman can learn to understand some of the causes of his customer's moods and apparent swings in emotion. In such situations the emotionally mature salesman is a strong person to lean on and is also discreet. Another common occurrence is for a customer to try out his ideas on a friendly salesman because he does not fear being ridiculed. These situations can be flattering to the salesman and harmless if he is aware of the nature of the relationship, but they can also distort his self-esteem if he lets the flattery blind him to his own weaknesses.

Developing interpersonal sensitivity. Salesmen typically need better theory than their commonsense notions about human behavior in order to understand interpersonal situations accurately. They can be taught to recognize the relationships between inner feelings and perceptions and outer events, and to choose among alternative courses of action. A salesman can be taught to have increased awareness of and sensitivity to emotional reactions and expressions in himself and in others. Without such awareness, the salesman's actions become incongruent with his conflicting emotions, which may be signaled to the prospect through nonverbal communications such as looking impatient or looking bored. In training, emphasis is placed on the salesman's development of sensitivity to cues furnished by the behavior of others and the ability to utilize this feedback in understanding his own behavior.

For example, suppose that a prospect says, "I think I'll shop around a while before deciding," and also that the salesman observed a look of adoration when the prospect viewed the product. The sensitive salesman would be aware that the prospect was mentally experiencing owning the product and that his communication was incongruent. This would indicate reassuring the prospect that it was a good competitive offer and reinforcing the idea that there was no need to deny oneself any longer.

Whenever a salesman talks to a prospect, he will unintentionally express something about his own attitudes. Since the buyer's confidence in the salesman is paramount in any persuasion attempt, the salesman should be completely honest and sincere. Once the salesman is aware of his faults he can attempt to correct them. If he cannot change, he is at least aware of these weaknesses and can avoid situations which will expose them. A sensitive salesman will remain on guard to control whatever self-defeating traits he may have—greed, feelings of superiority, and boastfulness, for example.

Training methods to increase sensitivity and improve human relations often take the form of role playing and reverse role playing. Often audio tape recordings are made to play back and critique afterwards. Video tape recordings used in the same manner provide the opportunity to observe nonverbal communications, which may or may not agree with the spoken messages.

BUYING INFLUENTIALS IN THE CUSTOMER'S COMPANY

When a salesman enters a new territory he is usually given some account cards which list previous calls on a few specific people, such as the purchasing agent, the office manager, and possibly the comptroller. The salesman will usually locate additional accounts in his territory with little or no background information. Because of normal turnover, even complete historical records become obsolete rather quickly. An essential skill for most sales jobs is the ability to determine who makes the buying decision, who else may influence the buying decision, and to what degree the various influences affect the ultimate action.

In a simple consumer purchase of a color television set, for example, the father may set a dollar limit and the mother may determine the size and style of furniture. The children may indicate a strong preference for a brand which their friends have. Neighbors may relate their good and bad experiences with various brands. The television repairman, who may have advised buying a new set instead of having costly repairs made on the old set, may strongly indicate a brand preference from the standpoint of his future business. The salesman in the store may talk glowingly about a particular brand for which he receives an extra bonus for selling that week. Each of these influences is superimposed on the predispositions of the individual members of the family. Their past experiences will color or distort what they understand from each of the influentials to whom they are exposed. In addition to the effect of all these personal influentials are such nonpersonal influences as advertising, store promotions, the convenience of the store, and the economic value in relation to their financial ability.

In a business situation the personal buying influentials seem to become even more confusing. A receptionist may be influential in determining which salesmen get in to see the buyer. A department head may have need but not authority to place an order, so he is limited to placing a requisition with someone else. Another department manager may argue for or against a given proposition even though he has no personal or business interest in the purchase. A comptroller or treasurer may determine the priority of expenditures. Staff specialists, such as systems men, methods experts, and standardization committees, may exert some influence. Outside experts, such as a certified public accountant or an interior decorator, may voice an opinion of the product offered.

Studies have shown that in perhaps nine out of ten cases the initial purchase request comes from middle management. Users of the product initiate the request in one out of ten cases. Similarly, naming a supplier pool would appear to be a logical function of the purchasing department, with its bank of specialized knowledge;

however, studies show that in three out of four cases it is middle management who names the supplier pool. The rest of such decisions are handled by the purchasing department, and top management rarely takes any part.

Each sales manager should be able to identify by job title the many people who can influence a buying decision in his industry. A list of 20 to 30 internal buying influentials whose preferences may lead to the selection of a new supplier would not be unusual (see the list below). Besides the static relationship of the buying influentials at any given instant in time, it is necessary to consider the interaction of these people at different times and the considerable changes in which person wields the power. These influentials also change because of new experiences; they age; they get promoted or assume new functions; they retire; and company goals and directions alter their attitudes. This dynamic situation provides an on-going challenge which a salesman can be taught to deal with and handle in his stride.

Salesmen should be taught to recognize and cultivate friendships with every buying influential. Each of these people has an opinion

---

SOME INTERNAL BUYING INFLUENTIALS

The user—the person for whom the product is actually procured.

The specifier—the one who states the requirements of the product or service.

The constrainer—the one who limits the amount that can be spent or ranks priorities.

The information supplier—the one who gathers relevant data for others.

The screener—the one who determines which information or informants shall get through to any of the other influentials.

The kibitzers—people who volunteer unsolicited opinions.

The voters—the people who are officially permitted to participate in the decision making.

The vetoer—the one who has the power to override the decisions of others.

The buyer—the person who actually places the order.

---

of the importance of his own job and a self-image which he would like to have recognized by others. The salesman can be taught to treat the influentials as they would like to be treated. He should attempt to demonstrate recognition of their individual importance by listening attentively to whatever they might say and to encourage their development of sound opinions favorable to his cause. They all have predispositions which influence their opinion of others, as well as an organizational role which they attempt to play. By seeking out these buying influentials and by cultivating their friendship, the salesman can discover their ideas and attitudes that are relevant to his proposition.

Every job from office boy to the president of a company is important and interrelated with all other jobs. Production, engineering, sales, service, accounting, administration, and line or staff functions are vital to the smooth operation of any business. Therefore, while the salesman's message to each buying influential should be geared to his individual predispositions, at the same time, the various messages should be compatible with each other in the very likely event that the buying influentials get together and compare notes. Each buying influential should recognize the salesman as a truly friendly authority in his field who is there to help him and his company succeed.

The ability to recognize and cultivate buying influentials is easily taught and often pays immediate returns in exciting a sales force and gaining new orders. New salesmen quickly recognize its value, and cynical old-timers often get enthusiastically involved. Without going into teaching methodology at this point, suffice it to say that a classroom lecture and guided discussion are frequently all that are needed to begin the development of this skill.

CREATIVE THINKING

Creativity is not new to selling, but its potential has been hardly scratched. More and more companies are holding brainstorming sessions in their sales training programs, and creativity is fast becoming a mark of the professional salesman.

Contrary to popular belief, every normal person has a considerable amount of latent creative talent. The creative process is the constructive exercise of one's imaginative powers to develop a new idea. In a selling situation, imagination can help the salesman to visualize new applications and new target segments for his product, improved product features to give his customers greater utilization or satisfaction, new solutions to his customers' problems, and so forth. While the sales manager or trainer cannot be expected to teach creativity, he can certainly encourage the regular use of creativity to further its development in every salesman.

Relatively few salesmen use their imagination to the extent to which they might. Many either feel they do not have an imaginative mind or do not recognize how situations could benefit if imagination were applied to them. To be creative, a person must be able to look at a situation without the normal constraints. For example, when told to connect four dots on a piece of paper, the less imaginative person will probably draw a square. Another person, using his imagination, may draw a circle with the dots on the circumference, or even some more elaborate figure, of an animal, for example.

Brainstorming. The manager who is interested in developing his salesmen's creativity encourages his men to dream up as many imaginative ideas as they can without exercising value judgments. For example, the marketing manager of a manufacturer of boxes held a brainstorming sales meeting in which he asked the salesmen for possible uses of their product. His only rule was that there would be no criticism or judgment of anyone's suggestion. The first 20 or 30 suggestions concerned novel uses of boxes, but then someone suggested that the material be used as flooring and wall covering. Someone else suggested that the material be used for point-of-purchase three-dimensional displays. A third salesman suggested that it be compressed into fireplace logs, while a fourth suggested adding a plastic coating to that it could be used in making livingroom furniture. Within the hour allotted for the session, several hundred creative ideas were put forth by the salesmen.

Brainstorming sessions do not have to be limited to a few strange characters on Madison Avenue. When the rule-book and constraints are thrown away, salesmen can use their minds as imaginatively as any other group of people. The group process tends to release inhibitions, and almost every salesman gets caught up in the creative spirit. Many an idea suggested in jest at such a session has turned into a multi-million-dollar market. Indeed, the industry created by the point-of-sale display idea noted above is now estimated to gross two billion dollars per year.

The alcoholic beverage industry, using similar methods, has identified target segments of the market which were poorly served or neglected in the past. Market research showed that Mexican Americans prefer a lime taste in their beer, while young Americans prefer a sweet fruit taste to their malt beverages. The modern marketing concept is based on serving the customer's need, and creativity in market research is turning up many new opportunities for making profits.

Using creativity in the sales situation does not mean developing something new under the sun; rather it means identifying an idea or process which is new to the salesman's industry. For example, a teaser campaign to introduce a new product might be appropriate in an industry that had not used this technique in twenty years or more. A series of announcements or interesting pieces of mail might very well stimulate the prospect to look forward to the new product. But competition is quick to imitate success, and novel ideas rapidly become boring. Therefore, the sales organization which encourages creative thinking is more likely to build a series of novel campaigns to stay well ahead of the traditional followers in an industry.

In a similar manner salesmen can be encouraged to use a creative approach to developing prospect lists, handling various phases of a sales presentation, and solving customer problems. The collective input of all the salesmen without critical evaluation will often include hundreds of ideas which can help every salesman.

Subconscious creativity. Much of a person's thinking occurs in the twilight zone just below the conscious level. In this area the artificial restrictions and constraints do not operate very well, and the mind is free to associate thoughts that it otherwise might keep separate. Consequently many people have found it practical to "forget" about a problem for a while or to "sleep on it" before making a decision. Often they will hit upon a unique idea or solution when their minds are consciously on another topic. A chance remark by a friend may trigger the solution to a problem which had been put on the back burner to simmer a while. Many people go through life without thinking about the creative process, while others intentionally utilize this power of the subconscious mind.

Whether the use of creative thinking is encouraged by direct methods such as brainstorming or by indirect or delayed methods such as presenting a problem one day and asking for ideas a week later, the salesmen should be praised for all contributions. Of course, when a salesman uses a creative idea on the job and has success, this should be well publicized and praised in order to reinforce the use of the creative process. In other words, the creative effort should always be rewarded and never judged on the basis of its practical or commercial applications. Out of several hundred creative suggestions made, someone will decide which few are worth pursuing. Decision making is a different skill and should not be confused with the creative process.

DECISION MAKING

Because of the enormous complexity of many sales situations, complete information is rarely, if ever, available when a salesman must make decisions. Many salesmen are willing to decide on a course of action with very limited factual data because they are confident of their ability to adapt as a situation evolves. A few others are paralyzed and cannot take any effective action when faced with two or more equally good or bad alternative courses. In any case, salesmen are continually faced with making decisions and they are rarely given any training to develop this process into an effective skill.

In some situations, the sales manager removes the opportunity to make decisions (and to make mistakes) by telling the salesman where he must go, in what sequence he should make his calls, what he is to say on each call, and so forth. Many salesmen are not permitted to quote prices or delivery dates until either the manager or a service unit calculates and decides what should be done. This process may be essential in some cases; however, it does little or nothing to help the salesman improve himself.

At the other extreme are the sales managers who give a salesman a territory and instruct him to manage his own time and accounts to the best of his ability. They usually offer assistance to each salesman whenever and however he wants it, but the implicit message is for him to stand on his own feet. In this sense they are at least permitting a salesman to learn by trial and error. The manager's reward or punishment can help or hinder the learning process, but at best this is a tedious way to learn decision making.

Linear system. Decision making can be taught with various degrees of sophistication, and obviously the techniques and concepts should match the job requirements. A linear system may be appropriate for a young salesman who needs close supervision. In such a system, the salesman knows that when A occurs, he should do No. 16 in the sales manual. When B occurs, he should do No. 21 in the manual. When an account is classified AAA, he should call an average of once each week. The salesman is expected to classify each account according to prescribed rules and to review the classification of every account every six months, for example. Each decision is based on specific criteria, and the salesman is taught to recognize when a situation calls for a particular limited response and to take that action.

Closed-circuit system. More common perhaps is the closed-circuit system, in which a number of possibilities may occur, all of which are prescribed, and the salesman is directed to specific action patterns. For example, an experienced salesman may be permitted to negotiate sales contracts up to a preset limit, fulfilling quantity and price conditions. However, he must clear with the sales manager any purchase that either exceeds the maximum amount or varies at all from the established conditions. The salesman's discretion may be allowed in making delivery promises, accepting returns, or granting allowances for damaged merchandise, for example, but all such decisions must be made within fixed and predetermined criteria.

Open-circuit system. Senior salesmen and national-account salesmen are often permitted to operate under an open-circuit system. This involves a decision-making process in a state of continual adjustment. The salesman is given a number of guidelines but is permitted to disregard them when he feels the situation requires some exceptional action. Unpredictable events may occur for which there are no guidelines, and the salesmen is expected to decide on the spot what course of action to take. His decisions may legally commit his company to many obligations. While this may seem dangerous, it is often essential because the salesman on the spot may be the most knowledgeable man in his company and, therefore, the only person qualified to make an intelligent decision. Such power is normally granted only after the salesman has earned the highest respect of top management.

Depending on the type of sales job and the amount of discretion involved, various decision-making theories can be taught to the salesmen. The framework and conditions under which a decision is to be made may involve certainty, expected value, conditional value, or risk with uncertainty. For example, if the selling company does not match the competitor's bid, it will certainly lose the account. If the company matches the competitor's bid, it will probably scare him off and keep the account for years. If the company can meet the customer's delivery schedule over the next three months, it will earn a high place on his preferred supplier list. The bid price might depend on which competitors bid and on who makes the ultimate decision as to which of the various options will be required.

An analytical or scientific approach to decision making may be appropriate in some situations. In general the steps to a decision would include the following:

- Observe the situation.
- Identify and define the problem.
- Formulate the hypothesis.
- Experiment (solve model, test solution, develop controls and limitations of the model).

For many sales decisions the following format might be more appropriate:

- Define the problem.
- Gather the facts.
- Analyze the facts.
- List the alternatives.
- Select the best alternative.

Because of the many areas of uncertainty in complex sales situations, the cybernetic decision-making process may steadily improve the quality of the decisions. Cybernetic in this context is used to mean self-regulating and recycling. The steps in this process are:

1. In relation to specific company goals, identify and define the specific problem and establish the limits within which action will be considered.

2. Before taking any action, identify the information necessary to make the decision and the cost of obtaining that information.

3. Before obtaining the necessary information, develop alternatives of action by assuming the range of results.

4. Gather the data necessary at the level of confidence desired.

5. Project the short- and long-term consequences of each alternative.

6. Make a tentative choice based on company objectives, but recycle the entire process as new information, new personalities, or new situations demand.

These few examples are intended to illustrate the range of possibilities available to the sales trainer. The content of any program, obviously, should be tailored to fit the situation and the needs of the sales force. There are many excellent texts, some didactic games, and a few films which enable the instructor to translate a general theory into a practice which will be appropriate to his real situation. Of course, a knowledgeable trainer or sales manager must recommend such a program before a company can be expected to fund it. When appropriate, however, training in this skill can pay dividends far in excess of the development costs.

SUMMARY

Given the fact that a salesman who tries harder than his competitors will probably succeed more often than they will, the manager should isolate the factors that otherwise make the difference among salesmen. Often this difference is traceable to certain skills. If those skills can be developed through training and positive reinforcement on the job, then it would seem wise to spend considerable time and effort to do so.

In sales training, often the largest improvements in the performance of the sales force come as a result of developing a particular skill. Early tangible evidence of the positive value of training is, of course, highly desirable. In fact, however, skill training usually produces long-term benefits to the sponsoring company and to the salesmen themselves. A man who learns to swim can immediately enjoy doing things which a nonswimmer would be afraid to attempt.

If the man continues to practice regularly, he will be a good swimmer the rest of his life. Similarly, learning a professional selling skill will make an immediate and permanent positive change in the behavior of a salesman.

Many activities in life put a high premium on the ability to communicate effectively. In addition, the skill of persuasion used in positive ways can remove obstacles and build team spirit and cooperation in most group endeavors. It is difficult to imagine any salesman who could not benefit by perfecting these skills. This does not mean, however, that every company should train every salesman to develop these skills. Clearly such training takes a great deal of time and effort and brings no guarantee of immediate results for the manager and his company. Other areas of training may demand precedence, and a high turnover, for example, may indicate that extensive training will be transferred to another company. The sales manager and trainer should analyze the needs of each salesman and relate the cost of the training effort to the probable results. Perhaps some of the salesmen would benefit immediately and easily justify the effort, while others might be taught different skills or simple selling techniques.

The same logic is appropriate to the other skills discussed above: They are not necessarily universally applicable. On the other hand, it is a rare salesman, regardless of his experience, who is skillful in every area discussed. Any salesman who wants to improve himself should be given the opportunity and the encouragement to do so. Clearly a salesman's training should not end with his mastering the company training manual.

SELECTED MATERIALS

Critical Path. Chicago: International Film Bureau. 16 mm, C.

    Shows ways to facilitate work planning and control.

Effective Listening. New York: Xerox Corporation, Educational Division.

    This two-part audio tape lesson with student workbooks and an instructor's guide can be used to train individuals or groups. Each part takes approximately 90 minutes.

Film Guide for Sales and Marketing Executives. No. 133. New York: Sales and Marketing Executives International, 1972.

> *SMEI also distributes the records, audio cassettes, and books on salesmanship and sales management listed in its monthly magazine,* Marketing Times. *These include aids in building skills such as listening, speaking, writing, influencing human behavior, and creative thinking.*

The Gellerman Motivation & Productivity Film Series. Rockville, Md.: Bureau of National Affairs Films.

> *Gellerman, Argyris, McClelland, Likert, Herzberg, and other top behavioral scientists, in "meet the expert" style, discuss and illustrate current theory and practice.*

Kepner, Charles H., and Tregoe, Benjamin B., *The Rational Manager: A Systematic Approach to Problem Solving and Decision Making.* New York: McGraw-Hill Book Company, 1965.

> *This subject is best taught in the Kepner-Tregoe seminars conducted by licensed and franchised instructors.*

McGraw-Hill Films Catalog. New York: McGraw-Hill Book Company.

> *This free catalog lists various training films for business and industry.*

Morrisey, George L., *Effective Business and Technical Presentations.* Reading, Mass.: Addison-Wesley, 1968.

The National Managerial Tests. Beverly Hills, Calif.: Roundtable Films. 16 mm, C.

> *This film tests principles and techniques of influencing human behavior in business.*

Nichols, Ralph B., *The Complete Course in Listening.* New York: Dun & Bradstreet, Manager Development Division.

> *An audio tape series with workbooks by one of the outstanding authorities in this field.*

Olympic Training Film Digest. New York: Olympic Film Services.

> *This monthly publication is available to subscribers. Olympic Training Film Profiles, another subscriber service, reviews training films and assists in locating films of appropriate content and level of sophistication.*

Some categories are creativity, decision making, letter writing, listening, motivation, and personal enrichment.

Superscope Library of the Spoken Word. Sun Valley, Calif.: Superscope, Inc.

Series of audio cassettes are available on many topics. Of particular interest is the psychology series, which includes lectures by Abraham Maslow and George Bach.

CHAPTER 5

Essential Knowledge
for Successful Selling

MOST INITIAL SALES training is designed to get the newly hired salesman into the field as rapidly as conditions will permit. Obviously,
product knowledge becomes primary in these situations, and traditional sales training centers around the product and the sales proposition. This includes the product and its features, the normal accessories and services, the entire sales agreement, the extra customer
services designed for the selected target market, and knowledge of
the manufacturer or supplier as well as the market and competitive
offerings. A salesman can never know too much about his industry,
his company, and his entire sales proposition (although he can use
too much information when attempting to sell some prospects).

After his initial training, a junior salesman should know how
to study his territory and identify likely prospects. He should
know what to do when he is about to face recurring problems such
as getting past a receptionist or handling a particular competitive attack. The well-trained salesman should know the various purposes
of a sales call other than routine order processing. He should also
know at least the titles of the many buying influentials he can contact within a single account and how to adapt his sales message to
suit the various people he may visit.

The primary reason for the salesman to understand and know
the entire sales proposition is simply to be able to communicate
with the prospect. If the salesman knows all the facts, he can make

an adequate presentation in language easily understood by each individual buyer, adapting the message to each prospect's specific needs or problems. Positive statements can be made instead of meaningless generalizations. The well-trained salesman can give accurate answers to questions, understanding and fully satisfying the prospect's objections. From a thorough knowledge of his proposition, the salesman will gain the self-confidence necessary for him to look and act the part of a friendly authority. Finally, a well-trained salesman in the new marketing concept can act as an intelligence agent for his company, bringing back marketing information to improve the product, services, or market position.

Sales managers and trainers can predetermine the minimum amount of knowledge which a trainee should possess before he is permitted into a sales territory. They can test the trainee's knowledge (with or without aids such as a sales catalog) within a specified time limit.

Those in charge of this initial sales training should be wary of a common pitfall in teaching and testing product knowledge: the use of stock numbers or technical terminology. One does not use Chinese to communicate with an American who understands only English. A father does not use polysyllabic words when teaching his four-year-old son to ride a bicycle. A technician, scientist, or engineer uses simplified models and examples to illustrate his theories and designs when asking nontechnical men for their financial backing. Similarly, a salesman who knows his industry, his company, his product, his proposition, and his customer does not use technical language. An accounting desk may be known to the salesman as a No. 4042, but to the prospect the stock number by itself means absolutely nothing, and the title, "accounting desk," does not communicate much more. The well-trained salesman will be able to paint a word picture so descriptive that his prospect will easily visualize the desk in operation in his own office.

PROSPECTING AND REVERSE-ORDER PROSPECTING

A problem common to many salesmen is deciding where to go on a particular day to talk to someone who is interested in their products.

Finding prospects, judging their interest, and getting in touch with the right person often seem to be more than half the sales effort.

The importance of knowing where the market is located for a particular product or service cannot be overstressed. If management does not identify groups of customer targets, then the salesman should be taught to do so. He should also be taught how to identify buying influentials within prospect companies, to minimize wasted time and increase his selling effectiveness.

Finding and Qualifying Prospects

Most selling companies have lists of customers who buy over and over again, as well as of those who once purchased some merchandise or service but did not stay active and of noncustomers whom they would like to serve. These lists are very often incomplete and out of date because of the constant movement of companies and of personnel within them. The local post office can provide a list-checking service that will help keep a mailing list up to date.

Outside of the company records there are numerous sources of prospect names. Mailing lists are prepared by name brokers and can be as broad or narrow as desired. Lists are available, for example, of auto registrations by make, college graduates, doctors, nurses, dentists, and voter registrations by precinct. Names can be obtained from published business directories such as Moody's, Standard and Poor's and Dun & Bradstreet's. Often trade journals and magazines will sell their mailing lists of names, titles, and addresses. Since there are literally thousands of such publications, each designed to appeal to a specific group, an appropriate list probably exists for most products imaginable. The U.S. Department of Commerce and many state departments of commerce provide a wealth of information simply for the asking. When the names of prospects are grouped geographically, as by ZIP code, the salesman can increase his daily number of calls by as many as two or three times the average because little travel time is wasted between calls.

If the prospects are in a mercantile endeavor, Dun & Bradstreet will probably have complete listings of them by city, county, or township, showing the company size, line of business, sales volume, principals and their titles, and other useful information. Prospecting by the Standard Industrial Classification (SIC) code number can be very useful in many selling situations. Each line of business has a separate number, and related businesses have similar numbers, so that a clerk can leaf through such a directory and pick out only those names which apply.

For most sales organizations, the next step to teach salesmen is qualifying prospects. The criteria will depend on the industry and the sales manager's experience, but some typical measures are the amount of annual sales of the prospect and the number of his employees. Three basic questions should be asked about each name on the list: First, does the person or company have need for the product or service? Second, does the prospect have the ability to finance such a purchase? Finally, is he willing to purchase, assuming the benefits can be demonstrated?

By asking these three questions, a salesman should be able to group or rank his prospects. For example, some names on his list may have an obvious need for his product and may have an excellent financial rating, while others might require some probing to discover their needs and might be marginal financially. Some prospects may be in a growing industry where people are willing to spend money now to gain the benefits of his products, while others may be in an industry which is depressed and may feel more secure saving their money or credit line and doing without the needed products.

In some industries, salesmen are taught to contact existing customers to obtain the names of their friends who might also be interested in the sales proposition. Often a new customer is enthusiastic about his purchase and communicates his genuine interest to others. The telephone and direct mail can often be used to make inquiries about distant and inactive accounts. The many ways of developing and qualifying new prospects may not be obvious to the new salesman. He should be taught several methods of prospecting to help him make additional legitimate appointments.

Reverse-Order Prospecting

Almost everyone knows some "lucky" salesmen. They make fewer calls than average but sell more; they talk to a prospect about a small order and suddenly get a big order. However, the very fact that this happens again and again should make one suspicious of their so-called luck.

Many methodical salesmen apply the law of averages and use sheer numbers to offset their poor luck: they make 100 calls in the expectation of finding ten prospects and ultimately getting one order. The "lucky" salesman makes 20 calls, develops ten or more prospects, and closes five to ten orders. Sales managers constantly urge their salesmen to make more calls each day to find that small percentage of the market that needs their product. But in private, sales managers admit that they would love to hire a dozen more "lucky" salesmen to replace all the plodders they now employ.

The "lucky" salesman makes fewer calls because he does a lot of brainwork before he attempts the legwork. First he will do some general research on the customers' industry. Then, given a list of 100 names, the trained salesman will analyze their possibilities for a legitimate use of his product and will further check out a number of the companies. Narrowing the list down to 20, he then ranks them as to probability and approaches the prospects in *reverse order*. Starting with the smallest buyer in terms of potential order, the trained salesman will use his first call as a dry run to test his theory of approach and sales presentation. In the process, he learns the common objections, the normal applications, and the points the buyer considers of interest. After this call, the salesman revises his approach and presentation and then calls on the nineteenth company on his list, learning still more. Long before he calls on the company ranked tenth, he will have developed a more thorough knowledge of the situation than all his "unlucky" competitors. Within his narrow specialty he will even be more knowledgeable than many of the buyers he will contact.

The trained salesman thus becomes an expert in his field, well versed in the legitimate applications of his product and the valid objections to it. Depending on how quickly he perceives the important points and adjusts his selling techniques, some of the companies numbered 20 to 11 on his list will become prospects. In his calls on the top ten companies, he will have the necessary confidence that comes with knowledge, and his closing average will increase dramatically. By the time he reaches the company with the largest potential, he is confident of his approach under various conditions and will have learned much about this particular buyer. To gain selective exposure, he will appeal to the area in which the buyer is known to be most interested. He will often be able to incorporate the details of a recent sale into his final presentation.

Compare this reverse-order prospecting technique with that of the "unlucky," methodical salesman who rushes out to make 100 quick calls, looking for the ten who may be interested in his story. Even if his stamina holds out, his discouragement at being told no by 90 intelligent business people will be hard to hide. Should he find the interested few, this salesman still cannot compare with the man who has expert knowledge of applications, objections, and methods of presentation. One need not wonder why the trained man is successful and the other is not.

PREAPPROACH PLANNING

Preapproach planning is designed to eliminate the "cold" call, the one that lacks human warmth and reveals little knowledge of the prospect's needs. If the salesman reveals that he has not looked into a particular prospect's situation or taken any trouble to dig for facts and analyze them, the prospect naturally feels he is simply another statistic to the salesman, who honestly couldn't care less which company is served, as long as someone gives him an order that day.

As we have said, it is normal for a man to fear strangers. Many people have been conditioned not to trust salesmen and will set up some form of defense against them. People are naturally skeptical about a new salesman or an unfamiliar company, or about any new or unknown product, particularly if some claims seem exaggerated or if its quality or value is impossible to measure. If a large expenditure is involved, people tend to vacillate between spending and not spending and to worry about what is the right thing to do. In addition, they may be irritated at being disturbed or taken away from other activities, particularly if the salesman has used subterfuge to gain admittance.

Because of these barriers to his first sales call on a prospect, the salesman must learn to plan his initial interview very carefully. First, he must direct his attention to the specific customer targets on which his company has decided to focus. Most often a company will pick its target market on the basis of its special ability to serve a customer need better than its competitors. This advantage may be due to the location of its plants, its unique type of production, its product features, distribution channels, market outlets, strength in promotion, or the area of excellence of its personnel. Since each company, even in the same field, is slightly different each will have a different view of its customer targets. The trained salesman knows his customer targets and why his company is in an advantageous position to serve them.

Prospective customers normally have many doubts, and salesmen should be taught the history of their company in order to be able to answer such unspoken questions as:

- Is the concern reliable?
- Is the concern physically and financially able to handle my orders?
- Is the concern really interested in my type of small (or large) order?
- Will my competitors buy at the same price?
- Will delivery be prompt?
- Will this concern be around in a few years when I need replacement parts?
- Is the company known to provide extra services?
- Will it make good on complaints?

These and other unspoken doubts, if left unanswered, will tend to detract from any sales message and hinder or possibly prevent persuasion. If the firm is catering to a highly select market that demands a great deal of free service, then the price of the product must cover these extra costs. Attempting to sell the product in an area where buyers are primarily concerned with a low purchase price would probably prove very frustrating.

To decide what is best for a prospect, salesmen must know what he will do with the product. They should be taught to find out who will use the product, how it will be used, and how long it will be used. The selling price is rarely the total cost of a product; other factors may include delivery charges, installation costs, the normal cost of operating or using the product, and the cost of cleaning or repairing the product over its useful life. For some products, the cost of time lost when the product is waiting for service, its trade-in value, the cost of storage when it is not in use, and possibly the cost of space required for its optimum use are also relevant. A careful analysis of what a prospect expects is necessary to determine which similar products really offer the benefits that are important to the particular prospect.

As has been mentioned, the salesman should be taught to identify the various buying influentials, the executives within a prospect company who will be in charge of various phases of acquiring and using a product. Often old customers in the same industry can supply much of this information. The prospect's house organs may also provide current information, and a few well-planned telephone calls can usually clear up confusing job titles and duties.

Salesmen can be trained to have a good understanding of the general business conditions in their industry and how national economic and social developments affect it. They can be informed about population growth, location, and movement and trends in income for target segments of the population. Government action affects most industries through direct intervention and other controls. In addition, government spending and financing often have an indirect effect to which salesmen should be sensitive and which they can apply in their daily selling activities.

A well-trained salesman, with knowledge of his market, his target prospect, and his own company and its products, is not apt to make a cold call. He is in a position to gear his approach to a specific person with a definite and constructive purpose. A carefully planned approach brings a salesman much greater success than a trial-and-error approach.

APPROACH AND INITIAL-BENEFIT STATEMENTS

The salesman should be taught to analyze the purpose of his initial interview with each individual prospect before he attempts to see the prospect. What degree of conviction does the salesman hope to achieve on this particular call? In some lines of business the salesman wants to close a sale on the first call, so that he will want to know only what will move people who are already predisposed toward his product to take action and buy. However, many initial sales interviews cannot realistically be expected to result in an order. Instead, the salesman's first visit normally has other purposes, and the salesman should be taught at least nine general areas to consider before attempting to approach a particular prospect for an interview. For each area, the salesman should learn to make an appropriate initial-benefit statement, offering the prospect a benefit for granting some of his precious time. The benefit should be at least equal in value to the interview time requested.

Obtain information. One purpose of an interview, other than to cause immediate buying action, is to obtain information. Specific areas of interest might include how the prospect uses a product or substitute products, how he feels about quality and price generally, and what competitors are active in the account. When planning an interview to obtain information, the salesman should search for areas of similarity between himself and the prospect which he can later develop in getting to know and understand the prospect personally. In his initial-benefit statement, the salesman might ask for a ten-minute appointment to see if there are ways in which he can save the prospect processing costs, reduce waste, speed up production, or otherwise make the improvements his product can provide. He plans his initial contact with a number of probing techniques in mind and he plans to build friendly mutual respect between himself and the prospect.

Discover the prospect's problems. A second purpose of a specific call is to discover problems which a prospect may have by scouting the area and encouraging the prospect to discuss his business. Often such a visit includes a tour of the prospect's office and physical plant. Thoughtful silence on the part of the salesman indicates that he is really studying the total operation. Should he observe an apparently wasteful or poor method of operation, he might ask why the prospect does it that way, but whatever answer the prospect provides, the salesman remains uncritical. For example, he might say, "Yes, now I understand. That's interesting." This professional attitude will make it possible at a later date to bring up the same point with precise facts, figures, and interesting illustrations. He plans his first call with an initial-benefit statement such as, "Mr. Johnston, I don't know if we can serve your company or not, so rather than waste your time,

I wonder if I could visit your plant first. If I see something that is clearly worth your investigation, I'll call for a personal appointment." Prospects are often flattered by such an unexpected contact and willingly arrange the inspection visit.

Develop the prospect's awareness of his needs. Often customer needs or problems are obvious to the expert salesman, but they are unnoticed by the prospect, and a third purpose of many sales calls is to develop the prospect's awareness of these needs. New equipment and techniques are constantly being introduced which can materially affect the profits of a customer. Small companies grow, and their needs change as their size changes. Pressing operating problems often prevent management from stepping back and reevaluating their systems and methods of operation. The salesman, as an authority in his field, can advise the prospect on the latest developments in his area.

If the purpose of the visit is to develop awareness in the prospect's mind, the planned discussion should center around his opinion of events and how they relate to the current situation. The interview is intended to bring out some of the salient points regarding new circumstances, with some indication of the disadvantages of continuing in the old manner. This type of sales interview is often referred to as seed planting, that is, planting in the prospect's mind the germ of an idea that will gradually grow and ultimately lead to a sale. The initial benefit offered might be to discuss some new trends in the customer's industry or new uses for certain products which his competitors may have attempted.

Offer a service. A fourth purpose for a specific interview is to offer the customer a legitimate service, such as a free survey or study of his operation, his inventory situation, or his financial needs. It might be an offer to help construct effective advertising, to promote store traffic, or to control stock. Clearly, no attempt to sell should be made during this type of interview because there is not sufficient data on which to base an intelligent decision. The initial benefit offered is a free audit of some operation to reassure the prospect that everything is in order or to point out where things might be better.

Submit recommendations. A fifth purpose of a sales interview is to submit recommendations. Many products can be legitimately offered on a regular and routine basis, such as specialty papers to printers and publishers. Since groups of customers in the same line of business, for example, often have common problems and seek solutions to fit their particular needs, the salesman can often learn of new methods and procedures from one customer and pass this information on to his other customers and prospects. Whenever the salesman can suggest improvement, he serves a legitimate function for the buyer and is a welcome visitor.

Provide nonsales information. A sixth purpose of an interview is to provide nonsales information. An effective salesman builds his image as a friendly authority whenever he can with his prospects and customers and takes an interest in their problems even when his products are not directly involved. Customers have occasional requirements which are not easily met, and the service-oriented salesman is quick to find facts and do preliminary research to help them. Articles in trade journals, newspapers, and magazines may be of interest to certain customers, who appreciate the salesman's interest and personal attention to their needs.

Offer a free trial. Many products are difficult to evaluate before they are used in a real work situation, so a seventh purpose of a sales call is to offer a free trial use of the product. While this is very similar to direct selling, the emphasis here is to convince a prospect not to buy but merely to try. A salesman need not be as talkative or dominant when he is honestly willing to let the product speak for itself.

Handle a complaint. An eighth and less obvious purpose of a sales interview is to handle a customer complaint. Salesmen should be taught to visit a complaining customer quickly to clear up any misunderstanding or correct a bad situation. Once the salesman shows sincere interest in correcting whatever seems wrong, the buyer is inclined to like the salesman. Effectively handled, this situation often provides the opportunity to sell additional products, either then or at some future date.

Cultivate the friendship of buying influentials. A ninth purpose for a sales call is to discover and observe the influence of other buying influentials, from secretaries to top executives, and to cultivate their business friendship. This is commonly done during a coffee break or at a business lunch. Since the business friends of an executive may have some influence over his ultimate buying decisions, it is often well worth the salesman's time to get to know these other people.

PRESENTATION AND CUSTOMER INVOLVEMENT

Normally, a good sales opening refers directly to the benefits that will accrue to the buyer or to an area that has been a problem for him, showing the prospect at the outset that the salesman is thinking primarily of him. Similarly, the salesman should indicate that he has studied the prospect's needs and is qualified to discuss them from an informed point of view. The prospect is much more likely to listen to and trust a salesman who has studied his individual needs than one who spouts generalizations that he suspects are canned or stereotyped. A trained salesman, knowing the purpose of the interview, the buying influence of the person to be contacted, the initial objectives to be obtained, and the various approaches which he may use, will thus design his presentation to communicate with the particular prospect. This involves seeing the sales proposition from the prospect's point of view and using words and phrases which are meaningful to him.

Salesmen are frequently taught to give a complete sales presentation, mentioning the common features of most products in the field as well as their product's exclusive features. The intention is not to overwhelm the prospect but simply to make him familiar with all the benefits of using the product. It should be obvious, however, that the prospect's knowledge or lack of knowledge determines how much information should be presented. A few well-thought-out questions regarding the prospect's areas of interest and knowledge, interwoven with the sales message, can work wonders in saving time and making the presentation more effective.

Normally, a sales presentation is designed around one major reason for a customer to buy. Of course, the salesman should be prepared to discuss any point raised by the prospect, but he does not use every point he is prepared to discuss. This is particularly important in repeat buying situations. In selling to a department store, for example, the salesman might focus his entire presentation on a back-to-school sale, a new consumer-advertising program, or a traffic-building idea.

In many situations there may be a series of two, three, or four points which the salesman is trained to stress. Listeners find it difficult to follow or remember a large number of sales points, however, and for maximum impact, the salesman should be taught to use a limited number of crucial points. He may get to "in the third place" but no further. It is usually more effective to offer illustrations and examples of a few points.

Because a sales interview may be terminated at any time, most experienced salesmen prefer to begin a presentation with their strongest sales point. They play their ace because they may never get to make a second point. Of course, without interruption they will proceed down the list and summarize by again stressing the major sales point.

There are occasions when the reverse order might be appropriate. For example, if a prospect visits the showroom, the salesman can be more thorough and he may wish to build a series of points up to a climax which would move the prospect to buy then and there.

Each sales manager will have a preference about the order of sales points to be made under given conditions. But whatever the order, a salesman should be trained to give a planned sales presentation rather than wandering from point to point at random. Otherwise, extraneous material will enter the presentation and consume too much of the available interview time.

Finally, salesmen should learn to remain flexible in planning a sales presentation. By observing his client's reactions, the salesman should know when to add more proof or to cut the message short and attempt a trial close. Although a prepared sales presentation may prove sufficient, the salesman should be taught to adapt to the individual prospect and to the immediate demands of the situation.

DEMONSTRATIONS AND CUSTOMER PARTICIPATION

Salesmen are often taught how to demonstrate a product but they rarely understand the many purposes of a demonstration and when to use it. Actually, the timing of a product demonstration depends primarily on the purpose to be accomplished and secondarily on the situational aspects at the moment of the sales contact. A dramatization or demonstration can be used to attract initial attention or to regain lost attention, as well as to focus attention on a particular feature of the product. It can be used to increase the prospect's understanding of a complex product or service or to obtain greater concentration on the salient points of a presentation.

Some demonstrations are designed to change the prospect's state of mind from ambivalence to conviction; while he may doubt the salesman's word, seeing is believing. A demonstration under realistic conditions is much more vivid than the eloquent words of a salesman, and the prospect is not apt to forget what his own senses tell him. Moreover, a demonstration may illustrate a point in much less time than it would take to tell the same point. For example, a quick sketch of furniture in a room is much easier for a prospect to understand than a lengthy verbal description of the various furniture pieces and their position in relation to each other and to the walls, windows, and doors.

A prospect will often attempt to carry on other activities while listening to a salesman talk, in the honest belief that he can do both things well at the same time. Rather than argue the point, the salesman can be taught to demonstrate his product or service in such a way that the prospect will devote his full attention to the sales presentation. A variation of this problem arises when a prospect is honestly interested in the sales proposition but the telephone and business associates continually interrupt the presentation. If the demonstration is vivid enough, business associates are more apt to watch quietly than to interrupt, and the prospect himself may ask the switchboard to hold his calls for the next few minutes. As an alternate course of action, the salesman can try to get the prospect away from his normal work station by showing him how the product really works in the shop, the plant, the warehouse, the selling department, or wherever it is normally used.

Another type of demonstration involves taking the prospect to visit another customer's business to show him the product in use and to point out the benefits to the user. In many companies the salesman can invite a busy prospect to his showroom for a demonstration either before or after the lunch period or outside the customer's normal working hours. Busy people are often the best prospects because once they see the product demonstrated, they quickly appreciate any timesaving factors and are personally motivated to obtain such benefits for themselves.

Sales trainees can be taught that to be most effective, a demonstration should be related to the individual prospect's problems and should show how the product can best satisfy his needs. A well-planned demonstration forces a salesman to deliver an orderly talk, and even a mediocre salesman will find the results rewarding when a planned demonstration replaces his straight sales talk. On the other hand, a successful salesman who can adapt his demonstration to each prospect's individual needs will find the added dramatization produces excellent results.

The sales manager might suggest, if not require, that an audio-visual presentation or product demonstration be used when the sales proposition must be made to a group of buyers simultaneously. The purpose of a group demonstration is to convert raw data—facts, figures, and concepts—into a form that an audience composed of people with different interests can grasp quickly and favorably. Therefore, the salesman should learn as much as possible about the general aims, interests, abilities, and capacities of the various prospects. This will make it easier to eliminate technical terms that are not familiar to the audience and to omit details which are of no interest to them. A planned question-and-answer period, both before the demonstration to cover what the audience will see and after it to summarize, is often substantially more persuasive than a simple demonstration.

Salesmen should also be taught to get the prospect to participate actively in a demonstration. If a prospect gets involved in using the product, he can no longer sit in cold, detached judgment; he automatically becomes part of the selling team. The prospect's cooperation in the demonstration tends to make him want it to succeed because a convincing demonstration will in part reflect on his ability as a performer.

A prospect is more easily persuaded when he acts the part of a satisfied user of the new product. He will tend to internalize the reasons for buying the product in order to make his acting more realistic and believable. Once the prospect shows or acts out the benefits of the new product, he is well on his way to being convinced that acquiring it is the best action he can possibly take. The understanding that comes from participation changes his simple awareness of the product into conviction, leading to a desire to act, to purchase the product.

Because prospects often hesitate to participate in a demonstration, the salesman should be taught to plan the prospect's role so that it will seem natural and not an imposition. For instance, he can ask a prospect to assist in a demonstration in order to help save precious time. In a similar way, any operation which requires more than two hands can be used to involve the prospect in a natural manner.

The salesman should also be taught to turn a skeptical attitude into positive involvement by asking the prospect to check something for himself so that there is neither distortion of facts nor room for any error. For example, if a fire extinguisher is to be demonstrated in a large garbage can, the salesman might start the fire and ask the prospect to stand by with the extinguisher for safety. Once the fire is blazing, the salesman can ask the prospect to prove to himself how easily the extinguisher works. Having used it, the prospect will know with the certainty of direct personal experience how quickly and efficiently it works; no simple verbal presentation could ever be as convincing or as impressive to the buyer.

HANDLING OBJECTIONS AND REINFORCING THE POSITIVE

A very popular but often incorrect belief is that after the demonstration and presentation end, the prospect offers his objections, and then the real selling begins. While this may happen on some occasions, prospects often object early and throughout a presentation, not just at the end, and they do so for a variety of reasons. A salesman should be taught to understand the unspoken reasons behind objections and to deal with them by using an appropriate technique chosen from a number of strategies.

Why Prospects Object

When salesmen are taught some of the major reasons why prospects object, they are then better able to decide how to handle the situation. They can be taught to probe for clues to separate the excuses from the real objections and to determine whether an objection is based on reason or emotion. The strategies used to deal with rational and emotional objections are normally quite different. Real emotional objections often must be handled tactfully and indirectly, but if an objection is real and rational, the salesman can analyze the prospect's statements directly for logic, project them into the future, and determine likely consequences. He can also suggest alternate ways to achieve greater satisfaction. These methods can be used openly, with the prospect's full knowledge and participation.

Emotional objections. Emotional objections are often unspoken and not always conscious in the prospect's mind, but they may be very real and represent a considerable obstacle to any sale. For example, we know that people tend to suspect and resist suggestions made by strangers. Many people want to feel that the salesman is honestly looking out for their welfare before they are willing to conduct any business with him. Clearly, the salesman has to be sincere and offer friendly advice in order to build his image as a source of reliable information.

Closely related to the fear of strangers is the fear of the unknown in anything new. The prospect knows from experience the advantages and disadvantages of behaving as he now does, but he cannot know with comparable certainty what will happen if he changes his behavior to buy something new. Rather than choose the new course of action, the prospect tends to do nothing. He may attempt to belittle the sales proposition as trivial or without any meaningful consequences for him. This kind of objection suggests that the prospect needs reassurance, and the salesman should be taught to reinforce the positive consequences of the buying action.

Another fear often below the conscious level is that of hurting existing friendly suppliers. Buyers and salesmen often develop friendships and loyalties, and even professional purchasing agents feel it is not right to switch suppliers unless there is a major problem with a current one. They do not want to hurt their friends. The new salesman may be effective if he points out how conditions have gradually changed, and while it may have been wise in the past, it is no longer appropriate to stay with an old supplier. The cost of loyalty may be disproportionate to the benefits received.

Other objections may be related to the timing of the salesman's calls. A salesman who begins a contact with a pleasant welcome but after a number of calls has offered little or no help to the prospect can quickly become a pest. A salesman who insists on telling his story when the prospect really does not have the time exhibits his over-eagerness to sell and lack of empathy for the prospect. On some occasions, a prospect may have the time to listen to a salesman but his mind is preoccupied with another business or personal problem.

He may be resistant to interference in his thinking process but not necessarily against the salesman's proposition. If he is pushed or cajoled at that moment, he may very well rebel against the salesman personally. At another time, when he has resolved the other problem, he may welcome the same sales proposition.

Rational objections. Assuming the prospect has a need for a product and finances to acquire it, then there are two main categories of rational or logical sales objections. In the first are objections due to a lack of information. The prospect may say no because he doesn't understand the presentation or it doesn't seem complete or logical. Such objections say, in effect, that the value offered is not equal to the sacrifice required.

The second category of rational objections has to do with the prospect's expectations regarding the selling situation. For instance, often a prospect will consciously desire to bargain. If the salesman is too firm and refuses to negotiate the price, the prospect may feel that the best part of buying is being denied him. The price actually agreed on is really less important than the enjoyable and rational process of bargaining. Another possibility is that a prospect may desire to be wooed. A man about to place a large order may feel that he deserves to be wined and dined by competing salesmen. By putting off a decision, he prolongs and extends his pleasure.

Answering the Objections

Sales managers can usually classify the most common objections for their industry and their particular products, and can then teach salesmen a number of methods to handle them. The techniques suggested below are generalizations which should be tailored to the manager's industry, his company, his salesmen, and their products.

Agree and counterattack. This popular method of handling objections is often called the "yes, but" technique because the salesman seems to agree with the objection and then goes on to refute it, neutralizing the point or overwhelming it with other sales points. He might use any of the following phrases: "Yes, I'm glad you brought that up, but you see . . . ." "I understand. On the other hand . . . ." "It does appear that way; that's why . . . ." "I thought so, too, at first. Then I learned . . . ."

Turn objections into sales points. This technique is also known as twisting the objection. Common phrases used by salesmen to convert buying objections into reasons to buy include: "Of course you're busy! That's exactly why I wanted to see you . . . ." "Being overstocked won't help you make a profit and it may cost you future sales if you lack the latest styles . . . ." "I'm glad you're not in the market now because you can look at it without pressure . . . ." "Yes, we do charge more because tests have shown . . . ."

Ask why. This technique can often separate excuses from real buying objections. The prospect makes a definite statement and the salesman asks why—for example: "I never heard that before. Why don't you like . . . ?" "That's strange. Why do you say . . . ?" "I don't understand. Specifically, what is it about . . . ?"

Admit the objection if it is valid. When a prospect's objection is both real and valid, it may be wise to praise the buyer for his astuteness. In return he is apt to accept other sales points which he might have argued against. Honest concession on minor points may very well win the sale. The salesman might reply: "Yes, we do require a higher down payment. We've found that this eliminates costly returns . . . ." or "Yes, our deliveries are running two weeks behind. Don't you think this might indicate . . . ?" or "You're pretty sharp, and that point might be important in some cases. Do you think . . . ?"

Postpone the answer. Some objections are voiced prematurely, and immediate answers will not carry the degree of conviction they should. A trivial objection can often be covered in the normal course of the interview, and it is a good idea to avoid a direct clash early in the sales presentation. To delay his refutation, the salesman might say: "That's a good point, and I'll cover it in a minute, but first I'd like to show you . . . ." or "At this point it appears that way, but I haven't shown you . . . ."

Deny the objection. Perhaps the most dangerous technique for a new salesman is to deny the objection because any direct contradiction of the belief of a prospect is likely to close his mind completely. When an objection is so important that it cannot be admitted or overlooked, the salesman should consider a direct denial, but he should also provide the buyer with some way to save face. The following phrases might be used: "Apparently someone has given you misleading information. You see, the facts are . . . ." "Either you are kidding me or I left out . . . ." "I'm sorry I didn't make myself clear on that point. The way it really works is . . . ."

However an objection is handled, the salesman should be taught to make the prospect feel satisfied, at least temporarily, so that his mind will continue to receive the sales message. A well-trained salesman will realize that objections are normal and may often indicate that he is close to earning an order.

CLOSING AND OBTAINING AGREEMENT

A sales trainee is often observed for many months regarding the number and type of sales interviews he conducts and his competence in handling the sales presentation and answering objections. Much of this observed behavior provides evidence of his potential as a salesman and clues to areas in which he might need further training. However, the acid test for a new salesman is the total orders and profit he generates in a given period. Closing the sale becomes his primary objective.

The trial close. One technique which should be taught to new salesmen in most industries is building a trial close into the basic sales presentation. A trial close is merely a test of the effectiveness of the sales presentation and the prospect's willingness to buy at that point. The results tell the salesman what he should do to make the message just right for a specific customer at that moment. Most trial closes are offerings of two or more positive actions. For example, a salesman offering items in several colors may ask the prospect, "Do you like the green or do you prefer the brown?" If the customer chooses one of the alternatives, the salesman moves directly into the close because the buyer has indicated he has decided favorably. On the other hand, if the buyer objects to picking a color at that point, the salesman can continue with his presentation naturally and smoothly. If the salesman asks, "Would you like these items delivered in a rush, or is our normal two-week delivery sufficient?" then he can continue the presentation no matter what negative answer the prospect may give. A positive response, of course, indicates that it is time to stop talking and write up the order. A trial close helps the new salesman particularly because it gives him an indication of the degree of the buyer's conviction at that point.

Obtaining Agreement

New salesmen are often ill at ease when it comes to the crucial moment of asking for the order. Rather than risk hearing a prospect say no, they rationalize their way out of the interview by promising to bring more information on their next visit. This creates doubts instead of building the customer's confidence.

A well-trained salesman will plan his strategy and maintain a positive service attitude throughout his contacts with various buying influentials. He needs only a few guidelines for successful closing. While these may vary from company to company, typically they include the following five points:

1. In the final stage of an interview, tactfully keep the conversation centered on the selling proposition.

2. Allow the customer to indicate the kind of information he needs to make a positive decision and the speed with which he can absorb it.

3. From the thousands of facts not used, keep some selling points in reserve to tip the balance at closing.

4. Give the customer an opportunity to buy through sharing the conversation and listening for buying signals.

5. Sell the right item in the right amounts for that individual customer.

Closing a sale is important, but the overall objective of the salesman should be his long-term contribution to profit. Repeat sales and customer referrals should be his goals because they more than make up for quick orders that may boomerang. The customer who knows he is ordering the right item for his particular use and the right quantity for optimum benefits will be loyal and not easily won over by competitors. In addition, he will refer other prospects to the salesman, who has thus earned his confidence.

Techniques for Closing

Sales managers can usually create a series of closing techniques which are appropriate for their own companies. As before the following techniques are intended only as starting points from which a manager can begin to train his salesmen.

Assume the sale is made. When a salesman establishes friendly relations with the prospect and they seem to have a meeting of the minds, this method is a natural and easy way of closing without pressure of any kind. The salesman assumes the sale is closed without actually asking for the order, and the buyer goes along with the salesman and is relieved of the difficulty of making a decision. One of the following phrases might be used: "If I may use your phone, I'll call this in right now and arrange for delivery." "I'll put you down for 200 units right away and back-order 100 per month." "The jacket looks fine. Try on the pants and the tailor will mark the length for you." "I'll put this through right away. Was there anything else you need today?"

Build a series of acceptances from minor to major points. In this technique, small blocks of logic are put together to form the presentation. The salesman attempts to get agreement on the importance and desirability of each small benefit of his proposition as he goes along. The prospect agrees that the product is desirable and really will provide the promised benefit. In this form of close, agreement is built into the entire presentation, and each minor acceptance reinforces the final major decision, as in this example: "Of course you want an attractive home. Of course you want to protect your children's health. Of course you want a nest egg for retirement. Since this product will help you realize all these benefits, it is logical to obtain it as soon as possible."

Summarize the selling points. When a prospect appears to want the product but is hesitant, a good closing technique might be to summarize the selling points. The salesman lists all the sound, logical reasons for ordering, placing the greatest emphasis on those benefits which seemed to have the strongest appeal for this prospect; this provides a brief and effective review.

A variation of this technique is the use of a T-account, or a two-column summary, for example, of "buy" versus "don't buy" or "Product A" versus "Product B." This is a physical enumeration of the two-sided argument used in persuasion. Clearly, to be successful, the salesman should demonstrate that the benefits of buying his product heavily outweigh the other alternative. When this technique is used with discretion, it can be very effective in persuasion.

Get a decision on a minor point. Many prospects are reluctant to make any major decision even when it appears to be in their best interest to do so. This may be very frustrating to the new salesman, but a slight change in technique will often bring success in closing the sale. Once the salesman recognizes the problem he should avoid requesting a major decision and should instead attempt to close on a minor point. While it may be impossible for some men to decide on a major purchase, it is relatively easy for them to make quick and firm decisions on optional accessories to tailor a product to suit their individual application. For example, the salesman may ask, "Do you prefer this machine with the manual or the automatic feed?" When the major decision is avoided and attention is directed to a minor decision, the sale is then assumed closed as in the assumptive technique above.

Devise a contingency. In this method, the salesman restates his proposition so that the positive decision to buy depends on something else that may or may not happen. The prospect agrees to buy only if the possibility becomes a reality and the emphasis in selling is on that contingency. Phrases used in this technique might be: "If you can pass the physical, then you will want . . . ." "If I can secure an exclusive outlet for your store, then your initial order will be . . . ." "If my plant will modify this product to suit your production line, then you want delivery by . . . ."

Refer to an impending event. Closely related to the contingent technique is the impending-event method of closing a sale. In this technique, the event will definitely occur and the prospect will suffer a loss if he delays in buying. For example, the trade-in value of an old car will drop every month the buyer waits, and he will have to pay that much more in cash to obtain his new auto. The salesman may combine this impending event with the contingent technique by explaining how expensive repairs might be necessary to keep the old car in shape while the prospect is hesitating.

Impending events include increased labor and production costs, government taxes and controls, seasonal changes in the weather, graduation dates, and the irreversible aging of people, and the salesman argues that buying now will prevent losses of money, health, appearance, comfort, convenience, and so on. When used legitimately, this technique of closing can be very effective.

Try the SRO technique. The standing-room-only technique is used to capitalize on the common human trait of wanting something that is a proven success. The Broadway show that is sold out in advance of a performance puts out a sign that reads SRO, and more people than ever will try to get tickets for future performances. In selling, this technique may be appropriate when, for various reasons, supply is limited. Whenever demand temporarily exceeds supply or a stock item is running low, this may be sufficient reason for some prospects to order.

A variation of the SRO technique is used in selling the last few items of a commodity that cannot be reordered. For example, when a manufacturer is about to discontinue a line of products, the close-out need not be a losing proposition. The few remaining products can be made more attractive with promotional activity that offers them on a first-come, first-served basis until the supply is exhausted.

Call in another salesman. This method of closing is often called the two-man close or the turnover or TO technique and may be appropriate when the salesman cannot get along personally with the prospect. When a salesman realizes that he is not communicating properly, but that the prospect is still undecided, he calls in a second salesman under the pretext that the second man is more familiar with this type of problem or product. Commonly used in selling in a showroom that handles walk-in prospects, it can be used in outside selling in the same manner as long as the prospect is still undecided. When carried out diplomatically, the prospect benefits by this technique because he can communicate more easily with the second man and the entire transaction becomes more pleasant.

PROVIDING CUSTOMER SERVICES AND BUILDING GOODWILL

The first order placed with a salesman is likely to be a tentative action viewed by the customer as a test of the salesman's claims. The buyer is temporarily changing his behavior from either not using the product or obtaining it through a different salesman. He has thus moved from a familiar situation into an area of uncertainty and unknown danger. He may have stopped buying from his old supplier, possibly hurting old business friends, without the security of a long and pleasant experience with the new supplier. As a result, the buyer may be filled with doubt, fear, and anxiety.

New salesmen should understand this crucial transitional period and be prepared to deal with it. Some salesmen become so elated when they get an order from a customer that they literally pack their briefcases and run. To these men, the correct application does not matter, nor does the amount of the order. They are so relieved that the customer did not say no to their sales presentation that they want to leave before he can change his mind. Their fear of a cancellation is so great that they will avoid any further contact with the customer until after the merchandise is delivered and the bill is paid.

Unfortunately, merchandise returns are costly, and attempting to resell a customer who feels he has been treated unfairly is very difficult. The customer depends on the salesman for expert advice in his field. He is legitimately entitled to that service, and all salesmen should know this before they attempt to sell any client or prospect.

The salesman should be taught that when he first sells a new account, both he and his company must perform almost perfectly. He should assure the buyer that his decision to change was wise and will be rewarding. All claims and promises of benefits should be fulfilled beyond the buyer's expectations. Because of this extra service and the high selling cost to obtain that initial order, many suppliers actually lose money on the first transaction. These suppliers are willing to take the loss because follow-up orders will continue to mount, and the total profit causes the initial selling and service costs to dwindle into insignificance.

When the salesman understands this long-range viewpoint and acts accordingly, the buyer's behavior becomes less and less tentative. His initial doubts and fears prove to be unjustified and gradually fade away because the rewards are as promised. The new salesman is reliable, trustworthy, and pleasant, so the buyer can feel assured and relaxed about dealing with him and can turn his attention to other problems. His buying behavior becomes habitual, practically automatic, as the new friendship replaces the old. The salesman's responsibility from then on is to continue to provide excellent service so that the buyer will not readily reopen the issue of choosing suppliers, and any competitive challenges will be both expensive and discouraging to other salesmen.

The salesman's efforts to build goodwill are aided by a common psychological phenomenon. This is the normal tendency to forget unpleasant things that occur and to remember the good events. For instance, when old army buddies reminisce about their service experiences, they remember the fun but tend to forget the monotonous routine and uncomfortable events. A well-trained salesman can easily take advantage of this selective forgetting.

An industrial salesman, for example, can be taught to provide extra services for his accounts. These services may include developing an automatic reorder system based on a minimum stock allowable, with built-in lead time. They may include helping the customer solve problems not related to the salesman's offerings. Over a period of years, industrial salesmen often become authorities in their field and in their customer's industry as well. Effective industrial salesmen go out of their way to help their accounts in any legitimate way they can, whether or not they may get an immediate order. In this way, the effective salesman builds customer loyalty. Over a period of time, occasional errors in ordering or shipping may occur, but the loyal customer will tend to remember the extra services rendered, to forget the occasional errors or problems, and to remain loyal.

Large direct-sales organizations such as International Business Machines Corporation spend much time and effort building goodwill. They will teach their customers' personnel how to obtain greater use of the computer, for example. The cost of building this goodwill exceeds the annual budget of many large universities, but there is usually little or no immediate benefit to the selling company. However, over the years IBM's customers tend to forget the occasional problems and high prices while they remember the training and extra services.

A large international manufacturer of ladies' foundation garments taught its salesmen to sell the concept of an inventory-control system to large department stores. Their system was designed to prevent a store from running out of stock in 98 percent of the requests. The system increased the stores' immediate sales and, perhaps more importantly, it also prevented loyal customers from shopping in competitive stores. However, each department store had to tie up more capital in inventory and provide valuable store space for the complete range of sizes. Over a year or two, a relatively short period of time, the department stores quickly forgot the disadvantages of this new system and openly boasted of its advantages to them. They developed this positive attitude toward the manufacturer by forgetting the negative aspects of the inventory-control system.

The same psychology applies even when repeat sales are not expected. Satisfied customers make the best salesmen because they enjoy pointing out the benefits they have received and encourage their friends and business associates to buy from the same salesman. An important customer may well become a center of influence and provide many leads to other sales. In selling home improvements such as aluminum siding, for example, one job well done can lead to others in the same area. Conversely, a new customer who feels the salesman has misled him can cause so much trouble that additional sales in that neighborhood become difficult, if not impossible. Many intangible services are sold initially on a casual or temporary buyer-seller relationship, which trained salesmen cultivate over the years into a mutually trustful client-adviser relationship.

SUMMARY

Initial sales training is usually designed to impart knowledge which will enable the new salesman to operate effectively in the field. Training objectives can be established and standards of achievement can be measured fairly objectively. This initial training need not be limited to the traditional product knowledge but can be broadened to include many basic selling techniques. New salesmen should know what to do before they are faced with many common and recurring selling situations.

The particular areas of knowledge cited in this chapter were meant simply to be illustrative of the kinds of knowledge which are basic to successful selling. Each sales manager or trainer should analyze his own company needs and identify the techniques that are most important for his salesmen to know. Since training takes time, effort, and money, priorities should be established and reasonable goals set. Initial training has a tremendous effect on the lifetime performance of many salesmen; thus it should be carefully planned. Continuous upgrading of the salesmen's knowledge is also indicated in a competitive business environment.

The order in which various subjects are taught should not necessarily follow the on-the-job sequence. Normally, it is wise to begin with subjects which are familiar to the trainees and gradually work into unknown areas. In the process of job hunting and interviewing, most new salesmen will have learned something of the products and typical customer contacts in the field. In this case it would seem natural to begin with product knowledge and the presentation, followed by demonstration. For some companies one particular area of knowledge may be critical, and this could be the high point of the training program. When the critical area is mastered, everything else may fall into line quickly and easily. Many good sales training programs end with prospecting and preapproach planning. These subjects often serve as an excellent review of the entire training program and come at the time when the new salesmen are about to face real-world situations, so that the theoretical knowledge is most relevant. Clearly, preapproach planning can be as important to training as it is to selling.

SELECTED MATERIALS

BNA Films Catalog. Rockville, Md.: Bureau of National Affairs.

> *This free catalog lists 16-mm sound and color motion pictures on management development and sales training.*

The Dartnell Corporation Film Catalog. Chicago: The Dartnell Corporation.

> *These films specialize in sales training aids, sales management, and sales promotion materials. One classic inspirational film of note is Vince Lombardi's* Second Effort, *which has supplementary materials of a motivational nature.*

The Dun & Bradstreet Business Course in Sales Training. New York: Dun & Bradstreet, Business Education Division.

> *The course, consisting of twelve study units each requiring an average of four hours, stresses understanding of the basic motives behind human thought and action. Ideal for role playing with groups of salesmen, it is adapted to each company's products and services.*

"Marketing Aids for Sales/Marketing Executives and Salesmen," *Marketing Times*. New York: Sales and Marketing Executives International.

This section of the SMEI monthly journal lists correspondence courses, a programmed course on fundamentals, capsule lessons, records, books, and audio cassettes.

Pederson, C. A., and Wright, M. D., *Salesmanship: Principles and Methods*, 5th ed. Homewood, Ill.: Richard D. Irwin, 1971.

This textbook provides an excellent traditional approach to basic salesmanship.

Schiff, Jack, *Professional Sales Technique*. New York: AMR International.

This complete self-study training course for individual salesmen includes 12 audio cassettes and a programmed-instruction textbook by one of the best-known and respected men in this field.

CHAPTER 6

Sales Training Methods and Techniques

IF TRAINING OBJECTIVES are clearly stated, then the subject matter to be taught and the person who does the teaching will each influence the choice of methods. For example, top executives obviously cannot devote a substantial amount of their time to training new salesmen on a regular basis. A corporate president may be willing to address a class of sales trainees, but he will be able to give them only a few minutes. On the other hand, if salesmen are to be trained to concentrate on high-profit items, an executive from the comptroller's office may have to spend several days working with them on quantitative computations.

The amount of time the trainees are scheduled to be in the field or on other work-related assignments, such as the sales-service desk, will also influence the choice of methods in scheduling related classroom activities. A group of sales trainees meeting all day for three consecutive days, for example, presents different training problems than does a similar group meeting every Friday afternoon for six consecutive weeks.

Another variable which should be considered before choosing a particular training method is the experience level of the trainees. All new salesmen have had some experience which will help make the training meaningful, whether it is in shopping, negotiating price, or attempting to persuade others to their point of view. Some new men may have had direct selling experience, and others will have influenced a buying decision. If the person responsible for sales training ignores this experience and treats all participants as if they were starting from zero, he may engender hostility, inhibiting the learning process. An instructor can draw on the experience of his class in a number of ways, and this will also influence his choice of methods.

Today's young salesmen are apt to be action-oriented and to prefer to learn new skills by observing them and then trying to perform them on their own. Generally, they become discouraged if they are compelled to be passive for long periods. They are often poor readers for the same reason; thus, many good textbooks cannot be used on the job or for evening assignments. On the other hand, these same young men are better educated than prior generations, and more sophisticated socially; consequently, what was effective sales training in 1955 may not be appropriate in 1975.

One common pitfall which sales trainers should avoid is the reliance on one "good" method to the exclusion of most other methods. Trainers like to do what they know best and avoid methods about which they know very little. For example, a good public speaker may feel very comfortable giving a formal lecture to a group of sales trainees. He may indeed impart a great deal of valuable information, and the trainees may have a high degree of recall on subsequent testing. The temptation for this instructor, then, is to use lectures to teach all subjects. If he is not thoroughly familiar with the use of role playing to build certain skills, he is not likely to use that method, even when it is more appropriate than giving a lecture.

Various teaching methods have evolved over the past few years which incorporate new technological advances not previously available. Each method has certain general advantages and disadvantages, and the experience of many outstanding trainers has provided some guidelines in the choice of methods. A sales manager or trainer planning a program should not provide many different methods simply for the sake of variety but should select the most appropriate method for achieving his objectives in each phase of the program.

INFORMAL LECTURES BY GUEST EXPERTS

Most businessmen can speak for an hour or two with the authority of personal experience on their own special topic. Many can also enthusiastically and effectively communicate a large amount of information to a group of sales trainees in a relatively limited time period, but it is a rare instructor who is able to present day after day, a better synthesis of content than is found in most sales manuals.

Experienced sales trainers agree that an informal lecture is a good method to motivate trainees at the beginning of a new subject because it can be used to clarify areas which seem to bother all trainees. To maximize two-way communication and enhance the learning process, the lecture should be given in a permissive atmosphere which encourages interruption with pertinent questions and discussion. The sales trainer can enrich the formal subject matter of the course with information from his own experience or from outside readings.

One large manufacturing corporation with many divisions used this method for the initial orientation of new salesmen. All salesmen hired in the previous six months were required to attend a two-day program at corporate headquarters. Speakers were invited from each major division, as well as from many corporate departments, such as accounting, law, and research. Each speaker was asked to describe briefly his functional area, what it could do to help salesmen, and what salesmen could do to help it. Question-and-answer periods were encouraged.

After the first program, several interesting things happened. Every unit that sent a speaker asked if some of their nonsales personnel could attend the next orientation program. Every speaker asked for feedback to improve his presentation at future programs. Many units below the division level asked if they could be put on future programs. The salesmen's orientation program quickly grew to a one-week program for all new supervisory employees. Better speakers arrived at each new program, and their visual aids became highly professional.

After new sales trainees attended the one-week program, they knew more about the corporation than most other employees knew after many years. The trainees were also caught up in a spirit of optimistic growth and unlimited future with the corporation. Each speaker communicated honestly and sincerely by answering all questions and fully discussing any negative points raised. Corporate officers whose names and formal titles were known only from the annual report became warm, friendly people known by their first names and by sight. A respect and camaraderie was built in 40 hours of informal lectures which most other salesmen had not been able to achieve in a career with the same—but to them unknown—company.

One need not work for a large corporation to use this technique. A sales manager with as few as five salesmen can create such a program with a little imagination. For example, a senior salesman can be asked to cover the subject of selling large accounts. A service clerk can cover order processing and delivery problems. Many local customers are often willing to help train salesmen by participating in meetings as guest speakers. Sales managers from noncompeting companies are often available on an exchange basis.

The major weakness of the lecture method is that it frequently puts the learner in a passive situation. One or more mediocre lecturers can easily bore an audience. Therefore, in planning to use this method, the manager should seek out speakers who have the best knowledge of the subject matter; who will be credible to the audience; who can handle the formal presentation as well as the question-and-answer period; and who are willing and able to prepare a number of visual aids or demonstrations to enliven the presentation.

While some lecturers like the audience to take notes, experienced training directors usually prefer the trainees to maintain eye contact with the speaker and to listen for the major ideas or points. If detailed information is to be memorized, then handouts are appropriate, but they should be distributed after the presentation. If they are given out beforehand, the salesmen will listen to the speaker part of the time and read part of the time. This disruption of attention frequently inhibits learning.

For those managers who prefer more active participation by the salesmen, there are modifications of the lecture technique such as conferences, seminars, and workshops. In a guided conference, for example, one or more speakers give brief lectures to introduce various points which could have been covered in a single lecture. The salesmen are given many opportunities to contribute their thoughts throughout the program; however, the conference leader or several members of a panel are prepared to direct the conversation to cover certain predetermined points. Usually, the conference leader can prepare his summary of the discussion days before the program is conducted, much as a formal lecturer would.

CASE-HISTORY PROBLEM SOLVING IN TEAMS

Requirements of a Good Case History

A case history used for educational purposes has to be a real, documented experience. This seemingly arbitrary definition has important implications for the training director. For example, it ensures that realism will be brought into a theoretical or abstract subject. All the events in the case really did occur, and the facts and opinions were those actually stated, even though they may often be contradictory. Many insignificant facts appear in a good case history, just as they do in a live situation. The opinions expressed by executives, however silly they may seem, are those actually stated at the time of the case. The student is forced to separate the wheat from the chaff.

Certain case histories allow students to be assigned to go to other sources to credit or refute statements or reports in the case with whatever information was available at the time. This is useful for teaching salesmen to develop sources of information beyond what they hear from several buying influentials in a single prospect company. When contradictory information presents an either-or choice, the temptation is to compromise between the two. In reality, outside information may support one position or neither position. Thus, the salesman who knows how to develop outside sources of information can make much more intelligent decisions about problems or difficult situations than the one who simply listens to two biased but opposite opinions.

Real, documented experiences are also useful to persuade either naive or cynical sales trainees that customers and prospects really do behave in a certain manner. When the manager or trainer knows that the case situation is real, he can be emphatic. Conversely, if the situation is fictitious or fictionalized, trainees may think that people do not really do things in the way the instructor describes; hence, they may disregard much of the lesson.

The case-history method usually concentrates on a written documentation of actual situations. The objectives are normally to identify and understand the concepts demonstrated by the case and to develop principles for handling these concepts when they are presented in future situations. However, young salesmen often attempt to deal with the specific details of the case and to solve the specific problem rather than search for general principles or appropriate applications of them.

For salesmen with a minimum of experience, it is usually wise to begin with cases which clearly focus on a simple, easily identified issue. As the experience level moves upward, of course, more and more complex cases should be used, until the group can comfortably approach real-world situations. For example, to label a case "Motivation" may help the neophyte understand that limited subject. However, in the real business world the salesman may not know what kind of problem he is facing, and the manager is not at his side to analyze the situation for him or to point out what is significant.

Use of Case Histories

Traditionally, the case-history method has been confined to training sessions with small groups in order to permit the full participation of every person. Today, experienced training directors have successfully used this method with 100 or more trainees together in a large room by dividing the large group into a number of subgroups or teams. Three teams may compete against each other on one specific question, and many questions may be asked to bring out all the pertinent points. Each group is given time for a buzz session to exchange ideas and reach a consensus. Then a spokesman for the team reports to the audience as a whole and must defend his group's position.

Subgroups permit every salesman to participate actively, and various experience levels on the team encourage the new men to ask questions and the older men to contribute fully. By requiring the spokesman to be a different salesman each time, the danger that one man will dominate the subgroup is lessened. Normally a team spirit develops which encourages each man to pull his own weight and help the team succeed. When they are competing against one or more other teams, the men learn to listen closely to other reports, which may differ slightly, and everyone benefits by this exchange among subgroups.

A variation of the group or team method of problem solving is to require each salesman to submit a brief written recommendation independently. This causes every man to pay close attention to the input of his team members but allows him to illustrate his own unique contributions. Often reports expressing minority opinions result which raise interesting questions that might otherwise go unnoticed. Clearly, the number of men involved and the amount of training time permitted will often dictate how simple or sophisticated this method can be.

The Incident Process

A major variation in the problem-solving technique, the incident process usually involves a fictitious representation of reality. Sales trainees are typically told to imagine they were in a situation in which certain events occurred and customers or prospects voiced specific comments or questions. Then a trainee is asked what he would do or how he would respond. Group discussion may then cover the appropriateness of the salesman's response, and the group may develop principles from the discussion. Several possible responses may be discussed by the group, and the trainer may then suggest certain principles and ask the group to develop applications.

The consumer products division of a large manufacturing corporation combines the case-history method with the incident process in sales training to make the case alive, current, and dynamic. Salesmen are given limited information concerning a real, documented experience. They must then buy answers to their questions to gain additional information. A series of questions relating to problem identification may be asked by the sales trainer, with groups debating the issues as they see them. After a series of buzz sessions, each group is told to report back in twenty minutes with a recommendation for action. About five minutes before the deadline, the instructor injects new facts into the situation. He may tell the group that a competitor has just reduced his prices 20 percent, for example. While the group may complain that they were almost finished, the incident illustrates changes that occur in the real world while the salesman delays making a decision. Once again, depending on the time allotted, a series of artificial incidents can be introduced, forcing the group to go back into a conference and revise their recommendations.

There are two areas in which the training director should use caution regarding the mixing of the true case-history method with the artificial incident process. First, the sales trainees should clearly understand that the case history is a real, documented experience. If they are in doubt about this, the entire learning process may be destroyed. Second, the type of incident which is introduced or the number of incidents should be such that the salesmen are not frustrated to the point of discrediting the entire exercise.

Approximately 300 sales and sales management textbooks are published every year, and most contain excellent case-history material or incidents which can be used in sales training. For more complete and fully documented cases, the Intercollegiate Case Clearing House at Harvard University periodically publishes and sells at a modest cost a description of all cases in their ever-expanding files. In most sales organizations many classic cases are available to the manager or sales trainer who is willing to dig for them.

PROGRAMMED INSTRUCTION FOR INDIVIDUAL SALESMEN

In many sales organizations, new men are hired and trained one at a time. In a relatively stable sales force, a new man may be added only when a need is foreseen or after it actually arises. A large sales force dispersed throughout the country may hire and train on a local basis, which necessitates training one or two new men at a time.

Professional sales training seminars such as those sponsored by the American Management Associations and the Sales and Marketing Executives International are usually excellent, as are a number of privately sponsored sales training clinics. Unfortunately, these programs are not offered on a continuous basis, and usually the local sales manager cannot wait for the next convenient seminar. Even when the budget and time permit sending a new man to an outside sales training program, the manager is still faced with the need to educate the man regarding the specific products, company, and industry and any other unique areas.

Historically, sales managers have been forced to use the buddy system to train new men under these conditions. This is simply the assignment of a trainee to observe and assist a senior salesman both in the office and in the field. Under directed and controlled conditions and if time permits, this can be an ideal learning situation. However, in real life, routine situations occur again and again, long after the trainee has learned how to handle them, while a challenging new situation may occur only once in two or three months. Besides learning many good things, the junior salesman also learns the informal limit on the number of calls per day, and perhaps he learns to drink martinis at lunch or to take a full day off to play golf once in a while. Inadvertently, the senior salesman teaches the new man many ways to beat the system. In addition, one new man may learn quickly, while another may take much longer to understand what he is observing. The sales manager may reduce all situations to what the average sales trainee should learn, thereby boring the quick learner and hurting the slow learner.

Use of Programmed Instruction

One training method which adapts to the individual's speed of learning is programmed instruction. In its basic linear format, it presents information in relatively small, simple units. The trainee is then asked a few questions testing his understanding of the material. If his answers are incorrect, he is told why they are wrong and asked to go back and repeat the unit. In this method the learner sets his own pace and is taught only the material contained in each unit, presumably only the good things.

An advanced format of programmed instruction involves branching rather than linear or straight-line progression. In this format, a wrong answer may direct the student to a different lesson altogether to clear up a specific area of confusion, rather than having him repeat the same lesson. After he has mastered the diversion or branch area, the student is led back to the most advanced point he had achieved and continues forward.

There are many programmed-instruction packages which can be used to help train salesmen. These commercial products may begin with basic sales techniques and proceed through college-level marketing concepts. They may be simple reading assignments with paper-and-pencil tests or sophisticated combinations of video tape demonstrations, textbooks, and computer terminals where the student can communicate back and forth with instructions, questions, and results about decision inputs. Many experiments are currently being conducted on these sales training packages, with new variations offered regularly. A sales manager would be well advised to check with other users before asking a neophyte salesman to work his way through such a package.

An office products sales organization with several hundred local sales offices uses programmed instruction to train all new salesmen in their local offices. The corporate training staff created its own package, which is sent to each new man in a suitcase weighing forty pounds. He is told to read certain material and listen to certain tape recordings. As soon as he feels ready, he is to ask to be given a test. If he achieves a predetermined score on each section, he is told to proceed; if not, of course, he must repeat. This programmed-instruction package is designed to prepare the average new salesman for a centralized training school in three weeks. One man may master the material sooner and be sent to the skills school right away, while another man may take one or two weeks longer and be delayed from attending the national school. However, every new salesman who is sent on for further training has mastered the basic information to an acceptable level.

In a similar manner, programmed instruction is often appropriate as a device to review or update the knowledge of experienced men in the field. Monthly booklets or audio cassettes can be mailed out by the sales manager with response sheets to be returned as soon as completed. Usually, a high grade—if not a perfect score—is required, and salesmen learn to take their time and get the answers correct before sending the response sheets back to the manager. Some salesmen will return them quickly, while others may take several weeks before they master the material. Each man sets his own pace as the group achieves the learning objective.

If salesmen have not used this form of training earlier in their careers, they may distrust it and withhold their cooperation. If they are compensated only for their volume of orders, clearly they will feel no obligation to participate in any training which appears to involve extra work on their part. As in most educational programs, the participants should be motivated to learn before they are subjected to the lesson. This may be difficult for a sales manager whose men are widely scattered and come together to meet only once or twice a year.

One national sales manager made programmed instruction mandatory for all new salesmen, and they continued receiving instructional packages after being assigned to field territories. Older salesmen, after seeing the great success of these young men, volunteered their names for future mailings of the packages. These same older salesmen had not taken the time to read and digest update bulletins in previous years. On occasion, reverse psychology may be necessary to motivate experienced men to use programmed instruction.

CORRESPONDENCE COURSES FOR MEN ON THE ROAD

Correspondence courses have been available for more than a hundred years and consequently are usually overlooked in considering various sales training methods for men in the field. The courses are lengthy and require considerable practice and thought between lessons. The better schools and organizations assign the same instructor to each student throughout the course both to personalize the corrections and criticism and to identify repetitive mistakes which may require individual instruction. Most people do not have the perseverance to stay with a correspondence course lasting six months or more. For this reason, correspondence courses are not appropriate for every salesman.

On the other hand, many salesmen who are on the road regularly cannot attend evening classes or full-week seminars on subjects which they have a strong personal reason to learn. For example, a salesman who wants to get into management may be told by a friendly sales manager that his written reports and sales letters indicate a serious weakness in his writing, and he will not be considered for management unless he can show tremendous improvement. Since it is very difficult to teach oneself how to write properly, this salesman on the road may feel totally frustrated. A knowledgeable sales manager or training specialist can recommend an excellent writing course, for example, the one offered by Dun & Bradstreet, Inc., entitled "The Language of Business," which has twelve units and takes about six months. If the salesman has the fortitude and drive to stay with the course, his sales letters to customers and his reports to management will probably show a dramatic improvement in two or three months. Beyond providing this immediate benefit to his company, the salesman will realize the personal satisfaction of doing something vital to further himself.

Home study works well for the strongly motivated learner, because the salesman himself selects the best time of day for him to study. Thus he can concentrate on each lesson without the normal pressures and interruptions of the regular nine-to-five business day. Good correspondence courses usually include case-history illustrations which emphasize practical applications of the principles being taught. This encourages the salesman to stay with the program to its satisfactory completion.

Many good correspondence courses are offered in sales training, retail management, credit, accounting, personal investments, and several other subject areas. Newer sales people tend to be eager to participate and learn new methods and techniques, while experienced salesmen are often skeptical. Once involved, however, most salesmen enrolled in these correspondence courses become very enthusiastic. When several are enrolled in the same course, they will often make time to hold their own group sessions on individual lessons.

Most nationally recognized concerns giving correspondence courses offer the sponsoring company some control over the training process. For example, they may make monthly reports to the sales manager on the grades of the salesmen enrolled in a particular course. When a number of salesmen are enrolled together, graded papers can be returned to a designated supervisor, ensuring that he knows who is actively participating and benefiting from the course and who is giving it only lip service.

The cost for the better correspondence courses is generally well below the cost of a live seminar or college course of equal quality. Strangely enough, the interaction between the instructor and the individual salesman is usually greater in the correspondence course because it is on a one to one basis. Corrections of lessons and tests use language and illustrations from the salesman's own industry. For these reasons, a correspondence course for a salesman who is motivated to learn a particular subject is often one of the best investments of training dollars.

AUDIO TAPE PROGRAMS

While sales training programs using phonograph records have been available for many years, record players are bulky and safe storage of records is a problem. Modern technology has resolved this problem by providing magnetic tape recordings and compact, lightweight playback units. The reel-to-reel type requires the user to thread the tape on the playback unit, which may be difficult for some salesmen. With the cassette type, the tape cassette is simply plugged into the unit and the user's hands never touch the tape. Cassettes can be mailed safely and can provide rapid dissemination of information to salesmen in the field. One cassette can hold from 30 to 120 minutes of material, half on each side.

The advantage of the audio recorded message over a written message is that there can be emphasis through inflection, volume, pitch, hesitation, pacing, desk pounding, background mood music, or appropriate background noise. These variables provide many more cues than the written word to help the salesman correctly understand the intended message. Cassettes made by practically any manufacturer can be played back on any machine because the speed has been standardized.

There are several hundred sales training cassettes on the market today, and since they are easy and inexpensive to make and reproduce, there are likely to be a thousand or more very shortly. Thus it is necessary to guard against the danger of programs of questionable value produced by fly-by-night operators. On the other hand, nationally known private concerns such as Xerox Corporation and Dun & Bradstreet, Inc., associations such as the American Management Associations, and public institutions such as colleges and universities have an image to protect. These organizations have the financial resources and prestige necessary to attract the best people to produce their educational cassettes and they sincerely test their products before offering them to the general public.

Another problem of which the sales manager or training director should be aware is the poor listening habits of most salesmen. Many experiments have shown that the average person remembers less than half of a ten- to fifteen-minute talk immediately after hearing it. The longer the talk or the period of time before testing, the lower the percentage of recall. This suggests that if the manager simply mails out cassettes for his salesmen to play back, very little education will occur. Of course, methods to increase the effectiveness of the cassettes should be built into the total training program.

For example, there are several very good audio tape programs which teach salesmen effective listening habits in as little as three hours. Follow-up studies show that these good habits are still in force among the majority of the students one year later. These programs normally offer a pretraining test to provide a bench mark and a post-training test to measure the improvement objectively. After a motivational beginning, the tapes proceed with the lesson, incorporating a series of stops for the listener to participate actively with a written response. They usually come with concise written summaries to reinforce the spoken message. A training director or sales manager would be well advised to begin any audio tape training series with a program for building effective listening skills.

Other formal courses vary in length from a single half-hour program to 40 half-hour programs. For example, at Florida Atlantic University an undergraduate marketing course is offered on 40 cassettes which the student can study at his own pace. Tests have shown the audio tape series to be as effective as the same professor either live in the classroom or viewed on television or film. Most good formal audio tape courses provide a workbook with blanks for the student to fill in as he listens, in addition to visual aids and some reading material. Often the workbook uses programmed instruction to reinforce the spoken word. A long course may include textbook reading assignments and possibly a written term paper. Regardless of length, good audio tape courses provide some form of active participation by the salesman. He becomes mentally and physically involved in the learning process.

At the same university, a formal program has been designed to train retail sales clerks in five sessions using half-hour-long audio tapes. In this program, the sales clerk hears the principles from an instructor and then is asked to apply his new knowledge. He listens to a typical situation in a retail store with natural background noises recorded on the scene. The tape is stopped at each crucial point for a written response from the sales clerk. Preliminary test results show a promising improvement in total dollar sales per clerk and in add-on sales of accessories or unit sales per clerk.

Many informal audio tape programs, usually in cassette format, can be tailored to the needs of the individual salesman. Some are motivational, for example, and help the salesman out of a slump. Of these, the better ones ask the salesman to take some immediate action, such as making a list of his ten best prospects, writing down one of his strengths and resolving to take advantage of it, or writing down one weakness and resolving to improve himself in that area.

Informal sales training cassettes are available commercially on most common sales techniques, such as prospecting, opening a sale, presenting the proposition, handling objections, and closing. Others cover public speaking, writing business letters, and a number of psychological topics to help the salesman to understand himself and others better. Many cassettes are intended to be inspirational in nature. These are usually on quite a low level, glorifying apple pie and waving the American flag. While the sales manager or trainer may like the philosophy they express, these tapes are of questionable value for sales training because too often they produce little or no change in the salesman's behavior. Of course, some salesmen may need an occasional reminder of their true worth, and an inspirational cassette probably can't hurt.

Perhaps the most advanced technique of using audio taped messages is the sales-tape-of-the-month concept. These tapes are usually highly informative and tailored specifically for one sales organization's internal use. For example, a large insurance company maintains a battery of these audio tapes in the home office. Field agents over the entire United States are asked to phone in during predetermined hours. They dial a number that connects them to the recording, and when they hang up the phone, the tape is rewound automatically.

Another company, with 160 salesmen selling to 7,500 dealers, mails out tapes regularly with new product information, sales tips, company news, and some humor. The branch sales office schedules informal meetings for the salesmen to discuss the ideas presented on the tape. In this manner, every salesman is made aware of company developments almost as they happen. Written sales memorandums that are half read and quickly forgotten are a thing of the past.

One company with 3,000 salesmen gives each one a three-ring binder and then mails out to them one audio cassette every other month, along with short written messages appropriate to each tape.

The binder also has pockets to hold the six tapes for that year. These tapes contain excerpts from the company president's public speeches, new product information, sales tips, contest rules and prizes, and occasional recognition of a few individual salesmen. By creating their own audio tapes, this company modifies its ongoing sales training to fit changing economic and competitive conditions.

The educational value of audio tape programs is usually enhanced by building in various opportunities for the learner to be actively involved—for example, stops for individual written responses or for group discussion when a number of salesmen are trained in one meeting. Frequently, workbooks, quizzes, and outside readings are appropriate to further involve the salesmen.

In a public-speaking course for its salesmen, one large paper company recorded each man's first five-minute talk before training. Without their knowledge, a certain amount of blank tape was passed between each man's first talk. As the program concluded, each man's last speech was taped back-to-back with his first talk. When both were played back to the entire class, the improvement was both obvious and dramatic. Every salesman was justifiably proud of his personal accomplishment, which helped to reinforce the desired change in behavior. All sales trainees want to know how well they are doing, and the imaginative use of audio tape can dramatically show them their progress.

Sales managers and trainers can build a library of sales training tapes appropriate to their particular needs. Most reputable organizations provide a money-back guarantee to reduce the risk in purchasing the wrong tapes. After a period of time, however, it would be wise to review the tapes before letting trainees use them. Audio tapes can become outdated as easily as sales training manuals.

The use of audio tape recordings for sales training in the field is covered in Chapter 9, "On-the-Job Coaching."

VIDEO TAPE AND FILM PROGRAMS

In the past it has cost upwards of $50,000 to produce the master negative of a good training film. This cost has prohibited most organizations from making their own films, and the limited size of the potential market has enticed only a handful of producers. The American Management Associations, the Bureau of National Affairs, Roundtable Films, the Dartnell Corporation, and perhaps a very few others have led this field for a number of years.

With today's technological improvements in the video tape recording process, converting from tape to film is relatively inexpensive. The final product, called a kinescope, is a regular 16-mm film of reasonably good quality. Commercially produced color kinescopes, made from broadcast-quality 2-inch-wide video tape, are almost equal in quality to color films made from master negatives.

In addition, thousands of video cassettes are now being sold that permit the user to plug in a prerecorded video tape cartridge and play it back through a large-screen television receiver without having to thread a film or tape. Both color and black-and-white programs cost considerably less than film, and the picture quality of these pretaped shows is equal to that of a live commercial television broadcast.

Rapidly advancing technology already has permitted most companies to produce their own sales training video tapes, cassettes, kinescopes, or films at a very reasonable cost. Because it is now relatively easy to create programs, almost anyone with a small amount of capital can produce his own. As a result, many visual sales training products on the market are of questionable value. The same cautions about buying audio tape training programs apply to the purchase of video tape programs. Also, building a library of training films or video tapes may be more expensive than building one of audio programs because sounds do not become dated rapidly, but clothing styles and automobile models, for example, quickly date a visual program. What seemed appropriate in 1973 may seem ridiculous in 1978, thus interfering with the educational process.

Making Video Tapes in the House

A common problem facing sales managers and training directors is whether to make their own tapes or buy them. If a company requires slick commercial tapes in order to be accepted by the salesmen, then broadcast-quality equipment is desirable. Script writers, directors, professional cameramen, stagehands, lighting and sound engineers, professional actors, and a host of others are necessary to produce a commercial-quality product. Companies that occasionally need productions of professional quality might consider such alternatives as color motion pictures, rental of the local television broadcasting facilities and personnel, or the services provided by professional production firms.

For most sales training purposes, semiprofessional productions using one-inch tape are readily acceptable by the salesmen. With reasonable preplanning, a sales manager or senior salesman can demonstrate and explain new product developments or sales techniques appropriately for the group being trained. The absence of professional actors can be offset by the sincere conviction of the real manager talking about products and systems he really knows about.

Television shows convey a sense of immediacy because the audience cannot distinguish between a live program and one that was video taped hours, days, weeks, or months previously. To preserve this immediacy, training tapes should not refer to future plans or current events such as this year's world series or the success of the city's pro football players. Furthermore, in a series of training tapes, each session should be independent of the others. When making two tapes on the same day, it may seem logical to refer to what has been covered earlier or will be covered later. However, the playbacks to trainees may be a week or a month apart, or trainees may see one program and not the other; thus, some points may not seem logical.

What appears on the television screen is often more important than what the speaker is saying, and the viewer will quickly tune out mentally if the scene is boring. A variety of camera angles and visual aids helps maintain viewer interest. Since television is a visual medium, its impact is greatest when it is used with action—that is, when the camera shows action behind the speaker or concentrates on the action alone, in effect substituting the action for the speaker. If narration is used for the presentation, a trained commentator is desirable.

Sales training tapes can be made in the house on subjects such as company orientation, selling knowledge and skills, and work habits. Decision making under conditions of uncertainty in marketing has been successfully taught using a case-history format with built-in stops for group discussion at critical areas. In short, the creation of video cassettes or kinescopes for sales training is limited only by the user's imagination and his willingness to innovate.

Using Visual Programs Effectively

The use of prerecorded television or film sales training programs in the classroom has been researched fairly well. Before presenting a visual program, the manager should prepare the salesmen for what they are about to see. By directing their attention in advance to certain portions of a program, he can substantially increase learning.

As mentioned, stopping the program at intervals or critical points to permit discussion or other active participation also enhances the learning process. If a salesman develops a mental block because he has seen something on the screen that bothers him or that he does not understand, a brief discussion may help him. Since the rapid rewind feature permits easy replay, any portion can be reviewed immediately and doubts or controversy resolved as quickly as possible. Experiments with training films have shown that programs stopped for the purpose of answering questions or reviewing a scene produce significantly greater learning than programs shown without interruption.

Various viewer-participation techniques, such as responding aloud or in writing to questions on the screen, can also increase learning. A series of studies using television instruction found that learning increases significantly when opportunities for viewer participation are provided at various points in the presentation. Recent studies by the author and others at Florida Atlantic University have shown that trainees learn and retain substantially more when discussion follows the viewing than when it precedes or when there is no discussion whatsoever. Finally, reviewing programs over succeeding days also can significantly enhance some sales trainees' learning process. Reviewing is particularly appropriate when the program presents many important points in a relatively short period.

Visual training programs are especially effective when the manager wants to convey the meaning of nonverbal communication symbols. For example, very successful sales training tapes have been made by some companies showing an incident in which the salesman does a number of things incorrectly. Trainees quickly spot the evasive look or lack of eye contact, the bored slouch or poor body posture, and so forth. This incident process usually produces a lively discussion among sales trainees. Such a lesson can be reinforced by a second part which shows the salesman as a model of correct behavior. Some sales trainees are particularly susceptible to imitating the correct behavior of the successful salesman in a training film.

When there are a number of intelligent approaches to a complex situation, a panel of experts can be video taped or filmed discussing the issue. Such a group cannot be expected to visit every small training class, but the recorded version can be shown again and again as long as it is topical. A variation that is also successful is the use of three salesmen demonstrating in separate sequences how they would handle the same difficult situation. This leads the viewer to judge the approaches, and subsequent group discussion can point out the advantages or appropriateness of each. If only one of the techniques demonstrated is correct, learning can be reinforced by a final sequence illustrating the buyer's reaction to each salesman.

The use of video tape to provide instant replay of role playing is a highly specialized training application. Because it is so complex and important, the next entire chapter is devoted to this specific method. Another application of video tape, on-the-job coaching (as contrasted to classroom use), is also covered subsequently, in Chapter 9.

COMPUTER GAMES

The simulation technique, long used in sales training, attempts to approximate real-world conditions and requires the salesman to take some action under a specified on-going situation. With the computer now available to more companies, highly complex situations with many variables can be created. The computer can predict in a few minutes what would happen over a time period such as three months if a given course of action were taken.

Computer-simulation games are used to develop the abilities of salesmen to analyze situations, to make decisions under varying degrees of uncertainty, and to appreciate the impact their recommendations to a customer will have on his business. Salesmen often enjoy computer games because they are directly involved and because the profit-and-loss statement generated by the game enables them to measure their own performance.

There are computer games tailored to a number of different products, services, and industries. (See the partial listing at the end of this chapter.) In addition, there are at least three basic formats which can be used, depending on the unique training situation.

An industrial manufacturer selling paint directly to retailers, for example, uses a sales training game based on real case histories. The salesman analyzes his retail customer's situation and recommends retail management action to help his customer increase business and to win the account's loyalty. In this company seven or eight salesmen serve as a team to advise one retailer on how to improve his P&L. The salesmen experiment with the variables a retailer must consider, such as advertising, pricing, and inventory management, and implement their ideas with quarterly decisions for each variable. The computer calculates what would result from these decisions and compares quarter-by-quarter progress. Each team plays against the computer but there is no interteam competition.

An electronics manufacturer plays a similar game with the sales teams actively competing against one another. Each team attempts to increase its share of market and its profits at the expense of its rivals. Because each team does not know what its competitors' actions will be, it must make decisions with only partial information. The computer then calculates the total impact on the market and its effect on each individual team. This game is played for the equivalent of either twelve quarters or five years to encourage long-range planning.

A third variation is structured on analyzing the potential value of various customers and prospects and deciding how often a limited number of salesmen should call on the different accounts. Other variables, such as the amount to invest in sales training, advertising, and sales promotion, must also be considered. This format is designed to teach salesmen some basic concepts of sales planning and territory management.

Each of these formats can include special options for the instructor to test the team's ability to respond to the unexpected. For example, the instructor can enter a new competitor into the market or arrange for certain good customers to be transferred to a competitor. The instructor can often manipulate the market research information to overstate or understate the real situation. The variations possible with the computer are infinite.

The major disadvantage of computer games played by a team of salesmen is the likelihood that one or two dominant men will make all the team's decisions, while the other men coast or totally ignore the learning situation. On occasion two strong salesmen on the same team may lead groups of opposing opinion, paralyzing the team. Clearly, these problems can be resolved if each salesman can operate as a one-man team; however, individuals will probably need more time to make each decision. In addition, the computer would have to have adequate storage space in the memory bank for many more inputs, and there would have to be sufficient processing time.

Often the true educational value of a computer game is in the group discussion at the completion of competition. Each team can be asked to report its initial objectives and how well they met them; what short- and long-range plans were made and what controls were used to monitor the progress; and finally, what the team would recommend for the future. By analyzing what actually occurred, the salesmen can derive certain principles and applications which should be helpful back on the job.

A MULTIMEDIA APPROACH

Each method discussed above has its strengths and weaknesses, and each seems to be more appropriate in some areas and less appropriate in other areas. In reality, any one method used alone is not likely to be effective. Most textbook publishers are approaching this problem by creating separate divisions to produce films, video cassettes, programmed-instruction workbooks, and so forth. Computer games often have student textbooks and related reading assignments. Unfortunately, each division is set up as a profit center and must succeed or fail on its own efforts. There is no synergistic effect, with each division contributing to produce results which are greater than the sum of the parts.

Thus, the sales manager or training director is faced with the problem of creating his own multimedia approach to sales training. In other words, he should not consider *either* television *or* a guest expert; rather, he should consider what combination of educational components will produce the optimum benefits for his salesmen within the time and budget constraints. Above all, he should ensure that whatever the salesmen learn will be meaningful to them in the real world.

The person responsible for training salesmen should facilitate the learning process by:

- Developing rapport with the salesmen.
- Arousing the salesmen's curiosity and interest.
- Being aware of the objectives and limits of a course.
- Challenging the salesmen's mental capacities.
- Measuring progress objectively by means of behavior changes.
- Providing a multimedia approach to utilize the best methods and facilities available.

In this way, he will make it easier for the trainees to become mentally and physically involved in the subject matter.

SELECTED MATERIALS

Espich, James E., and Williams, Bill, *Developing Programmed Instructional Materials*. Palo Alto, Calif.: Fearon Publishers, 1967.

Gerlach, Vernon S., and Ely, Donald P., *Teaching and Media: A Systematic Approach*. Englewood Cliffs, N.J.: Prentice-Hall, 1971.

Graham, Robert G., and Gray, Clifford F., *Business Games Handbook*. AMA, 1969.

Readings introduce the games approach to training and demonstrate how games are used by particular companies. An extensive bibliography is included, along with a summary of over 200 games currently in use and their training objectives.

Hendershot, Carl H., *Programmed Learning: A Bibliography of Programs and Presentation Devices*. Bay City, Mich.: Hendershot, 1970.

This loose-leaf catalog of all programs currently available is kept up to date by periodical supplements.

The Language of Business: How to Read It, Write It, Understand It. New York: Dun & Bradstreet, Business Education Division.

This correspondence course of 12 study units averaging five hours per unit requires about six months.

Rowntree, Derek, *Basically Branching*. Palo Alto, Calif.: Fearon Publishers, 1962.

Teaching Machines and Programmed Learning. Washington, D.C.: National Audiovisual Center, National Archives and Records Service, General Services Administration. 16 mm, B&W.

This 28-minute film provides an orientation to teaching machines and programmed learning for instructors. B. F. Skinner, Arthur A. Lumsdaine, and Robert Glaser discuss theories, materials, and machines.

The Video Play Program Catalog. ¾ Inch "U" Videocassette Edition. Ridgefield, Conn.: C. S. Tepfer Publishing Company.

Videocassette/Cartridge, Recorder/Player Directory. Vol. 4, No. 9 (Sept. 1972), p. 13. Ridgefield, Conn.: C. S. Tepfer Publishing Company.

Original equipment manufacturers' listings of models on the market at that time or projected to be marketed by June 1973 are given, and format, options, and prices are described.

CHAPTER 7

Sales Training Using Video Instant Replay

To ILLUSTRATE THE practical value of sales training or to make a particular subject more meaningful, direct observation of a real sales interview in a prospect's office is extremely effective for most sales trainees. Ideally, each trainee should observe one very effective salesman making several calls of the same kind, such as prospecting. The trainees should be thoroughly prepared to observe closely those activities which illustrate the principle being taught. After every trainee has witnessed several interviews, he should be able to deduce certain generalizations, and a class discussion can reinforce this learning.

Unfortunately, most effective salesmen do not have the incentive to spend a great deal of time with trainees. In addition, when the salesman and the buyer know that they are being observed, their behavior and speech may be guarded. In contrast, people who like being in front of an audience will go out of their way to give an outstanding performance. It is almost impossible for anyone to behave naturally in a sales interview when he knows he is being observed and judged by a third party.

Another problem is that the model salesman must make his regular calls even though the trainee is with him. On a given day the men might call on one prospect, two accounts that order regularly, and one account that has a serious complaint. The trainee will have difficulty making the intended generalizations from such a variety of observations. Of course, the problem is compounded when each trainee observes a different salesman.

To overcome these difficulties, effective salesmen are often asked to come into the classroom to demonstrate their selling technique on a particular phase of an interview. The demonstration has greater meaning for the trainees when the experienced salesman tells what he will do beforehand and accepts questions after the demonstration. The entire group of trainees observes the same performance, and usually the trainer summarizes the key points at the end of the training session to reinforce the desired learning.

Role playing has been effectively used to dramatize a selling demonstration because it provides an opportunity for interaction between buyer and seller. Structured role-playing sessions can also introduce unforeseen events which the men must deal with on the spot. Assignment of roles may vary: An effective salesman may play himself, with the trainer playing the part of a particular type of buyer. Or individual trainees may play either or both parts, and groups of trainees can help one man prepare for the interview. Role playing is most commonly used to involve the sales trainees actively in the learning process and to reinforce by demonstration specific points already covered.

Audio tape recordings of role-playing situations allow subsequent analysis of only the spoken communication, while video tape recordings capture both spoken and visual communications. In fact, video tape usually records much more than the trainer can possibly discuss in the scheduled time.

Video tape, however, is not always an easy medium to use in training. Often it requires more preparation on the part of both instructors and trainees than other media, and it does not necessarily save class time. For example, replay can easily consume two to three times the number of hours required for role playing without critique or feedback. Moreover, video recordings often involve both the instructor and the trainee on a highly emotional level, which makes the medium difficult to use objectively. Fortunately, most sales trainees enjoy seeing themselves on instant replay, and some excellent training has occurred with this medium.

ROLE PLAYING

Presenting a Desirable Model

When someone demonstrates a technique to trainees, he becomes a model whom the trainees are encouraged to imitate. They will, however, observe more than just the desired technique. For example, an experienced salesman, or the sales manager himself, when taking a part in a role play, may show signs of amusement as he toys with his prospect, or may exhibit an unconscious tendency toward braggadocio. His mannerisms, facial expressions, body posture, and gestures will be perceived by the trainees both consciously and subconsciously. Many trainees will try to imitate the poor traits as well as the good traits.

Role playing, unlike conventional acting, requires the participants to take actions and speak lines spontaneously instead of following a predetermined script. This places demands on the person handling the camera that a professional television cameraman would find very difficult, if not impossible, to meet. In taping the role play of a sales interview, for instance, he may simply aim the camera to take in both players and leave it that way. This shot, which would approximate a view of two people from across a room, might be ideal to establish the situation, but it could not possibly show the quizzical raising of an eyebrow. If the cameraman is to capture the actions that the trainer wants to emphasize during the replay, he should be instructed during the pretaping planning session to anticipate certain facial expressions at critical times or to be on the lookout for certain meaningful gestures. If he is adequately prepared, he will be ready to vary his distance and lens setting according to the spontaneous developments of the role play.

Sometimes the emotions of the cameraman (or of the person who selects the picture to record if there are several cameras in operation) interfere with the presentation of an ideal role model. If the cameraman resents the actor, for example, he may subconsciously focus on a minor distracting movement, such as repetitive scratching of the ear, rather than calling attention to the desired action. An actor's nervous twitch, drumming of his fingers on a desk top, or locking of his jaw muscles may seem amusing to the man working the camera but may easily destroy the educational value of the instant replay. On the other hand, if these mannerisms are nonverbal indications of impatience or resistance on the part of the person playing the buyer, they may be exactly what the trainer wants to have recorded in close-up. Unfortunately, the cameraman is too often a trainee who does not have proper preparation or instruction regarding the actions which are desired and the actions to be avoided. In these cases, the trainee will focus on what he believes to be important or what he thinks is comical, and the video tape may not picture the intended ideal behavior.

Acting

The person invited to role-play the expert is normally a salesman well established in his field. He is often known for his willingness to cooperate in teaching sales trainees, which is highly desirable. None of these traits, however, ensures that this person will perform acceptably before the camera. In a professional studio with three or four cameras going simultaneously, a good television director might be able to make the actor look professional by recording the appropriate view. In-house productions for sales training purposes usually have only one, or at best two, cameras, so the actor must play to a camera.

Instructional television is an action-oriented and person-to-person medium. This requires the actor to play the part of the friendly authority talking directly to one trainee. For example, when he is demonstrating a product in a role-playing situation, he should direct all his gestures and eye contact toward the camera. The close-up view recorded for replay will not show the prospect if the trainer wants his trainees to watch the demonstration.

Another difficulty in acting for video instant replay may arise whether the actor is an experienced salesman or a sales trainee. When faced with a new situation, it is normal for a person to revert to behavior which has been effective for him in the past. Thus one person may become overly aggressive in a televised role play. Another man may become very cautious and quiet. A third person may act the comedian for his audience. In these situations, the instant replay of the video tape does indeed reflect what the person normally might do under new and strange conditions. The replay, however, does not necessarily reflect what the trainee might do or the experienced salesman actually does in a prospect's office without anyone observing. Sales trainers using this technique should be aware of this important distinction.

Paraphernalia

In a real sales interview, the effective salesman would probably make use of a number of charts, graphs, written testimonials, and possibly a pad of paper to sketch layouts or to summarize a number of points. If the content of these visual aids is to be stressed rather than the general way in which they are used, then using them spontaneously in the role-play situation will probably be of no educational value. When their content is not critical, visual aids should be prepared especially for video taping. For example, when the salesman is about to show the prospect a written document, the camera can zoom in toward the piece of paper. Then the camera can black out for a second and a large chart can be substituted which will have information printed large enough to be seen on replay. As the salesman speaks, one line at a time can be exposed so that the audience will focus on the proper item. The same principle would apply if the salesman were to show the prospect a miniature, model, or blueprint drawing. Whenever possible, the visual aids should be made to fill the screen, with the salesman speaking off camera.

If the salesman doing the demonstration is supposed to be addressing a group of clients and using a slide projector or an overhead or opaque projector, for example, the same preparations would be appropriate. The camera should not attempt to show the salesman, his equipment, and the reproduced message at the same time if the instructor wants his trainees to focus on the message. Any equipment in the foreground will tend to dominate the picture during replay. For these reasons, when using video tape to show model behavior, it is important for the instructor to prepare the equipment operators and actors and to design appropriate visual aids especially for the particular program.

SELF-CONFRONTATION

The most common use of video tape in sales training is to record a salesman or trainee in a role-play situation for instant replay. This technique gives the salesman an opportunity to see himself as others might see him: He literally confronts himself with a set of perceptual standards which normally are applied only to others.

Ego-Involvement Problems

Sales trainees and experienced salesmen confronting themselves for the first few times tend to be very anxious and often extremely self-critical. There is tremendous ego-involvement in watching oneself perform on instant replay. The trainee may be instructed to observe how he handled a particular question, but his attention is magnetically drawn to his nose or his receding hairline. Many salesmen have felt that their first few exposures to this medium made them more self-conscious performers rather than better ones.

A number of research studies have agreed that salesmen often experience a decrease in the effectiveness of their presentations after viewing the first one or two instant replays. Indeed, some salesmen abhor a video role-playing assignment because after previous role plays the sales manager and other salesmen have given them too much negative feedback, making them uncomfortable and embarrassed. For example, recently a sales manager in the paper industry refused to role-play in a management seminar because five years earlier, as a sales trainee, he had been chewed out in a role-playing situation. While his five-year sales record was outstanding, his one experience with instant replay had taught him to avoid being put in that defenseless position ever again.

Controlling the Feedback

Self-confrontation by instant replay can be a very constructive and valuable sales training technique. The first few evaluations of taped performances should emphasize the many good traits that each man exhibits. Little or no negative criticism should be permitted in this first phase of video sales training. After the men get over both the shock of seeing themselves and their preoccupation with self-centered trivia, they are ready for some carefully regulated constructive criticism. For example, the instructor might say, "That was a great response to the prospect's question, Charlie, but have you considered how you might have reflected his question so that he would have had to answer his own objection?"

When the salesmen can comfortably accept limited constructive criticism and get caught up in the spirit of helping one another, they may be ready for some personal criticism. Initial criticism might be concerned with body posture, eye contact, or eliminating a distracting gesture or other mannerism. The final level of criticism might reflect the way the salesman communicates his personal feelings in his words and actions. For example, he might feel superior to his customers, and perhaps justly so, but if they can sense this attitude it may hurt his sales.

The guideline for criticism is that the feedback should never tell the salesman more than he really cares to know about himself or more than he is ready to accept. When this point is exceeded, the situation may be uncomfortable, embarrassing, or totally destructive. Learning may be blocked, at least on a temporary basis, and permanent psychological changes may occur. When a trainee gets a flash of insight about a basic fault in his behavior, he has diagnosed the problem, but that is all. Seeing oneself in a horrible way can hardly be expected to advance a person's growth and development if he is not ready to deal with such revelations. In fact, to defend themselves against painful criticism, some salesmen commit all sorts of horrendous errors, making the video tape session a complete farce.

Protecting the Trainee's Ego

Experienced trainers use a number of techniques to soften the blow of instant replay and to protect the trainee's ego. One is to reverse the role play so that the salesman plays the part of the buyer. This seems particularly appropriate when training salesmen to be empathetic with their prospects. Another technique is to assign a case history to the salesman and ask him to play the part as if he were the salesman in the case. This permits the trainee to try out the new behavior patterns being taught but provides a defense against possible criticism. If anything goes wrong, he can say that he was doing what the man in the case probably would have done, certainly not what he personally would have done. A variation is for several trainees on a team to decide how one of the members will play a role. The team decision gives the individual role player a defense against any criticism. In a third method, called the bedlam technique, two teams of three men play the roles of buyer and seller. Any member of a team can respond for a teammate and save him. This technique divides the impact of self-confrontation.

The critique or evaluation of an instant replay should also be designed to protect the trainees. Each man can view the replay in private or alone with the instructor. When a group will view the tape, ground rules should be established to encourage positive comments and limited constructive criticism.

An experienced sales training director would not attempt to teach public speaking by having each trainee perform only once or twice. Similarly, self-confrontation through instant replay should be built into a program which enables each man to progress gradually according to his abilities and motivation. Saving video-taped performances that clearly illustrate steady improvement until the end of the training period will encourage most trainees to continue their efforts to improve.

Self-confrontation by means of instant replay is perhaps the most action-oriented and personally involving technique for classroom sales training. Handled with the precautions noted and a large measure of compassion for the trainees, it can produce highly rewarding results.

EFFECTS OF REPLAY ON THE LEARNING PROCESS

A sales trainer should expect interaction between the medium (in this case, video instant replay), the trainee's aptitudes and traits, and the learning objectives. However, if the unique features of video instant replay are not utilized to present the critical information, there is little reason to expect unique effects as a result of using this medium. Conversely, when the information is presented by means of features which are unique to instant replay, then unique effects may be expected. The unique attributes of instant replay will have a unique educational effect only if they arouse in the trainee a mental process which is relevant to the learning task at hand.

The sales trainee's attitude toward the value of classroom training, toward his instructor, and toward the instant replay of his video-taped performance all affect the learning process. Studies have shown that when viewing oneself on a television screen is potentially threatening, people prefer to be exposed to positive rather than negative information about themselves. If they are forced to listen to too much negative information, they tend to discredit and become hostile toward the source of information and will attempt to evade the message and to stop the communication process.

The trainee's awareness of his behavior in a role-play situation is usually distorted by his self-interest and his personal involvement in the training process. The accurate record of his performance provided by instant replay may contradict his erroneous perceptions and be threatening to his self-esteem. Nevertheless, a number of studies showed that this supposedly threatening characteristic of instant replay does not impede the desired learning or intended behavior change. On the contrary, viewing oneself often enhances changes in the desired direction. The problem then is one of arousing in the trainee an appropriate mental process to facilitate acceptance of new and partly negative feedback about himself.

Preparing the Trainees

A review of the research literature indicates that two conditions are present when trainees change their behavior as desired. These conditions were not present in those studies which reported defensiveness, rejection, or other indications of learning inhibition. The two conditions are that the trainees know what behavior is expected of them before the role play, and that they have accepted the criteria and are willing to modify their behavior to meet expectations.

When these two conditions are met, the instant replay and critique tell them how close their behavior came to meeting the accepted standards. Under these conditions, defensive reactions are not likely to take place.

The effects of video instant replay on the learning process, therefore, can hardly be attributed to the medium alone. For optimum contribution to the learning process, the sales trainees should be properly prepared so that they understand and accept the standards of behavior expected of them and really want this form of training feedback. Finally, the criteria of judging the changed behavior should be identical to the learning objectives stated before the training began.

If the trainer wants the salesman to be able to find out what his prospects sincerely feel about their needs, for example, the learning objectives might be stated as follows:

1. To be able to use six or more probing techniques comfortably while role-playing a 15-minute sales interview.

2. To be able to recognize sensitive areas and to probe more deeply into these areas without offending the prospect.

3. To permit the prospect to dominate 50 to 60 percent of the 15-minute interview.

4. To listen well enough to recall correctly at least 80 percent of the prospect's major points immediately after the interview.

Trainees should be shown how they will personally benefit by learning the particular techniques and motivated to do the best job possible. They may hear lectures about the techniques, read assigned materials, and perhaps view a film on this subject and participate in a discussion afterward. When the manager feels that they are ready for the role play, he should carefully explain the expected standards of behavior and precisely how the trainees will be judged. When all sales trainees understand and accept the criteria, they can proceed with the role play and instant replay. Used in this manner, the medium will enhance the learning process with a minimum of defensive reactions.

Contrast the positive effects of such preparation with the effects of a training program reported in *Sales Management* (May 1, 1972). The director of training wrote that he usually gives his salesmen 15 to 20 minutes to read a five-page case study or to watch a video-taped interview. Then the men are instructed to elicit valid and informative answers by using a probing technique in a role play. They are given about five minutes to think about what they are going to say and then they proceed directly to the video-taped interview, which rarely lasts longer than 10 to 15 minutes.

"Highly directive managers get into trouble right away, and gladly wind it up in less than five minutes," he writes. He is "disturbed" that many of his managers do not probe properly. He cites an extreme and unusual example of one man breaking down completely, illustrating "the extent of self-awareness that can be generated by a remarkably simple technique." But using inadequately considered methods of training can only inhibit the learning process and turn many good salesmen against the medium and probably against sales training in general.

PROBLEMS TO CONTEND WITH

Many of the difficulties that companies experience in using video instant replay are the fault not of the equipment but of the people who control its use. Among these problems are the performers' anxiety, the time allocations, the attitudes of the equipment operators, and the control of the critique. If the instructor does not consider these factors when planning to use video tape in sales training, they can defeat his efforts to use the medium successfully.

Performers' Anxiety

Although some salesmen and trainees look forward to their first experience with video tape, many do not. Anxiety on the part of the performers is a common problem, and care should be taken to make the actors more comfortable in this new situation. The most common method of reassuring a performer is promising him a private critique with his instructor. This spares the salesman the possibility of making a fool of himself and having his errors corrected publicly. Most salesmen seem more willing to admit their faults in a private session than before a group of peers.

When time limitations prohibit private replay sessions, the instructor should carefully explain the entire training procedure. The trainees should be assured that no one will be abused or psychologically attacked and that all video tapes will be erased after the training sessions are completed. As noted earlier, each trainee should understand how he can personally benefit from this new experience. He should agree with the expected standards of behavior and he should know precisely how he will be judged. The time taken to alleviate the trainees' anxiety before the taping session is well spent, for it increases real learning.

Insufficient Time

Even with a carefully controlled procedure and a climate of compassion for the trainees, there is still a strong possibility that the trainees' ego-involvement will interfere with the learning process. As mentioned previously, trainees watching their first few performances on video instant replay focus their attention on aspects other than those intended by the instructor. Subsequent performances may show a decrease in effectiveness in the areas under study. Once this fascination with themselves has passed, the trainees learn rapidly from instant replay.

The sales manager or trainer should plan to have each trainee on camera long enough to become comfortable when role playing. Replay of the performance should be unhurried so that the trainee will have enough time to understand and accept his deviation from the desired behavior. This is especially important because the trainee is unable to defend himself by the normal means of faulty recall and faulty perception, since instant replay precludes such denials. The average sales trainee should perform at least three or four different times if video instant replay is to increase his learning.

If the manager has prepared objective criteria upon which he will base his evaluations, he can measure the salesman's progress in each successive role play. For example, he can count the number of times the salesman interrupts the prospect or blocks communication. With a stop watch he can clock the amount of time the salesman talks and the amount of time he is silent. He can give an objective test of recall before each playback, to determine the improvement in the trainee's listening ability. Objective measures of this type permit the instructor to pace the critiques and to determine when a trainee is having difficulty with a point or phase of training.

Attitudes of the Cameraman

The camera neither creates nor corrects distortion. Generally, if instant replay interferes with the learning process, it is the instructor's fault: He probably has not learned how to use the equipment properly and cannot introduce the camera into the training situation comfortably. The person assigned to do the camerawork can interrupt, disrupt, and destroy good role-playing situations. He can ridicule, irritate, and embarrass the trainees, or he can encourage, support, and reassure them.

The problem is not essentially one of the cameraman's technical proficiency. Rather, it concerns his attitude toward the medium and the way that his attitude affects his communication with trainees. The man behind the camera can hide or underplay certain details or he can focus the camera to call attention to various actions, gestures, expressions, and the like. Thus, instant replay can be used as a strong form of punishment, a way of getting back at a particularly obnoxious trainee.

Under normal training conditions, camera angles and close-up shots are used to highlight points of importance to the individual learner. For example, by closing in on a distracting gesture or focusing on a bored prospect, the instructor can draw the trainee's attention to specific aspects of his presentation. The process of selecting what will be recorded for playback should be controlled objectively rather than by emotion, whim, or pure accident. Selective editing of part of an event can be crucial in determining the educational effectiveness of video instant replay.

Uncontrolled Critique

Perhaps the most sensitive area in video instant replay for sales training is that of controlling the critique and evaluation. Some trainers are so impressed by the amount of student interest generated by self-confrontation that they concentrate on determining the degree of interest rather than the degree of learning. Consequently, instead of learning the basic information or developing the skills being taught, trainees become preoccupied with competing against each other in a game or defending themselves in an ego-damaging situation.

A sales trainee with strong inferiority feelings or doubts about his own abilities tends to attack others to prove they are not superior to him. If the critique is permitted to develop freely, without guidance and controls, this kind of trainee will search for any error or indication of a performer's weakness, whether or not it relates to the intended learning process. His attack may take the form of a vicious blow against the defenseless role player who has made an obvious mistake or it may take the form of a joke about the performer's shiny bald head.

Clearly, criticism should be limited to comparing the taped performance with the objective criteria established and agreed on before the role play. Moreover, it should be channeled into constructive suggestions which are offered as alternative ways to handle the situation more effectively and will help the trainee in future performances. Finally, as stated earlier, criticism and evaluation should heavily emphasize the positive aspects of each trainee's performance. This will reinforce the tentative new behavior as well as build an atmosphere of friendly cooperation in the learning environment.

BENEFITS OF VIDEO TAPE RECORDING

Perhaps the only thing worse than misusing video tape in sales training is being denied the privilege of using it. Real and tremendous benefits can accrue to sales trainers using this exciting medium. Nine out of ten users of video tape equipment report that the cost of their equipment is well justified and the benefits clearly outweigh the effort involved in trying to use it effectively.[1]

The consensus among sales trainers is that video tape recording increases trainee interest and participation. It is virtually impossible for the trainee to sit back passively or mentally tune out the picture on the television screen when he is the performer. The self-interest of the trainees is so strong, in fact, that many of them ask for permission to practice with video recordings outside the normal business hours. Experienced salesmen often want to come back in the evenings during a week-long training seminar to perfect their taped performance. Very few sales training methods can generate this kind of spontaneous involvement and interest.

In sales training, instant replay improves performance by providing an opportunity for more candid self-analysis. When the typical salesman or trainee is merely told of a minor fault which detracts from his effectiveness, he may shrug off this negative feedback. Unless the instructor wishes to make a big issue of this minor fault, the entire topic is quickly forgotten, and there is little behavior change. With instant replay, however, the student can see how his minor fault really is distracting. In the proper learning climate the trainee will accept constructive criticism and gain insights about himself which he might otherwise reject. If he watches himself again and again in the same video-taped performance, he will notice additional things which he missed on the first replay. This medium can provide a trainee with more information about himself than he can assimilate

[1] *AMA Research Report No. 93* (1968).

in a single viewing. Because of the unique nature of instant replay, there is no delay between performing and reviewing the performance. The trainee can see what he has done correctly and what he has not done or done poorly while he is still in the learning state and highly concerned with meeting acceptable standards of behavior.

Video instant replay provides positive reinforcement of tentative behavior patterns which the trainee is trying out for the first few times. For example, if he is told about reflective techniques in a seminar, he may feel that they will insult his prospect. Later, when he attempts to use a reflective question in a role play, he may feel ill at ease. But when he sees the instant replay, the situation may seem quite normal. The prospect not only accepted his reflective question but went on to elaborate or explain what he meant by a previous statement. When the positive results of his tentative behavior are immediately reinforced by instant replay, the trainee will use this technique with more and more confidence until it becomes part of his habitual behavior.

Because video tape can be erased and reused hundreds of times, it is a valuable yet inexpensive tool for self-instruction. Once the trainee knows the criteria he must meet or the model he is to imitate, he can practice his performance again and again on video tape. Instead of unknowingly making the same mistake over and over, he has immediate feedback to show him what he must correct.

Timely presentations and commentaries on fast-breaking events can be recorded on video tape advantageously because there is no delay for processing time. Executive announcements of changes in company policy, for example, or of promotions or the progress of a sales contest can be taped and shown immediately to salesmen or sales trainees. Used in this manner, video tape can convey a sense of urgency or news value characteristic of television but lacking in other media.

Similarly, a presentation at a small executive meeting can be taped and later shown to an enlarged audience of salesmen and trainees. For example, the new advertising campaign may be officially presented to only a few executives, but its impact may depend heavily on the field salesman's cooperation in implementing the strategy. If the presentation has been taped, several copies of the tape can be made quickly and inexpensively and shown at regional meetings the same day. Sales trainees will feel they are an important part of the organization if they too can watch the televised presentation.

New products and modifications and improvements of existing products can often be demonstrated on video tape to advantage through magnification or models. Technical experts can explain the changes and customer benefits to every salesman, when their presence in many regional sales offices would not be possible. The conviction that comes from seeing and hearing the expert on television cannot be easily duplicated by a printed memorandum over the signature of a stranger. Thus video tape can be an inexpensive way to update materials and keep sales messages current.

As noted earlier, a library of video tapes or video cassettes can be created containing executive presentations appropriate for company orientation and sales training topics. An outdated tape can be corrected in part or erased and remade completely with no material cost. Viewing such current tapes leads every sales trainee to feel that he knows the executives of his company personally and has the latest information available.

Of course, video tape recordings share many of the advantages of film. For example, both media foster better preparation of the instructor or guest lecturer's presentation and more effective use of dramatization and visual aids. Because the message and information will be used a number of times, the speaker is likely to take the time and effort to do an outstanding job, whereas he might make a quick, informal, and occasionally inaccurate speech to one small group of sales trainees.

When film or tape is used, motion itself may be an essential part of the learning process, particularly in the understanding of sequential events. But all the parts of an action are not necessarily relevant to the point being made, and film and tape permit the elimination of nonessential elements as well as the contraction or expansion of time to suit the specific educational goal. For example, to walk a sales trainee around a plant or a large piece of equipment might take a considerable amount of time, but the film or tape need show only the important parts of the tour. An event which takes hours or days to occur in real life can be shown in a few minutes on the screen. Conversely, something that happens rapidly can be shown in slow motion to permit better comprehension.

Finally, video tape and film both allow control of the sound that accompanies the picture. Real background noises can be toned down or eliminated, and a narrator's voice can be recorded over a conversation or instead of it. Thus the sound message can be tailored to fit the learning objectives and to call attention to the appropriate part of the lesson.

The benefits of using video tape or cassettes in sales training are probably limited only by the imagination and creativity of the people using this exciting medium—except that time and money constraints obviously can determine the amount of training and the equipment the instructor can use.

SELECTING THE RIGHT EQUIPMENT FOR THE JOB

The rapid and continuous technical developments in the field of video recordings make it impossible to recommend one method or brand as best for sales training. The quality of the recorded picture is steadily improving while the cost of the systems is decreasing. Most manufacturers of video recording equipment are attempting to simplify the operation and lower the cost enough to make their units attractive to the mass market of homeowners. Color video cassette playback units are being sold nationally for under $1,000. When several competing manufacturers get into mass production of these units, the retail price will probably drop dramatically. As video tape dominated the market in the 1960s, the video cassette is likely to dominate it in the 1970s.

For a few hundred dollars above the base price, the cassette playback unit includes an apparatus which permits the user to record whatever he can receive on his regular color television set. These units will also accept a program from a television camera, and this complicates the equipment selection problem. An inexpensive black-and-white camera can be purchased with optional accessories, but color cameras are relatively expensive at this time, which all but precludes their use with the inexpensive cassette system.

Before investigating the equipment on the market, the trainer or sales manager should carefully define his training objectives. When he has decided how video instant replay will help achieve his training goals, he is then in a position to list the most desirable product features. For most role-playing situations the instructor will want a zoom lens on his camera to show a performer's facial expressions close up, for example, or to bring out the details of a full-page magazine advertisement. He will probably want a system which will require only normal room lighting. If he needs to show actors walking or otherwise moving about, he will probably want individual microphones for each performer rather than a single all-directional table-top mike, for example. If all the equipment is to be used in the classroom, then compactness would not be particularly important. Conversely, if the equipment is to be transported around the office or to a series of hotel rooms for on-the-road training, then ruggedness and compactness become more critical.

The sharpness of detail should be tested before any purchase is made. Rather than view a demonstration tape made by the equipment manufacturer under ideal lighting and sound conditions, the trainer should arrange to try the equipment under the typical conditions in the area where it will be used. Most suppliers today offer either a free demonstration or a rental arrangement which permits on-location testing of their equipment. Often, some or all of the rental charge can be applied to the subsequent purchase of the video equipment.

For some sales organizations dual sound tracks may be desirable to record in two languages on the same video tape. This feature gives the user one picture and his choice of either of the sound tracks. It also permits a trainee in a field office to record a presentation and send it in to a central training location for review. The instructor can then record his comments and evaluation on the second sound track, relating them to the picture, and send the tape back to the salesman in the field.

When the trainer anticipates that his role-playing sessions will include three or more performers on camera at the same time, he would do well to consider having two or more cameras. This would require a small monitor for each camera at a central point and a switching device that enables the operator to record whichever picture he wants the instant he sees it. If the trainer plans to spend some time preparing instructional video programs for which the final tapes must be nearly perfect—for example, programs showing model salesmen demonstrating ideal practices—he should investigate recording units which allow him to edit the final recording electronically.

Because training time is limited, rapid forward and reverse are considered essential features by most sales trainers. Of course, if the video recording is to be used on different machines, compatibility is also essential and should be demonstrated before the system is purchased. While service contracts and guarantees are normally offered on most video equipment, breakdowns can occur during a training session; thus local service and/or replacement on loan may be the key factor in the final selection of both the manufacturer and the local dealer or servicing organization.

Color video equipment is desirable if the additional cost is minimal; however, very few sales training directors feel that it contributes anything to the learning process in the typical role-play situation. It is very difficult to isolate the educational value of color television in classroom sales training, although color obviously improves the entertainment value of most instant replays over black-and-white. In the 1970s, mass production of color video equipment may reduce its cost enough to eliminate this question.

To produce sales training tapes of a permanent nature and a quality that is comparable to commercial broadcasting requires a lot of good luck and the professional services of script writers, lighting and camera technicians, an experienced television director and supporting editorial personnel, sound engineers, and so forth. When a situation arises that justifies an elaborate production of high quality, the rental of professional production facilities and personnel might be the most economical way to achieve it.

On the other hand, all sales organizations can probably benefit by using inexpensive video equipment and instant replay on a day-to-day basis. The total investment may be less than $2,000, or less than half the average cost of training just one salesman. By using some imagination and creativity, sales training directors can produce half-inch tapes for audiences of their own salesmen which more than meet the needs of the situation. As the number of salesmen to be trained, the level of sophistication to be achieved, and the consequent cost of training increase, most medium-to-large sales organizations should be able to justify purchasing one-inch tape equipment, with its higher quality and greater number of features. For under $10,000, most sales organizations have been able to produce high-quality in-house training programs.

Sales managers and training directors should be aware of the danger of becoming too enamored of this medium. As with many hobbies, there is always something new and exciting to buy, and technological improvements will constantly make older equipment obsolete. When the old equipment satisfies the training objectives, however, it need not be replaced by the latest equipment. Maintenance and service costs should dictate the economical time to purchase new video equipment.

SUMMARY

For a number of reasons, it is difficult, if not impossible, to assign trainees to observe one effective salesman in action with a client or prospect. At best, several trainees, each on a different day, may go along with the same salesman as he visits his accounts. Because they will see different things, they may not derive the same general principles.

The next best thing to a field trip for sales trainees is usually watching the effective salesman demonstrating his technique in the classroom. All the trainees see the same presentation and the instructor can guide the subsequent discussion to arrive at the desired generalizations.

By role playing in the classroom the experienced salesman can demonstrate several effective ways to handle unforeseen questions and events in a prospect's office. In this situation, the effective salesman becomes the learning model and the trainees are expected to imitate his performance. This technique requires considerable time for preparation and performance, which is an imposition on most field salesmen. It is frequently better to have this role play taped so that it can be shown to a number of small training classes.

A series of video tapes can be created which illustrate the best practices of several effective salesmen. The tapes can be played straight through or stopped for discussion, partly rewound for instant replay, or used in any way that serves the purpose of the instructor. The unique feature of video instant replay allows the trainer to repeat selected portions of a performance at any point. This can clear up confusion which might otherwise be left unresolved.

When the trainees are involved in role playing with instant replay, they must deal with painfully accurate self-confrontation. Many salesmen and trainees are ill at ease in this new situation, and some fear being criticized or embarrassed if they do poorly. Because they frequently become so emotionally involved in seeing themselves on television for the first time, they may not pay attention to suggested improvements in their performance. When they repeat the role play, they may be even less effective than the first time. If there is too much negative feedback, the actor is apt to learn little more than to avoid this kind of training in the future.

By emphasizing the positive aspects of the performance, the instructor can help the trainee get over his self-consciousness and apply any constructive criticism to his future performance. Experienced sales trainers use a number of techniques to soften the impact of self-confrontation, and anyone using video instant replay for the first time would be well advised to consider some of their suggestions carefully.

The threatening characteristic of instant replay, the annihilation of the trainee's defenses of faulty perception and faulty recall, does not always impede the desired learning or intended behavior change. When the trainee knows what behavior is expected of him before the role play, and when he has accepted these criteria and is willing to modify his behavior to meet the expectations, then defensive reactions are not likely to occur.

When the teaching objectives have been stated precisely, the desired performance for various levels of achievement can be specified, criteria for measurement established, and the degree of learning quantified. Then modification of the trainee's habitual performance can be identified specifically, underscored, and measured both qualitatively and quantitatively on instant replay. This measured progress can guide the instructor as to how much negative feedback the trainee is willing and able to accept.

The four most common types of problems with video instant replay are attributable to the people who control the use of the medium. These problems are due to (1) inadequate emotional preparation of the trainees by the instructor; (2) allotment of insufficient time to enable each trainee to perform several role plays and to watch the instant replays; (3) selective editing that is determined by the emotions of the cameraman rather than the learning objectives; and (4) lack of control or guidance of the critique and evaluation sessions, which allows trainees to hurt one another psychologically.

The benefits of using video instant replay relate primarily to its unique attributes. Highly active and ego-involving, the medium appeals to the trainee's self-interest immediately after he has tried to perform an assigned task. The immediate feedback provides reinforcement of tasks done well and an opportunity for more candid self-analysis to further improve performance. Because the tapes can be erased and reused many times, video instant replay is a handy and inexpensive tool for self-instruction, provided that the trainee knows the criteria which he must meet. Other benefits relate to its use in rapid dissemination of information with a sense of currency or urgency characteristic of television. In addition, the medium shares many of the positive attributes of training films: It requires better preparation of materials, makes use of motion, can stretch or condense time, and holds numerous possibilities for the recording of sound.

Video recording equipment should be selected according to sales training objectives. Equipment can be rented or purchased on a trial basis, which permits the training director to use it as he normally would before irrevocably committing his limited budget. For most role-playing situations, video systems using half-inch tape, which cost under $2,000, will prove adequate. For in-house production of sales training tapes, the higher-quality one-inch video tape systems for under $10,000 are justified when the number of salesmen and the cost of training can offset the cost of acquisition. If training requires the production of broadcast-quality programs, then using outside professional television facilities and personnel is cheapest in the long run, since it is practically impossible for any organization other than a broadcasting station to maintain a full-time staff of professionals.

By using common sense, compassion, and sound training principles, the average sales trainer can have a great deal of fun with video instant replay and enjoy its many wonderful benefits. If he purchases only that equipment which serves his learning objectives, it need not be an expensive medium.

SELECTED MATERIALS

The Audio-Visual Equipment Directory. Fairfax, Va.: National Audio-Visual Association. Published annually.

> *Equipment specifications and prices are listed.*

Curl, David H., "AV Training," *Training in Business and Industry* (August 1967), pp. 13–15.

Dehon, William N., "Self Confrontation Via TV: Videotaped Feedback for Training at Sandia Laboratory," *Training and Development Journal* (October 1967), p. 43.

Eachus, Herbert T., *Self Confrontation for Complex Skill Training: Review and Analysis*. Wright-Patterson Air Force Base, Aerospace Medical Research Laboratories. September 1965.

Salomon, Gavriel, and McDonald, Frederick J., "Pretest and Posttest Reactions to Self-viewing One's Teaching Performance on Video Tape," *Journal of Educational Psychology*, Vol. 61, No. 4 (1970), pp. 280–86.

———— and Snow, Richard E., "The Specification of Film Attributes for Psychological and Educational Research Purposes," *AV Communication Review*, Vol. 16, No. 3 (1968), pp. 225–44.

Stoller, Frederick H., "The Use of Focused Feedback Via Video Tape in Small Groups," *Explorations: Human Relations Training and Research*. Washington, D.C.: National Education Association, National Training Laboratories, 1966.

Stroh, Thomas F., *The Uses of Video Tape in Training and Development*. AMA Research Study 93 (1969).

Technology in Education. Cleveland: School Product News, 1969.

> *AV hardware is covered, and case studies of good applications in schools and colleges are presented.*

CHAPTER 8

Developing Effective Attitudes and Work Habits

THERE SEEMS TO BE some controversy about including effective attitudes and work habits in sales training. Some people feel that attitudes cannot be taught, while others feel that anything can be taught to a trainee who wants to learn. This controversy is more apparent than real, however. In fact, sales trainees develop strong attitudes on the basis of their experiences in both formal classroom programs and on-the-job training assignments. The development of productive attitudes and good work habits should be a carefully planned part of the training and career development of salesmen.

It is not natural to want to cooperate, to want to work long and hard, to want to please the sales manager. It is natural to be selfish, to want to be physically and mentally comfortable, to be demanding of management. Men tend to learn the desirable attitudes as they mature and as they realize greater satisfaction by going along with the system rather than by being sarcastic, cynical, and hostile. This learning process can be encouraged and accelerated; it can be ignored and left to grow as fate dictates; or it can be discouraged and arrested or stopped completely.

Consider, for example, the sales trainer or manager who tells the salesman where he should go on a given day and what he should be saying and doing in his territory. This kind of training and control teaches the salesman to become heavily dependent on the manager. It also causes him to develop an attitude of irresponsibility—after all, whatever goes wrong must be the manager's fault for giving bad instructions or for communicating poorly. As long as this salesman does what he believes he was told to do, he will expect his monetary rewards. The attitude he learned from the manager is that he gets paid simply to carry out instructions. He is not to think or act on his own; in fact, no one cares what he thinks or feels as long as he does what he is told. When things go well, he can claim it was because of his superior execution of the instructions. This salesman has been taught to claim the good and disclaim the bad and not to confuse the manager with his ideas, feelings, and opinions. If he continues to work under these conditions, he will probably stay as dependent and irresponsible as a child. His attitude development will have been arrested at an early stage.

Consider, on the other hand, the trainer or sales manager who describes the goals to be accomplished and asks the salesman to recommend the process he would prefer to use. A formal classroom discussion of the advantages and disadvantages of various methods of getting the job done will show that some ways are more appropriate under certain conditions and other ways better when the situation is different. If the sales manager permits the trainee some limited discretion in trying out different ways of doing things, he will be encouraging growth. This manager converts the salesman's mistakes into opportunities for him to learn and to improve himself. As he gains the manager's confidence, the salesman is permitted to operate more and more on his own, seeking only occasional advice from his manager. The salesman gradually learns to be independent of his manager and to be responsible for his own actions. This is true growth and development. This salesman learns profitable self-management, which includes the attitudes and work habits necessary for success.

Desirable attitudes and work habits cannot be taught in isolation in one training seminar. The appropriate concepts should permeate the entire formal classroom training. And since older salesmen can reach plateaus of productivity or become cynical if management's words and actions teach them not to care, these concepts should continue to be stressed throughout the career of the professional salesman.

Sales trainers frequently approach this subject through a discussion of the salesman's job, presenting, for example, a job description that applies to all salesmen and states in general terms what the company wants to have accomplished by the job. They ask the trainees (or experienced salesmen, for that matter) to spell out in detail what the company should expect from their unique territories. Next, they discuss what the customer or target account wants the salesman to accomplish. Finally, these experienced trainers ask what the individual salesman can bring to his job in terms of his unique experience and abilities. This technique provides opportunities for each salesman to set many of his own personal goals. With the guidance of the experienced trainer, it enables him to assume some authority in designing his work, and encourages him to accept responsibility for his subsequent actions.

Another common approach to developing effective attitudes and work habits is a discussion of the cost of the various functions of a business. For example, on an order for $10,000, perhaps production and factory overhead cost $6,000. Shipment, installation, billing, and reserve for bad debt may cost $1,000. The remaining amount must cover research and development, advertising and promotion, and the selling expenses. Although oversimplified, such a discussion normally leads to the cost of a salesman's calls. The manager or trainer can ask each man to divide the cost of his salary and expenses for a typical month by the number of calls he expects to make. When the salesman realizes that his personal direct cost to the company averages $30 to $85 per call, he begins to appreciate his responsibility. By comparing this cost with the average contribution to profit of his orders, the salesman can determine what his closing average should be. Experienced sales managers and trainers direct this kind of discussion so as to bring out ways each salesman can more easily achieve his own and company goals. Each salesman is asked to identify and take advantage of one particular strength and to identify one personal weakness and commit himself to improving in that area. Thus, salesmen are taught that someone really cares about their individual growth and development.

While a manager cannot directly teach healthy attitudes and work habits, he can clarify the thinking of salesmen as to what is expected of them. He can clear up any misunderstandings about their profit contribution, for example. He can help motivate them to become more effective. When salesmen and trainees want to grow and develop, many opportunities will arise, in the classroom and on the job, to discuss better ways of doing things. There really is no excuse for forcing new salesmen to learn by lengthy and often frustrating trial and error on the job.

THE VALUE OF SALESMEN

Sales managers and sales trainers have usually proved their selling skills in the field, and they are justly confident of their demonstrated performance. They have learned to live with, if not to accept fully, the fact that most prospects will say no and that even the successful salesman will fail to get an order more often than he will succeed.

Traditional sales managers believe that the ability to close a high percentage of sales separates the "born salesmen" from the "losers," even though they may go through the motions of trying to increase a salesman's average and talking him out of a slump. However, no short-term hand-holding strategy will keep a rejected salesman from blaming the prospect's stupidity, his company's high prices or poor service, or any other problem that is easier to cope with than his dissatisfaction with himself. Rejection is a major part of the selling job, and salesmen, particularly sales trainees, should be formally prepared to understand and deal with it.

Modern sales managers have learned to recognize complaints of this kind and reluctance to call on sarcastic or abusive prospects as symptoms of a training need. Their initial and on-going training programs are designed to build the salesman's self-esteem and self-confidence in two ways: by reinforcing the special value of his efforts and by increasing his ability to accomplish something worthwhile on each sales contact, whether or not a sale is forthcoming.

The Special Contributions of Salesmen

To achieve the first goal, the trainer can ask the men to discuss how an effective salesman differs from other effective people in the company. Salesmen generally like this kind of discussion because it gives them the chance to be recognized for their unique contribution and importance to their company. Typically, the discussion includes many of the following points:

1. A salesman *is* the company to individual customers and to other people in general. Whether he is at work or at play, whatever he does or says, the impression he makes on people becomes the basis for their opinions of his firm.

2. A salesman in the field represents his company independently of immediate supervision. It is his responsibility to establish facts, interpret information, and act on situations according to company policy. He is on his own when he visits a customer.

3. Inner drive is essential to a salesman because he can work or loaf in spurts if he so desires. Most office and plant workers must process the work flow because any bottleneck is easily noticed and quickly corrected. The salesman's self-discipline causes him to work hard, be persistent, and show great initiative.

4. The salesman alone determines what should be done each day and on each contact with clients, and he alone can do it. With most office jobs, one simply phones in sick and someone else does the work. Many sales jobs require considerable traveling—driving in heavy traffic, for example—and if the salesman doesn't do it one day, no one else can handle it.

5. Most salesmen are authorized to make expenditures for the company and for their own needs. The proper and wise use of company funds is a responsibility usually reserved for the top few corporate officers.

6. Many sales jobs require mixing socially with prospects and customers. The salesman's diplomacy and social intelligence must be far superior to that required of people in the company whose jobs do not necessitate after-office-hours contact with customers.

7. Market research information can often be obtained most effectively by the salesman. He is closest to the customer and is often the first one aware of customer needs and competitive actions. Quick reporting of the proper information can influence top management decisions.

Each sales organization can build its own list of functions, duties, and responsibilities which recognizes the importance of the salesman. The manager should not assume the young salesmen realize these points, and in any event, it cannot hurt to reinforce their sense of self-esteem periodically.

Making Each Sales Call Count

The second way of building the salesman's self-confidence is by training him to achieve something of value on each sales contact, whether or not he closes a sale. The achievement can be made on any or all of three distinct levels. First, of course, is the progress toward a sale. One contact may be required to plant ideas with a prospect. A second contact may help further interest, and a series of contacts may be required to build conviction and finally produce favorable action. The salesman can easily learn to evaluate this level of achievement by role-playing one phase of an evolving sale. On a given contact, the salesman attempts to accomplish a measurable goal but not necessarily an immediate sale.

The second level of achievement involves using the psychology of communication and persuasion. Armed with this basic knowledge, the salesman may change the degree of sophistication of his goals. For example, the salesman may want to build the prospect's confidence in him as the source of the commercial message. He might do this by bringing the prospect some news about his industry or about competition. He might offer ideas and suggestions which will help his prospect's business. Each contact is designed to build the salesman's image as an honest and helpful source of information, a man to be trusted.

On the third level, interpersonal skills, the salesman can be taught to be sensitive to warming trends, to the deepening of mutual trust and understanding of problems. While a tough professional buyer may have been as rough and abusive as ever today, for example, he may also have given out more helpful information. He is beginning to level with the salesman. Conversely, when something goes wrong in an interview, the salesman can be taught to sense just where things began to go downhill and to make appropriate changes in his next approach. On each contact the salesman can learn something about the prospect's personality and professional role in his company. In other words, developing a good understanding of interpersonal relations becomes a measure of success independent of actual sales.

In these ways the salesman can accomplish something of value on every sales call. Each contact becomes one episode in a series of meetings and each future contact presents an opportunity to experiment with new ideas and concepts.

Self-evaluation

Finally, the salesman should be taught to evaluate himself on a regular basis. Each call should be analyzed afterward to determine the progress made and to decide on the appropriate action for the follow-up call. In addition, the salesman can set personal goals and measure his accomplishments in certain key areas of his job. For example, one salesman might set a target of calling on one new account every day and opening three new accounts each month. By setting reasonable personal goals and measuring his own performance, the salesman can appreciate his tangible progress and accomplishments. In this way, one rejection or one success is viewed not as the end but more realistically as one point along the way.

ORGANIZING SALES WORK

Setting Priorities

When a new salesman is given a territory he will often be given an account card for each existing customer and all known potential customers. He may want to call on each account in person at least once to determine for himself the value of every client. He may approach them in alphabetical order, by geographic groupings, by potential size, or in some other systematic way. Before long, however, leads, customer inquiries, deliveries, complaints, management directives, and many other things will intervene, and his original plan never gets accomplished. He may work long and hard, but somehow he is so busy handling urgent things that he never gets around to doing the things he planned to do.

Important jobs and urgent jobs. Salesmen should be taught the distinction between what is urgent and what is important. The urgent things that happen daily require attention, a decision, and usually some immediate action. A ringing telephone must be answered; a customer request must be attended to by a personal visit; a delivery must be scheduled. The sales manager wants to see the salesman "the first thing tomorrow morning." Such events are urgent but they are rarely important enough to require priority over everything else. But because they are urgent they get attention, and a very busy day may end up accomplishing very little that is constructive.

The salesman who is busy doing all the urgent things puts off the important things for another day simply because they are not urgent. He somehow never gets around to really analyzing his territory. He never has time to do the market research which will provide many clues to help sell certain accounts. He rarely takes the time necessary to work up several reasonable objectives and detailed plans or strategies to achieve them. He may eliminate a call on an account which is about ready to buy in order to see someone else who "wants to see a salesman right away."

Salesmen should be taught that the customer is not always right and that the sales manager does not have the right to destroy a planned day. Calling on an account of large potential value may be much more important than visiting a small account that phoned simply to get one more competitive price. Working up a strategy to win a new account may be more important than seeing the sales manager who simply wants to keep informed about the salesman's progress. Obviously, the salesman must answer all inquiries and see his manager, but not necessarily at the time they specify. There is nothing wrong with asking whether another specific time might be equally acceptable. Most people are reasonable in changing their requests when they are convinced that the salesman has other important things to do, and in most cases his customers and manager will respect him more as a result. Sometimes the requests will be important, and the salesman, clearly, will have to adjust his schedule to suit others. However, the salesman may never accomplish the important things if he automatically gives in to all the little urgent demands without question.

Developing a sales forecast. Developing a reasonable sales forecast and planning the sales strategy to achieve that goal in a specific territory is certainly one of the most important things a salesman can do. Practically every facet of a company, in one way or another, can and should be affected by a realistic annual sales forecast. Production can be scheduled, and standard unit costs can be determined more accurately. Raw materials or components can be acquired when needed, and the physical facilities allocated on an optimum basis. Cash flow can be predicted, and budgets determined to spend funds in an orderly manner. Advertising and promotional plans can be developed to help reach the targeted markets or to introduce new products. In the modern marketing concept, the customer's needs determine what products and services can be offered on a profitable basis. Thus, it is the salesman in the field who probably knows most about what is likely to sell in his territory. Other sophisticated inputs and treatment of the data may be used to assign final quotas, but this does not lessen the importance of the salesman's individual contribution.

Through the analysis necessary to develop an accurate forecast, the salesman will identify certain key target accounts in various parts of his territory. From his estimate of the value of these accounts and his knowledge of the specific products to be sold to them, the salesman can determine how often and at what time he should call on these key accounts. Seasonal variations, particularly in the prospect's business, may indicate the wisdom of making more frequent visits during certain seasons as compared with calling on a regular schedule throughout the year. In any event, this process of analysis produces part of the organizational plan for the territory and is more important than the petty, time-consuming, urgent events which have little impact on long-range goals.

Depending on the needs of a particular sales organization, sales forecasts may be made on the basis of sales dollars per account; profit contribution per account; product by account; or number of new systems or applications per account. Obviously, combinations of one or more of these forecasts can aid the salesman in organizing his sales work.

Expense forecasting. In addition to sales forecasting as an important planning tool for many organizations is expense forecasting. Expenses can be forecast for each account, indicating cost estimates for travel, entertainment, sales promotion gifts, and so forth. This requires the salesman to exercise some judgment in relating his investment of company funds, as well as his own time, to the expected return in profit contribution. Salesmen can be taught to do rather complicated forecasting of this nature, and the process helps them develop effective attitudes and work habits.

Market research. The salesman can be taught to plan and execute market research projects to gather information which will help him sell more effectively. Such data will locate the greatest potential in his territory for increased profitable business. For example, Dun & Bradstreet directories can be used to identify potential new accounts by their line of business and their size. Trends in buying and new applications of existing products can be identified through customer trade journals, existing customers, and other salesmen. In estimating the demand for a new product in his territory, the salesman can consult the sources mentioned as well as conduct a survey of a sample of potential customers. He can also contact trade or professional associations and many trade publications.

These activities are relatively easy to learn, but they are rarely urgent. During training, the salesman should learn to appreciate the value of obtaining good information and making careful forecasts. Unless this phase of training and development is given a thorough treatment, the chances are rather good that the salesman will quickly forget what little he may have learned. When the formal training period is over, the sales manager would be wise to reinforce the intended learning by showing a strong interest in each salesman's plans and organization of his work. Salesmen need on-the-job encouragement to implement these important skills; the return is seen in a favorable influence on their working habits as well as in a general increase in their effectiveness.

Time and Energy Control

Using the natural body clock. Most effective salesmen have almost boundless energy and are physically uncomfortable when they are idle. New salesmen, particularly, are willing and able to work long hours to make the most of their selling time. For example, after putting in a long, hard day, they will drive to the next area on their itinerary at night so as not to waste selling time. As desirable as this may seem at first glance, it is not necessarily the best use of their time and energy. When salesmen do not eat, sleep, and relax regularly, as the human body and mind require, they can easily become impatient with other people, quickly irritated over minor inconveniences, and less sensitive to the needs of other people, and thus less effective in their dealings with regular customers and new prospects. By pushing themselves too hard, salesmen can develop psychosomatic illnesses such as headaches, stomach disorders, and blood-pressure complications which can seriously affect their health.

Rather than waiting for symptoms to develop, it is much wiser to apply the principles of preventive medicine. Sales trainees can be taught to make optimum use of their time and energy and still stay healthy and mentally stable without the use of stimulant or repressive drugs. Medical authorities agree that man has a daily cycle in his body chemistry which causes him to be active and alert at one time and inclined to rest at another. One salesman may be full of pep at breakfast, while another does not reach his peak until noon or later, for example. Once a salesman discovers his own natural body clock, he can plan his daily activities as much as possible to take advantage of his energy peaks and to avoid highly demanding situations during his low periods. In this way he can reduce frustration and fatigue, which often cause errors and accidents.

Use of business hours. Studies have shown that, on the average, salesmen spend only 20 to 33 percent of their time in face-to-face conversation with their clients. Therefore, even the best, most persuasive salesman can benefit by controlling and reducing his nonselling time. Travel is essential, of course, but by preplanning the route and the mode of travel, the salesman can reduce wasted time and motion. Waiting time in customers' offices can be reduced somewhat by making appointments ahead. This time can also be used constructively to write reports, plan future calls, and gather additional information pertinent to the current call. For example, many magazines found in reception areas are addressed to individuals in the firm and may provide clues to their interests and attitudes.

Some salesmen race all day long trying to see as many clients as possible, and they become impatient and frustrated when they must wait to see a buyer. It is almost impossible for them to hide their annoyance from the buyer, and their attitude tends to be counterproductive. In the evening they may need to spend several hours trying to recall the events of the day and complete their records. These problems can be avoided if salesmen are taught to plan a reasonable work load for each day and to use their waiting time to fill out records while the details of the previous call are still fresh in their minds. If time permits, they can seek additional information about the people they may meet then or in the future. In this way their mood will be relaxed, and their approach to the particular buying influential will be friendly and will include something of interest to him. And, not incidentally, the evening will be pleasant, permitting them to relax and be refreshed for the next morning.

Salesmen can be alerted to the danger of spending a disproportionate amount of time on nonprofitable or small accounts. Where special service is the norm, salesmen can learn to utilize the supporting personnel in the home office to provide special literature and information requested by the smaller accounts. Since one never knows when a small account will become a large account, salesmen should be taught to be courteous and fair with all accounts. However, the time spent on each account should be used with discretion.

Use of spare time. Coffee breaks, lunchtime, and dinnertime can often be spent with prospects and customers to mutual advantage. New salesmen should be cautioned, however, that such time should be relaxing and pleasant. If the salesman must work at being nice and must carefully guard his every word in a customer's presence, perhaps his spare time would be better spent alone. It is very common for salesmen on the road to build lasting friendships with their customers, and this is an ideal way both to relax and to build customer loyalty. However, the situation should be natural and satisfying to both the customer and the salesman.

The salesman should be taught that when he is traveling, his spare time during the day is best spent relaxing to be refreshed for the next challenge. Evenings can be used partially for self-improvement activities—for instance, learning about competitive products, developing problem-solving techniques, studying changing conditions in the market and in customers' industries, and reading pertinent sales literature. The trainee should realize that self-improvement activities go well beyond acquiring additional sales information. The company expects him to be well informed on many topics of national and worldwide significance, as well as to develop interests in hobbies, sports, and politics and to fulfill his civic responsibilities. The company wants the trainee to become an interesting person whom people like to be with and give their business to.

Training for optimum use of time and energy. Experienced salesmen and new trainees out in the field can be taught to maintain a confidential record of their activities for a week or two. This will show them how much of their time is spent traveling, doing administrative work, handling urgent matters, and doing important things such as planning and self-development work. Many salesmen are shocked when their own measurement and evaluation show the amount of time and energy they waste on unimportant activities. This kind of revelation will often strongly motivate salesmen to learn how to use their time and energy more effectively. Such an attitude is very different from one based on the suspicion that management simply wants them to work longer and harder.

Modern sales managers want their sales force to be effective, productive, and healthy. Salesmen readily understand that conserving their time and energy operates both to increase sales and to make them relaxed and interesting people. Trainees can be taught to use brainwork in place of legwork and to prepare themselves for broader responsibilities. This approach departs radically from the traditional sales meeting and contest, which exhort the salesmen to make one extra call every day and to dedicate their entire waking hours to the selling profession.

The attitudes and work habits of salesmen usually reflect the words and actions of their sales manager and trainer. If the manager shows a sincere concern for each salesman's personal growth and development, the salesmen are apt to do as he recommends. But when the manager shows greater interest in the sales than in the men, the salesmen are apt to react negatively to his suggestions.

Route and Call Frequency

Organizing sales work should begin with a clear understanding of the company's goals (high volume and low unit profit, for example), followed by a realistic appraisal of the various market segments and specific accounts to be selected as targets. Many companies that have initiated studies of selling costs have found that as much as 20 percent of their orders produce no profit and in fact cause a loss when the salesman's time and expenses, inside administrative costs, warehousing, packing, delivery, and billing are included. Every territory should therefore be analyzed to determine which accounts can buy in quantities sufficient for the seller to operate profitably.

Classifying accounts. For the new salesman, analyzing his territory means classifying his accounts by size or potential and using the results to determine the number of calls which will achieve the business desired. For example, the largest accounts might be grouped in Class A, indicating weekly visits. Class B accounts might require visits every two weeks, and other accounts might need to be visited monthly, bimonthly, quarterly, or only semiannually. By dividing the total number of calls required in a year to cover all accounts (as classified) by the number of working days per year, the salesman can determine the minimum number of calls per day which he should average in order to cover the accounts exactly as management wants. This figure will also indicate the amount of time remaining each day to develop new business and to cultivate future customers that may require years to develop. New salesmen should clearly understand that they should not use this extra time seeing buyers who may be friendly but who cannot buy more. Putting in a long day calling on small accounts or on ones that are nearly saturated with the product is not as productive as working efficiently for fewer hours.

Having classified each account by potential, determined the frequency of calls per year for each, and established the minimum number of calls per day required to cover the territory, the salesman must then decide specifically where he will go monthly, weekly, and on each particular day. Depending on the nature of his business, the salesman may plan most of his time or as little as half his time, allowing the rest for the unexpected demands which may be normal in his industry. In any case, the trainee can be taught to plan intelligently to cover his accounts as his company desires.

Circular calling route. For purposes of illustration, assume a machine tool salesman has been assigned 300 selected accounts in upstate New York, and he has classified them according to potential. If 25 of these accounts are large enough to be visited monthly and are located in four or five different industrial cities, he can plan his calling route in a circular pattern to return to the first large account approximately one month after his initial visit. The remaining 275 accounts cannot be visited with equal frequency and must be broken down into groups, indicating visits every two months, quarterly, semi-annually, or annually. Each of these groups is then fitted into the basic calling route. If there are 18 Class B accounts, requiring bi-monthly calls, in the Syracuse area, along with five Class A accounts, requiring monthly calls, the salesman would visit each of the five Class A accounts once a month and nine of the 18 Class B accounts during each pass through that part of the territory. On alternate months he would again visit each of the five Class A accounts, but he would switch to the remaining nine Class B accounts. The smaller accounts are fitted into the schedule in the same manner, so that they are visited no more nor less than management desires.

Naturally, as conditions change, accounts can be reclassified for either more or less frequent visits.

Having scheduled, for example, eight days' work in the Syracuse area, the salesman should review the history of each account he is to visit, particularly with regard to the purpose and results of previous calls. He should then decide what the purpose or objective will be for each account and which person he should see. Equipped with this information, the salesman can review his sales presentations or approaches as he anticipates each situation and can fill his briefcase with the materials that he is likely to need for these particular calls. Finally, he will make the visits on his schedule for each day and utilize his remaining time to solicit new accounts or to cultivate customers that had previously been selected for that purpose.

Four-leaf-clover route. Some sales trainers prefer to teach the so-called four-leaf-clover pattern of coverage. In this routing system the salesman starts at the center of the four-leaf clover, covers accounts in one leaf on one day or in one week, and then goes to the next leaf for one day or one week. Only four leaves are used so that the fifth day or the fifth week can be spent on call-backs or special activities. Obviously, the size and shape of a territory, the means of transportation, the potential of the accounts, and their special requests will influence the specific routing system developed.

Maintaining flexibility. Sales trainees should be taught to approach their pattern of covering accounts systematically. However, they should be well aware that emergencies will interrupt their plans and that they will have to be flexible enough to handle an urgent crisis when it develops. Once the emergency has passed, they should go back to their systematic plan.

Whatever form a plan of sales calls may take initially, it may require some modification as time passes. The plan is designed as a tool to help the salesman conserve his time and energy. It is not perfect and should not be followed when its dictates seem contrary to common sense. If a salesman's training has taught him that this tool is basically of his own creation and that he is free to modify it to serve his needs better, he will be apt to use it constructively. Conversely, if he feels it as an ironbound constraint or a police action to control him, he is likely to fight the system, to his own detriment.

Planning follow-up. As mentioned earlier, trainees can be taught to make a note of what transpired immediately after each call, while all the details are fresh in their minds. At that point they should decide how to follow up on the account and what additional information they may need or what customer service they can perform on their next visit. Frequently some interesting literature or other information can be mailed to the customer between calls, and the salesmen should be taught to use home-office support for this purpose. Occasionally letters can be used to thank the client for his time and to put certain facts and figures in writing for his reference. For many people, the written word carries more authority than the spoken word, and a letter repeating an offer will reinforce the verbal message and may be much more convincing. The point is simply that the salesman can increase his effectiveness if he develops these good working habits.

USING RECORDS TO IDENTIFY POTENTIAL SALES

To become more independent of the sales manager, trainees should be taught to report certain information automatically and to maintain certain records to guide their own efforts. Clearly, management needs some information to control costs, but the major use of feedback from salesmen is in planning. The salesman is closest to the customers and is in a position to find out what they want, how they react to various marketing efforts, and how competition is operating, and to identify new trends in the customers' industries. In addition, the salesman can maintain various records to measure and evaluate his own progress and accomplishments and thereby improve himself.

If the trainer approaches this subject on a positive note, pointing out how record keeping can help the salesmen, they are apt to accept it. Conversely, if the subject is approached as a means of control or as a necessary evil, the salesmen are apt to avoid records and paper work. With the latter approach, required call reports become exercises in creative writing and serve no legitimate function. If a record system cannot be justified on constructive grounds, it should be eliminated.

Account record card. While records will vary in importance to different sales organizations, perhaps the most universally useful one is the account record card. This card normally shows the current status of each customer and prospect and compares sales to date with forecast data in each product category. Depending on the line of business, some or all of the following data might be included: name, address, phone number, names and titles of people to be contacted, location of home office and branches, last year's sales, sales forecast for this year, and sales to date this year by product category, credit rating, and sales expenses. Looking at the account card, the salesman can easily tell the exact status of his customer this year as compared with last year and as compared with his goals for the current year. Whether it is posted weekly or monthly, the card is a visual reminder to the salesman that he is on target or that he needs to take some special action or extra effort to achieve his goals. Of course, if he is ahead of forecasts, it is visual proof of his accomplishment, and this provides a psychological reward.

Call organizer. Another essential record for most sales organizations is the call organizer, or call record, which furnishes the salesman with a list of alternate buying influentials whom he should contact, a checklist of materials he may be able to use, and an indication of what occurred on the last call or two, so that he can plan each call with a specific objective. This record is often also used as the follow-up record, and after the call is made, it is filed at the date planned for the next call. Each week the salesman can see in advance some of the places he should visit and is provided with a quick review of each account.

The call organizer or follow-up record encourages the salesman to preplan every customer contact and reduce or eliminate cold calls. He may, for example, plan to obtain special information from the client, plant new ideas, review or revise an old quotation, or present a new application. Knowing what he wants to do, the salesman will be able to determine which buying influential he should see in order to have the best chance of success. Then, if the nature of the business lends itself to such a procedure, he can telephone ahead to establish firm appointments, thus reducing his waiting time. At this point, the salesman fits his follow-up calls into his route and his call-frequency schedule to achieve optimum effectiveness.

Other records. Obviously, many other records are used in different sales organizations. Most organizations require each salesman to maintain monthly or quarterly sales activity records showing dollar volume by product category. These records can be used by the salesman to see whether or not he is concentrating his efforts on higher-profit items, selling the complete line, or achieving whatever goals he and the sales manager had previously established.

For some companies the prospect list is an essential record. Probably the major source of information for identifying potential sales is the file of existing customers. They can buy more of certain items and services and can provide the names of other people who might be good prospects. These customers do forecasting and planning for the future of their own business operations. Thus, they are often sources of information about industry trends of which the salesman might not otherwise be aware.

Frequently, a list of the salesman's ten largest prospects is circulated among sales executives, so that they may help if they know something special about the account. They may have contacts whom the salesman cannot normally reach, and they may have helped the prospect in the past and be due a return favor. People throughout the selling organization cannot help the salesman unless they know what his target accounts are, and it is to the salesman's advantage to enlist all the aid possible.

In addition to the salesman's own records, many commercial and private lists are available, as noted in Chapter 5.

Training methods. In training salesmen to keep and use records, the emphasis should be on the value of records in simplifying their work and increasing their effectiveness. Merely to lecture about record keeping in a training seminar is probably insufficient. Trainers can build a series of case histories which involve decisions in planning, routing, setting objectives, and so forth. Each salesman can be given a copy of the relevant records and asked to recommend action. From the group response, principles can be evolved which will reinforce the intended lesson. After the trainees have practiced using the records constructively in a number of cases, they will feel comfortable using them. When they are assigned real accounts, it will seem natural to use the appropriate records for planning purposes and to measure their own progress. In this way record keeping can easily be made an effective work habit.

ATTITUDINAL SURVEYS

The grapevine is one source of information about salesmen's attitudes or morale; however, it is rarely accurate, and it can be misleading. Direct interviews between the sales manager and each salesman are not likely to yield much truth either. When the salesmen feel that their future raises may depend in part on what they say, they are inclined to tell the manager what they think he wants to hear. If the manager uncovers an unpleasant truth and states it as a fact, some salesmen may feel that his interpretation is a whitewash or that the manager cannot face the "real" situation. And while such objective measurements as rate of turnover, absenteeism, and overdue reports are excellent general indicators of past performance, they do not pinpoint specific areas which may need correction.

An attitudinal survey, on the other hand, can find out the beliefs and feelings of salesmen on a number of significant points, and such a survey should be the first step in planning how to improve attitudes. The survey usually contains questions to determine the salesman's general opinion of his company as a place to work. Then there are specific attitudinal questions about fairness in pay, opportunity for advancement, adequacy of training, and frequency with which the manager praises good work, for example. Finally, there are often questions on sensitive items such as the company's practices with regard to pricing, delivery, quality control, making adjustments, and so forth.

Many sales organizations find that by having the entire survey made by people who specialize in this kind of research they gain two important advantages: First, an outside organization can usually secure more frank answers to the questions. Salesmen are apt to feel greater assurance of anonymity if they are told that the questionnaires are to be checked and tabulated in an office of an outside firm and that no one from their own company will ever see the questionnaires.

The second advantage—an extremely important one—is in the greater experience the specialist has in interpreting the results. For instance, it would be difficult, if not impossible, for a sales manager to decide whether the following response to a typical question is good, fair, or bad:

"Generally speaking, how does this company rate as a place to work in comparison with other companies in our industry that you know about or have worked for?"

	Salesmen's Answers
One of the very worst	2%
Worse than average	5%
Just average	52%
Better than average	31%
One of the very best	10%

Comparing the above-average ratings to those below average gives a ratio of 41 to 7. Should the sales manager infer a high state of morale from these results?

He might, and in fact one national sales manager apparently did exactly this, according to a recent article in a national magazine. But he might not make this judgment if he had standards by which to judge the results.

Experience has shown that the salesman who says his organization is "just average" usually has relatively low morale or poor attitudes. If the last two responses in the example above are considered favorable, then the results might be compared with a standard as follows:

Our company	41% favorable
Standard response	63% favorable
One competitor	92% favorable

Such a comparison leads to a conclusion quite different from the first interpretation.

Results of attitudinal surveys are most useful when they can be compared to some standard or previous measurement. Standards vary from question to question, however, and the importance of any single response is relative to the importance of the subject. For example, a favorable response of 50 percent to a question about fair compensation is relatively better than a favorable response of 70 percent to a question about whether an instructor is entertaining.

A well-planned attitudinal survey can usually measure the variations between high producers and low producers, for example, or between new salesmen and experienced salesmen. This sort of sophisticated information helps to isolate problems and point toward likely corrective actions. In addition, highly trained interviewers, again from an outside organization, can conduct free-form or nondirective interviews with an appropriate sample of salesmen to gather detailed information which can also be used as a guide for effective remedial action. This input, together with the sales manager's direct knowledge and the sales trainer's experience, can help pinpoint the areas in critical need of improvement. For example, rumors may be accepted as fact by the salesmen, thereby causing poor morale. An informative meeting can be held to clear up misunderstandings.

SUMMARY

Sales managers and others concerned with training cause salesmen to form certain attitudes and to develop certain work habits. They may do so by intent and design, by neglect, or by ignorance. In any case, sales trainees will react to future demands on their time and energy according to what they have learned in both formal training classes and on-the-job training assignments.

A good training program will include a thorough explanation of and justification for the industry, covering its historical development and its contributions to society. It should also include a discussion of the uniqueness of the company which will enable the salesman to be proud of what he sells and the services he performs. His training should stress helping customers by serving their best interests.

The training program should clearly spell out the company's compensation plan and how each salesman's pay is symbolic of his personal contribution to the company, which includes providing work or employment for many people in production, administration, and service as well as creating future jobs and providing a return to those who were willing to risk their capital in his company.

To help build the attitudes that will enable the salesman to speak with confidence and enthusiasm, sales training should emphasize the independence of each salesman. Good training makes the salesman aware that he is personally responsible for what happens with a prospect. His success as a salesman and his career lie in his own hands, and it is within his power to make them as great as he wants them to be.

To this end, the salesman's unlimited opportunity for advancement should be emphasized. Trainers can give many examples of executives in the company who started in sales and moved upward to broader responsibilities. They can also mention leaders in the industry who rose from their sales organizations to national recognition.

Clearly, sales training should face the problem of rejection and prepare the salesmen to achieve something of value on every sales contact. The young salesman should learn how to evaluate each sales interview so that he can appreciate some degree of progress even though a sale may not have been consummated.

Studies have shown that poor planning and organization are a common cause of failure among salesmen. Without proper training, salesmen may spend too much time with friendly clients regardless of their business potential. They may also devote too much time to the many urgent but truly unimportant events which seem to occur daily, although they may work hard enough. A good training program should enable the salesman to understand forecasting, time and energy control, route and call frequency, and the correct use of records. However, more understanding is not enough; the new salesman should practice using these tools in training so that their proper use becomes habitual.

Many of the leading commercial training programs are effective because they require the trainee to develop a plan of action to take back with him into the real world of his job. Initial sales training should have this goal, and the sales manager's personal interest should reinforce the desired behavior back on the job. Salesmen should realize that their manager knows and cares that they are attempting to use and to perfect the skills and work methods that they were taught in training.

Finally, people concerned with sales training should be careful not to waste their efforts developing certain attitudes in trainees to combat imaginary problems while ignoring the real ones. One measurement—whether of a man's height, weight, intelligence, or attitude —means nothing unless there is a standard with which it can be compared. In the absence of a standard, several measurements should be made over a time span so that trends, improvements, or areas of increasing difficulty can be seen. The development of attitudes can be encouraged in the formal training period, but sales training cannot make up for ineffective management or poor company policies. The sales trainer would be well advised to identify and measure a problem before he attempts to use sales training to correct it.

SELECTED MATERIALS

Conflict. New York: McGraw-Hill Textfilms, McGraw-Hill Book Company. 18 mm, B&W.

An interesting discussion of the approach-avoidance system from the psychologist's point of view: Shape up or ship out (change your attitude or leave).

Gruenfeld, Leopold W., and Weissenberg, Peter, "Supervising Characteristics and Attitudes Toward Performance Appraisals," *Personnel Psychology*, Vol. 19, No. 2 (Summer 1966), pp. 143–52.

Hanan, Mack, "Make Way for the New Organization Man," *Harvard Business Review*, Vol. 49, No. 4 (July–August 1971), pp. 128–38.

Harley, Kay, "Team Development," *Personnel Journal*, Vol. 50, No. 6 (June 1971), pp. 437–43.

Ivancevich, John M., Donnelly, James H., and Lyon, Herbert L., "A Study of the Impact of Management by Objectives on Perceived Need Satisfaction," *Personnel Psychology*, Vol. 23, No. 2 (Summer 1970), pp. 139–52.

Krathwohl, David R., Bloom, Benjamin S., and Masia, Bertram B., *Taxonomy of Educational Objectives—Handbook II: Affective Domain*. New York: David McKay, 1964.

The book discusses attitudes of awareness, willingness to receive, acquiescence, willingness to respond, acceptance of a value, and commitment, among other objectives related to attitudes and measuring the degree of attainment.

Lawler, Edward E., III, "Job Attitudes and Employee Motivation Theory, Research, and Practice," *Personnel Psychology*, Vol. 23, No. 2 (Summer 1970), pp. 172–78.

Livingston, J. Sterling, "Myth of the Well-Educated Manager," *Harvard Business Review*, Vol. 49, No. 1 (January–February 1971), pp. 79–89.

Mager, Robert F., *Developing Attitude Toward Learning*. Palo Alto, Calif.: Fearon Publishers, 1968.

The book discusses the problem of defining attitudes in behavioral terms and procedures for developing such attitudes.

Wohlking, Wallace, "Attitude Change, Behavior Change: The Role of the Training Department," *California Management Review*, Vol. 13, No. 2 (Winter 1970), pp. 45–50.

CHAPTER 9

On-the-Job Coaching

ON-THE-JOB COACHING has long been used and widely accepted by sales executives, and many believe the field is the only training location that realistically portrays the selling situation. While it does have some limitations, on-the-job coaching is popular for a number of reasons. First, it can be used by any size and type of sales organization. It requires no special budget, time off the job, or expensive preparation. It is a very practical way to give a salesman individual attention without disturbing the rest of the sales force. It can be a relatively quick and inexpensive way of discovering a salesman's strengths and weaknesses. And it provides the new salesman with an opportunity to try out some classroom theory in the prospect's office under somewhat controlled conditions.

This method of sales training has its limitations, however. It is very time-consuming and requires one supervisor for one salesman. The person doing the training needs special incentives and relief from his other normal duties. Moreover, field coaching can be very expensive and frustrating if it is not preceded or accompanied by some off-the-job training. And it does not necessarily represent reality because the salesman and the prospect both may behave differently when the supervisor is not present.

While on-the-job coaching is normally thought of as taking place in the field or in the client's home or office, it can also include selling to real prospects in a showroom or at trade shows, for example. If the supplier has his own showroom, visiting clients can be assigned to a new salesman, whose behavior is observed by a sales supervisor just as it would be in the client's office. In this situation, video tape can be used unobtrusively to record the attempt to sell, and the tape can be played back for critique after the visitor leaves.

Some sales managers, for automobile dealers, for example, have audio-taped sales presentations and customer reactions by planting microphones in supposedly private offices in showrooms for many years. If used exclusively for sales training purposes, this method would be ethical; however, there is always the danger that the supervisor or manager might intervene to team up with the salesman against the client or to listen to a private conversation in the salesman's absence. Such methods are clearly unethical and should not be tolerated by professional salesmen.

Well-planned trade shows also provide an excellent opportunity to train salesmen on the job with real clients. Salesmen can be assigned to man a booth or exhibit, to entertain prospects, and to contact people at places other than the exhibit. The problems of making a trade show pay off are very similar to those of planning a territory to justify its costs. One rule of thumb for judging the effectiveness of a trade show is that each salesman in attendance should make as many contacts in one day as he would normally make in one week in his territory. The exhibit draws the attention of prospects, and the salesmen are then expected to make sales or develop interest for follow-up calls with the same percentage of success as in their territories. These goals and conditions impose pressures and time constraints which are similar to those of working a sales territory; however, one manager or supervisor can directly oversee several salesmen in the same day. Clearly, the salesmen should know the goals and how they will be measured; otherwise, they may think the trade show is a lark or an excuse to have fun on the job, or they may feel that working 10 or 12 hours per day is a form of punishment. On the other hand, good planning can make a trade show an excellent place for on-the-job training.

OBSERVATION

Preparation and Techniques for Coaching Calls

There are many good reasons for a manager to work with his salesmen on their calls; however, the coaching call is unique. On this kind of call, when the salesman begins to commit errors, the coach does not participate in any way. The salesman conducts the visit as he sees fit, in the silent, noninterfering presence of the manager. As a consequence, sales are often lost because the salesman is left on his own. Therefore, he should know beforehand that the manager will provide neither a crutch if he starts to falter nor a life preserver to save him if the sale appears lost. This policy can put an emotional strain on the manager because he has a natural tendency to help the salesman. Young or inexperienced managers often yield to the temptation to save the sale, but in so doing, they sometimes lose the man. There are ways to reduce the danger that the salesman will make mistakes, but sooner or later he must face the test of standing on his own, and this is precisely what he must do on a coaching call.

Prior to the day on which the coaching calls will be made, the sales manager would be well advised to tell the salesman the purpose of the observation and what behavior to expect on his part. The salesman can also be told very specifically what kind of calls the manager wishes to observe. For example, the manager may want to see how the man operates on a typical day with a complete range of accounts. He may prefer to watch the salesman spend an entire day out prospecting for new business. On occasion, the manager will want to see how the salesman handles steady customers, or how he handles big target accounts who have been buying from a competitor.

When a manager simply tells a salesman that he wants to observe him making whatever calls he has planned for that day, several things may happen. First, the salesman may feel that he is being picked on or being put on the spot unfairly. Second, he may feel that the manager is out to criticize him or to change his behavior. Some salesmen will feel that the observation is a great opportunity to demonstrate to the manager how good they are. In any case, the salesman's emotions will be aroused to the point of dictating his actions. He may invent a telephone message which requires him to alter his previous plan, for example. Rather than risk making a fool out of himself in front of the manager, he will call on the accounts whom he knows are friendly and receptive. Under such conditions, the manager will see only what the salesman wants him to see, and the odds are that the day will not be typical.

Some managers attempt to circumvent this problem by riding with the salesman for three or four consecutive days so that they are forced to call on a range of clients. While this may be an improvement over the one-day method, it requires much time, and the salesman's emotions will still strongly influence where he takes the manager. Observation under these conditions is seen as a police action, and the salesman will not knowingly break any of the rules.

Another variation which some managers use in field coaching is to exchange roles with the salesman on alternate calls. First, the manager attempts to sell while the salesman observes silently. Then, on the next call, the salesman is supposed to use many of the techniques he observed and try to sell while the manager remains silent. This system may be appropriate for some selling organizations; however, every client is unique in some way. The situations are rarely identical, and the salesman is likely to imitate the manager's techniques rather than do what might be more appropriate. Any failure is easily rationalized by the salesman as simply doing what he was told. When an order is obtained, the salesman may still feel he knows a better way— which may or may not be true—and once again, little constructive learning takes place.

When the observer or sales manager and the salesman have a mutual trust, the manager can level with the salesman. He wants to see how the man operates on his own under certain conditions in order to help the salesman accomplish his own goals. The manager has the responsibility of creating this friendly climate for growth and development, and when he is successful, salesmen will often ask to go on the type of call that has given them the most difficulty in the past. They think of the manager as the golf professional and ask him to watch how they swing in order to correct and improve their game. Under these circumstances, the manager is most likely to observe what the salesman really does when he is alone in his territory.

What to Look For

The sole purpose for observing a salesman's behavior on a coaching call is to determine his major strengths and to identify problem areas which training can help correct. After the manager has observed a number of calls, he may be able to see a pattern underlying a number of weaknesses or mistakes. For example, a salesman who fails to plan objectives for each call might show up as very flexible but not as effective as he might be if he made the planning effort. More often, the manager will recognize several problem areas, each relatively independent of the others. At this point, the manager should determine a priority of training needs by ranking the importance of corrections desired.

A checklist is frequently useful when a manager observes a salesman make a series of calls (for an example, see Checklist 1). The list should be tailored to the particular sales organization and should include the items taught off the job that the manager considers important. For example, probing techniques and listening skills might be more important for some organizations. In any event, the salesman is rated plus, zero, or minus on each item (except the last two) immediately following the call. A separate sheet is used for each interview, and the sheets are numbered in sequence. At the end of the day, the manager can quickly review each item to see where the salesman seems strong and where he might benefit from further training.

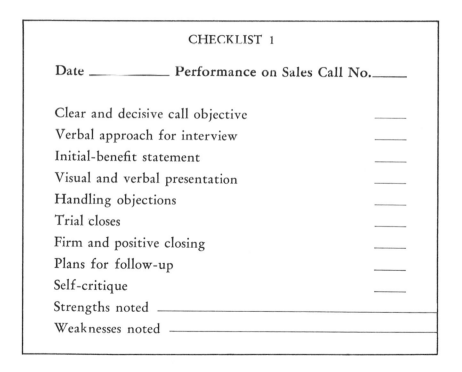

CHECKLIST 1

Date _____ Performance on Sales Call No._____

Clear and decisive call objective   _____
Verbal approach for interview   _____
Initial-benefit statement   _____
Visual and verbal presentation   _____
Handling objections   _____
Trial closes   _____
Firm and positive closing   _____
Plans for follow-up   _____
Self-critique   _____
Strengths noted _____
Weaknesses noted _____

In many cases, the sales manager—with the salesman's knowledge and approval—carries with him an audio tape recorder, which enables him to replay an interview to clear up any doubts about what the client or the salesman may have said. The tapes can later be given to the salesman for self-critique, if that is desirable.

GIVING FEEDBACK

Making Comments During the Day

If a knowledgeable sales manager travels with any salesman from eight o'clock in the morning until five at night, he can compile a very lengthy list of the faults he has observed. This is only natural. If the manager were to comment on every mistake throughout the day, the salesman would soon become discouraged. Even if the manager confined his comments to major mistakes, he might discourage the salesman. Any negative feedback to the salesman during the working day is very likely to change his subsequent performance.

In most cases, it is best for the manager to observe a number of calls before he provides any feedback to the salesman. In this way, the chances that the manager will make a false snap judgment are reduced, and the salesman will probably be encouraged to continue his efforts on his own. Most salesmen will do many things right on every call and probably not do as well on some things as the managers might like on all calls. However, if the salesman is totally unprepared, or if a weakness becomes painfully obvious during the morning, the manager might do better by calling a halt to the observations and having a serious man-to-man talk.

The salesman will usually ask for some feedback after each interview, even when he knows the rules of the situation. An effective technique used by many managers in this situation is simply to reflect the salesman's question back to him. For example, when the salesman asks how well he did in closing the sale, the manager reflects, "How well do *you* think you did?" Obviously, favorable comments can be volunteered by the manager when they are honest. If the salesman should press the manager for an opinion, the manager can reply, "I'd rather reserve judgment until I see a few more calls; then I'll discuss it with you."

Making comments acceptable. When the sales manager is doing the coaching, the prestige of his position is often enough to make his comments acceptable to the salesman. Normally, during the day they spend together, the coach has an opportunity to build the salesman's confidence in him as an authority figure. The kinds of questions which the coach asks about planning, for example, will communicate to the salesman that his observer knows what he is talking about. The stories he tells while they are riding together or having lunch will indicate the observer's sales experience and past accomplishments. The point is not to overwhelm the salesman but simply to build the image of the coach so that when he begins his critique, the salesman will be more apt to accept his suggestions.

When the salesman does something wrong and is obviously aware of it, the coach can comment sympathetically that he too has made many similar mistakes. If the salesman complains about the amount of time it takes to handle all the paper work, the coach can smile his understanding and avoid criticism or attempts to justify the system at that point. Throughout the day the coach is the friendly authority who is interested in helping the salesman personally rather than the public relations man speaking for top management or the policeman looking for petty violations.

The Final Critique

At the end of the observation period, many sales managers prefer to have the salesman himself begin the critique by describing what he has accomplished that day. The kinds of things he talks about will provide the coach with some indication of the salesman's self-awareness and possibly some blind spots. For example, one salesman may point with pride to the sheer number of calls he made that day. Another salesman may take pleasure in achieving good reactions from a tough account he has been working on for months and ignore the fact that the account has little potential in relation to the time spent.

The coach may also comment favorably on a number of things that he observed the salesman do well. For example, he might ask, "Did you realize when Mr. Johnston really got interested in your presentation?" By praising and probing, the coach can learn more about the salesman's awareness of human relations and the communication process. Occasionally, a favorable turn in a sales interview may be due to luck or the salesman's intuitive behavior. When the phenomenon is called to his attention during the critique, he may want to know more about it and how he can bring it about intentionally. Obviously, he will be receptive to this kind of suggestion from the coach.

After the salesman has discussed the good points of the day, the manager would be wise to ask the salesman what he feels are generally his strongest points, including those that may not have been illustrated that day. This question causes the salesman to think of himself in relation to other salesmen. His response should provide some clues about his readiness to face the truth about himself. His self-image will probably not square exactly with the manager's view of him, but it can be compared in general. If he omits some important areas, the coach can ask him directly how he would rate himself on these points.

Although the focus is on the positive—the good points of the day and the strengths of the salesman in general—some weaknesses will naturally come out in the conversation. In addition, the salesman will probably refer to some of the things he was not able to do effectively during the day. During this process, some of his hidden emotions may come to light. For example, in discussing his weakness in trying to close, he may say, "You know, it's strange because I never thought much about it, but I just realized that I don't feel comfortable forcing someone to make a decision."

Whenever the salesman can correctly identify his own weakness, the manager should be cautious in attempting to change the salesman's behavior. For example, if the man realizes that he is weak in approaching new accounts, the manager might decide he needs more training in this area. On the other hand, the salesman might decide he will avoid new accounts and concentrate on getting more business out of his regular accounts. In this case, training is not likely to change his behavior. Once the salesman admits a weakness, the manager might ask him what he thinks he can, or should, do about it. The coach is really asking the salesman if he is ready and willing to change his behavior in a positive way.

If the salesman does not admit to any weakness, he may justify his mediocre results by claiming that his territory is poor or that the general economic situation is bad, for example. Telling him that he is weak in an area and needs training will do little or nothing for such a salesman. He is not ready to accept the truth about himself. But the coach should not let the salesman off easy at this point. He might pinpoint one weakness which showed up on several calls and ask the man to explain how it occurred each time. If he is still extremely defensive, the manager might explain how other salesmen handle similar situations much more effectively. Finally, the manager can offer to prove his suggestions will work by modeling the appropriate behavior. This challenge can hardly be ignored. It is really a contingency close because the manager is saying, "If I can show you a better way to do this, will you admit your way is weak?" Once again, the use of audio-taped interviews will counteract the salesman's defenses of faulty recall or disbelief that he really did as the coach says.

The entire process is designed to isolate one area of weakness that is seriously holding the salesman back and that can be corrected by training. Going into every item on the typical checklist can destroy a poor salesman's self-confidence, and this serves no purpose. The coach will achieve more positive results by focusing the critique on one key area. He might say, for example, "Let's not worry about these other points for now, Charlie. Let's look at this one thing. I believe that if we can improve your opening, you'll see a tremendous jump in your sales figures." With constructive criticism, the coach helps build the salesman's self-confidence, and he is then able to concentrate on correcting the one area. As the man improves, the coach can move on to other areas, again, one at a time. Under these conditions, the salesman will take direction more readily as he realizes that the coach is steadily helping him to grow.

When coaching an effective salesman, the manager can be liberal in his praise; however, he should not overlook minor faults simply because the man is so good by comparison. The salesman may never realize he has an offending habit or a distracting mannerism or whatever his minor fault may be unless the coach calls it to his attention. The manager may prefer to treat this salesman as an equal and offer him a friendly tip or two in a casual way by pointing to future promotions. Every salesman is entitled to constructive criticism which will enable him to become more effective in the future.

DEMONSTRATING THE PROPER TECHNIQUES

On-the-job demonstration of desirable sales techniques is an appealing method of training salesmen because it seems relatively simple. But whoever does the coaching should be aware of the pitfalls in demonstrating sales techniques. Trainees will learn many things beyond the stated purpose of a given demonstration, and some of these things may not be desirable. The experienced and successful salesman uses techniques which a young trainee might not be able to imitate properly. On one call, for example, the coach might use a negative close by telling the prospect that he cannot afford the product. This technique might be very effective and appropriate for the client; however, the trainee, who lacks the self-confidence and experience of the coach, would probably get into difficulty if he tried to imitate the coach.

The coach may travel with one salesman on one day and with another salesman on the next day. This makes it very difficult for the coach to know as much as he would like to know about the accounts he will be visiting. While he will probably read through the account records and get a verbal briefing from the salesman before each call, to a great extent he will have to remain flexible and adjust spontaneously to the client. This is *not* particularly difficult for an experienced salesman, and the ease with which he accomplishes it may inadvertently teach the trainee that he need not spend much time in preplanning his calls.

In classroom training the coach can ask the trainees to picture a situation and make certain assumptions before he demonstrates a sales technique. To save time, he can take shortcuts or stop the demonstration whenever he chooses. But on-the-job coaching is the real thing and requires a performance which is near to perfection. To get the best results, it takes careful preparation.

Before each call the coach and the salesman should discuss the purpose of this particular visit. What does the salesman hope to accomplish? Which buying influential should they attempt to see and who might be a good alternate if that person is not available? When they are in agreement, the effective coach will then explain the technique he plans to use to accomplish the stated objective of this visit. This technique might involve an opening teaser or an initial-benefit statement, followed by a series of questions. Then, depending on how much information is obtained, it might involve a demonstration or a promise to bring back more information on a follow-up call.

When the salesman knows the plan of action which the coach will use, he can follow the developments with some degree of understanding. The coach can point out certain things which the trainee should be looking for or observing. Several contingencies can often be foreseen, and the coach would be wise to explain them. For example, the coach can explain that if the client is extremely skeptical, he will offer to conduct a free survey of the customer's needs before making any recommendation. If the client is mildly interested, the coach will offer a free trial of the product. If the client is very interested, the coach will attempt to close the sale on that same visit. By explaining the probable contingencies and his corresponding plans, the coach directs the trainee's attention to the client's actions.

If the salesman knows the intended flow of conversation or action, he can carefully observe how the coach directs the client's thoughts. But since any sales conversation must be a two-way dialogue, the coach cannot predict exactly what will take place. If the conversation begins to wander, he can demonstrate a tactful way of returning to the intended subject. In any case, trainees learn significantly more when they are told specifically what to look for beforehand than when they simply make general observations.

Finally, an effective coach will demonstrate how to end an interview on a positive note so that a return visit will be welcome. Clearly, it does the trainee little good to observe a hot-shot closer pressuring his client to the point where he becomes offensive. Most selling depends on repeat business, and it is important to have good relationships with all prospects.

The coach probably will not be able to tell the salesman how he plans to end the interview because so much depends on what actually occurs. However, he can ask the salesman to be thinking about how he would close the interview. When the time comes, the coach can demonstrate planting ideas, promising to get certain facts for the client, or any number of techniques designed to set up the follow-up call. In this manner, the coaching call begins with careful preplanning and ends with planning the next call on the same client.

During the actual visit, the coach should be careful not to yield to the temptation to show off or to go far beyond what was planned. Because of his sales experience, the coach is often able to establish a friendly, warm relationship with the client on a single visit. It would be natural for him to make certain assumptions and jump toward an order if it were his account. The purpose of the entire training procedure, however, is not for the coach to get orders but for the trainee to develop into an effective salesman. Clearly, there are times when orders will be received in the natural course of a sales interview. This is highly desirable, but the coach should concentrate on the purpose of the visit—that is, to demonstrate proper techniques.

After the sales call, an effective coach will ask the salesman to critique the visit. The things the salesman talks about are the ones he considers important. This will give the coach some insight into the salesman's maturity as well as his rate of learning. Did he observe what was intended or did he get sidetracked by some petty incidental? Did he understand some of the subtle but critical statements or silent pauses that may have influenced the entire outcome of the interview? Was he aware of where the coach followed the plan and where he deviated from it to adjust for something which was not anticipated? Did the salesman realize what valuable accomplishment resulted from that one call? Finally, the coach might ask how the salesman would have ended the visit. This will lead naturally to the salesman's plans for his own follow-up call.

When the salesman has completed his critique of the interview, the effective coach will reinforce the intended lesson by summarizing the important events and desired behavior patterns. Using this reinforcing process instead of simply assuming that the trainee knows the important points increases learning significantly. The coach might point out the key statements in the opening, the development of the prospect's interest, and so forth. He might also point out why he was silent in a given situation or that he nodded his head in agreement to encourage the client to continue talking. The effective coach will relate his actual behavior to his planned behavior to emphasize the need for careful planning. He will explain any deviations from the plan and point out the constant need to adjust behavior to suit the situation. The demonstration of proper techniques is not simply doing what comes naturally. It is preplanned, deliberate behavior requiring considerable self-discipline on the part of the coach.

SUPERVISION ON COACHING CALLS

In many organizations, it is a major function of the sales manager or sales supervisor to travel with his salesmen and help critique their sales calls. With the added aspect of supervision, the training situation can become very complicated. In a purely training function, the manager is the friendly, patient authority who is out to help the salesman to become more effective. In a supervisory function, the manager is out to maximize profitable sales at the lowest cost.

When the salesman knows that his future raises and territory assignments depend on the supervisor, he will not readily risk failure in the supervisor's presence. Rather than trying new techniques which may be more effective, the salesman will tend to repeat his standard techniques, which are at least safe. If the manager explains something to him in a quick or disjointed manner, he will say that he understands completely to avoid appearing stupid or antagonistic. Rather than admit that he has trouble in any area of selling and would like some help, the salesman is apt to bluff his way through. Rather than accepting any negative feedback about his sales performance, the salesman will likely become defensive and attempt to rationalize any mishaps which may have occurred.

The sales supervisor is also placed in a difficult position because the salesmen are not on the same social level with him. When he sees something wrong, he is expected by management to discipline the salesmen. The discipline may take the form of friendly advice, a mild chewing out, or an outright confrontation. The processing of expense reimbursement, for example, can be delayed in an attempt to force a salesman to comply with the supervisor's demands. The supervisor can threaten a salesman with turning in poor ratings or unfavorable recommendations unless he does what the supervisor wants. In contrast, the truly friendly supervisor who wants to give raises to most of his salesmen is faced with budget and policy limitations. For these and other reasons, the social distance between the salesmen and the supervisor is often greater than it need be. The salesman is often relieved to be rid of the supervisor at five o'clock, and the supervisor may feel the same way.

Some sales organizations resolve this conflict by having their sales trainers do only on-the-job coaching, with no responsibility for supervision. This can be an expensive specialization. However, these organizations feel that the long-term benefits justify this division of labor; as their salesmen develop, they more than pay back the cost of training.

More commonly, the sales supervisor attempts to play the role of big brother: "You do what I say to help me get promoted, and I'll help you get raises and a better territory." In this process the two men may develop a camaraderie which encourages an honest exchange of thoughts and good training. But such a relationship may also create a degree of cynicism because both men realize it is strictly a short-term bargain with each individual out for his own good. Company policy can reduce this risk by clearly stating that one of the essential conditions for a promotion is that the supervisor show the growth and development of the man assigned to him.

The Curbstone Conference

In a curbstone conference, which is probably the most common form of on-the-job coaching and supervision, the supervisor normally analyzes problems and procedures immediately after the sales call. With the salesman's active participation, they discuss what was planned, what actually occurred, how, in the positive sense, it might have been better, and what would be the logical procedure for the follow-up call on that account. An effective, constructive curbstone conference may take considerable time; therefore, the supervisor should plan to make fewer than the average number of calls for that day. Since immediate feedback after each call is apt to change the salesman's behavior, the alternative, of course, is to withhold all critique during the normal selling hours and to get together in the evening for the conference. This method has the disadvantages of a decrease in recall and the blending of impressions so that details are either forgotten or applied to the wrong call. The strong advantage of taking precious selling time during the day for curbstone conferences is that it provides immediate reinforcement of things done properly and immediate correction of things missed. This practical programmed instruction enhances the learning process.

The items discussed during the critique will, of course, vary from company to company; however, they will include at least some of the items in Checklist 2.

CHECKLIST 2

Questions for the Curbstone Conference

Was the precall objective realistic?

What additional information, if any, would have helped to plan the call better?

Was the timing of the call appropriate for the objective?

Was the buying influential the appropriate one to contact at this time?

What additional materials, if any, should have been brought along on this call?

Was the opening effective? How might it have been improved?

Could the presentation have been more effective? In what way?

Was the client encouraged to discuss his views openly and fully?

What does the client like about the sales proposition?

What does the client dislike about it?

Was proof offered to support the salesman's claims?

Did the client have enough information to make a sound decision?

Was the client asked for an order? How many times?

Did the client receive something of value for his time? What?

What was accomplished on this call?

What will be the objective when calling again?

The Follow-up Evening Conference

By devoting the daytime to education, the supervisor can concentrate on being the friendly trainer and gain some acceptance of his

suggestions. Before quitting for the day, experienced supervisors recommend that the salesman be praised and encouraged to continue
improving himself. In this way, the evening can be devoted to a more
relaxed conversation about the salesman's progress that would include
honest praise for the things he is doing well, honest criticism of any
failure to meet company standards, and discussion of the areas he
should concentrate on to become more effective. Salesmen naturally
expect such a discussion at the end of the day, and this follow-up
session can be informal and productive.

In the evening conference, the supervisor can discuss such things
as work habits, attitudes, and mannerisms, as well as the individual's
ambitions and self-reliance. Most of these topics relate to what the
company expects of the salesman and what he expects from the company. This is a time for open, two-way communication to encourage
complete honesty and to further understanding. The supervisor can
assist the salesman in problem solving on a tough account, suggest
corrective action when sales are in a slump, or encourage him to keep
trying harder than his competitors. Supervision and control of salesmen can be compatible with coaching and training as long as the
sales manager or supervisor considers developing the man to have
priority over getting orders. In the short run these two functions are
usually in conflict; however, the manager should be mature enough
to perceive the long-term benefits that will result.

COACHING FOR FUTURE DEVELOPMENT

Because on-the-job coaching is a one-to-one situation, it provides an
excellent opportunity to give the individual salesman full attention.
His work and the future of his career are subjects in which both the
salesman and his supervisor would naturally be interested. The immature salesman of any age is concerned primarily with short-term
goals. He wants to know how he can bring in more orders tomorrow,
go over quota, and get a raise in a few months. He is also willing to
skip his afternoon calls to enjoy a spontaneous party or a pretty girl's
company. The young, inexperienced salesman does not understand
that it will take time for him to achieve his goals, and his current
needs demand immediate satisfaction. He is relatively dependent on

his sales manager or supervisor for guidance and direction. Their control and discipline serve as his business conscience because he has not yet developed his own.

These traits are normal in a young salesman and are not necessarily bad or wrong. In fact, because the immature salesman is so dependent on his manager, he can be directed. Work habits and attitudes can be developed which will help him become more effective in the field. The young salesman has a strong desire to excel quickly and he has the energy required to work long and hard. If this desire and energy are controlled and directed by the manager, the young salesman can be very productive.

Controlling and directing the young salesman requires a considerable amount of personal attention and time on the part of the manager. As the salesman develops effective attitudes and work habits, the manager would be wise to begin weaning him from the manager's support. If he is cut off all at once, without having developed self-discipline or long-term goals, he may go astray and revert to childish behavior. The problem then becomes one of guiding the young salesman to develop his own long-term perspective and attain his goals.

Experienced sales managers suggest asking the salesman, if he could do or be anything he wanted, where he would like to see himself in business five years from today. The salesman's first reaction to this question quite often is some vague generalization such as the desire to be the best and highest-paid salesman with the best territory on the sales force. Upon reflection, however, the young salesman is apt to become more realistic and begin to think in terms of likely progression. For example, he might want to be a supervisor or a sales manager for a small district. In any case, the coach now has the opportunity to describe the training and experience which are usually required for that position—for instance, a proven sales performance record and the ability to manage one's own territory independently. If the young man really wants a certain promotion, he should know the price he will have to pay to achieve it. The coach may also play up the advantages and privileges which go with the desired promotion and where else it might lead in the organizational hierarchy.

When the young salesman has decided on a realistic goal, the manager can encourage him to take the steps necessary to attain it. In so doing, the manager gradually shifts the discipline, control, and direction to the salesman himself. When situations arise that cause the young salesman to ask for the manager's advice, experienced managers recommend reflecting the question and asking the young man how he would handle the situation. Soon he will not come to the manager without thinking of one or more feasible solutions. As his suggestions improve, the manager can tell the salesman to go ahead with his own ideas but to check with the manager under certain conditions. The developing young salesman will gradually earn the manager's confidence to the point of being given complete control over his own territory.

Older inexperienced salesmen present a more serious problem to the sales manager or coach; however, a similar approach can be effective. Because the older man has more experience in life, his time perspective—of the past, at least—will probably be more realistic. Experienced managers ask such a salesman what he feels life is all about. Once again, the initial response is likely to be general; in this case, it may be the desire to be healthy, wealthy, and wise. In one or in several different interviews, the manager attempts to get the older salesman to develop more specific goals regarding a life style which he would prefer to his present one. This will frequently include a job which is physically less demanding and in which his wealth of knowledge and experience can be put to better use.

The manager then has the problem of identifying positions within the organization which the older salesman can fill if he develops certain traits of independence—for example, senior salesman, national-account salesman, sales trainer, on-the-job coach, or sales supervisor. Once again, the manager explains the job requirements and the price the man must pay to get what he wants. By encouraging independent thinking and action, the manager can build the older man's self-confidence and rekindle his desire to accomplish something new.

Contrary to popular thinking, older salesmen can learn new skills. They can learn to use computer analyses and printout information, to make forecasts, to plan their own activities, and to carry out their plans independently. They can be assigned new duties involving customers and other people who relate to older salesmen better than to young. Because of their age, older salesmen are often more loyal to their sales organization, and this makes them ideal for many public relations assignments.

The rigorous demands of the selling profession do not lessen as a salesman gets on in years. All salesmen need encouragement, recognition, and praise on a regular basis. When older salesmen seem to reach a plateau of productivity, they are often reflecting the sales manager's attitude. If the manager has given up trying to change the older salesman's behavior, the man cannot be expected to change, to adapt, to meet new challenges.

The manager who sincerely cares for the individual will continually encourage each man to develop his potential capabilities. Many creative people do not develop their talent until later in life, after they have had considerable experience dealing with the mechanics of their profession. An older salesman often has a wealth of technical product information and a knowledge of customer applications which can be used constructively in the development of new products. Some older salesmen compensate for their lower energy level by intelligently analyzing the markets and using their effort where it will do the most good.

On-the-job coaching is a natural situation for helping each salesman to identify and set his goals realistically. The salesman cannot always do this on his own because of the day-to-day demands on his time and thoughts and because of his limited knowledge of the various opportunities within his organization. The sales manager or supervisor is in a position to guide the salesman's thinking by asking specific questions regarding career goals and by providing additional information. In this sense, the long-term goals of the coach, the company, and the individual salesman should blend into a mutual objective, with each component helping the others.

REINFORCEMENT OF NEW SKILLS

It is one problem to get salesmen to try a new way of doing something, to change their behavior patterns temporarily, and quite another to get them to behave habitually in a new way. Some salesmen have a desire to improve and may be willing to try something new if it sounds reasonable. Others want to please their manager and are also willing to try whatever he may suggest. Still other salesmen, who may be quite cynical, may fear displeasing their manager, and for this negative reason, they may be willing to carry out his directives to do something in a different manner.

For various reasons, the manager should expect the initial trials to have mixed or poor results. A salesman's first few attempts at a new behavior pattern are apt to be crude and mismanaged. If the manager was not convinced of the value of the new method before he instigated the change, he may readily give up at this stage. However, if he is sure in his own mind that the new system is worth learning, he should stay with the new process despite the negative initial results.

When the salesmen realize that the manager is insistent and is not about to forget the new requirements, they will try again and again. Some men may need close coaching and attention, and most will need encouragement because it is frustrating to fail. As some men succeed, others will renew their efforts, and most salesmen will then go along with the new system.

The manager should be aware that the new behavior, even when successful, is still tentative, strange, or uncomfortable to most of the salesmen. Many will be tempted to slip back into their old way of doing things. At this early stage, the manager or field coach should insist on continuous, conscious practice of the new behavior pattern. Direct observation on the job is very important at this point for two reasons. First, it communicates to salesmen that management is serious about the change; and second, it permits early guidance and correction if necessary. Salesmen out in the field alone should realize from management's actions that someone knows what they are trying to do and cares whether they do it correctly. This kind of reinforcement is usually necessary to encourage salesmen to keep up with the difficult procedure. With practice and positive feedback, the new behavior pattern becomes habitual and more comfortable than the old way of doing things.

Clearly, the sales manager doing the training and the sales supervisor or on-the-job coach should be in full agreement about the value of the expected change and its priority when calling on real customers. If the salesmen do not receive the reinforcement they need, some men will give up trying, and others may continue to practice the skill incorrectly. Without feedback, it is very difficult to acquire a new skill;

without a positive incentive, it is almost impossible. Changing one's behavior is not easy, nor is it always painless. The rewards should justify the hard practice and the little improvements that are steps in self-development.

The reinforcing process should continue long after the salesman has achieved the desired new behavior. He should be praised for good performance until the behavior becomes habitual. The most common pitfall for sales management in this process is to move on too quickly to another area or in another direction. Regular feedback from the salesmen themselves and from the field coach can be used to determine when the men are ready for another step in their development. Obviously, salesmen will learn new habits and develop at different rates. With on-the-job coaching, this is no problem as long as the manager is aware of, and accepts, the differences among salesmen.

SUMMARY

The entire process of on-the-job coaching is designed to help the individual salesman become more effective and able to manage his own activities independently within the guidelines or standards established by management. This sales training method can be applied to trainees, intermediate salesmen with limited experience, and senior salesmen. Because it is tailored to the individual, the pace of training can be different for each salesman, just as the subject matter might be different for each man.

Because the coaching job is very important, the man to fill it should be carefully selected. He should be dedicated to helping other people, acutely sensitive to other people's readiness to accept criticism, and willing to learn a great deal about training. Of course, the man selected should have a good knowledge of his own company and industry and acceptable experience in selling to the company's customers. Finally, his attitudes and work habits should be of such a demonstrated effectiveness that top management is willing to have new trainees imitate him.

The combining of supervision and training is a difficult and questionable practice, although it is very common. Men assigned to do both duties should be cautioned about the problems they will face and the ways in which they can lessen, if not eliminate, the conflict in the two roles.

While on-the-job coaching is commonly thought of as a short-term and sales-oriented procedure, it need not be confined to that level. Effective coaches help salesmen to identify long-term personal goals and encourage them to develop the necessary knowledge and skills to achieve their objectives.

The sales supervisor or coach is frequently the field salesman's main regular contact with his company. As such, the coach is usually the person responsible for implementing desired behavior changes by continually observing, correcting, encouraging, and providing a model for salesmen. The supervisor is thus often in the critical position of being the only one who can reinforce the desired learning. How he carries out this duty can determine the success or failure of the entire process of on-the-job training.

SELECTED MATERIALS

Borwick, Irving, "Designing Training Programs: Parity or Parody?" *Management of Personnel Quarterly*, Vol. 8, No. 4 (Winter 1969), pp. 40–46.

Gennan, Martin J., "Employee Perceptions of Promotion," *Personnel Journal*, Vol. 50, No. 3 (March 1971), pp. 213–17.

Harrow, Herman, "A Critical Look at Criticizing," *Supervisory Management*, Vol. 14, No. 5 (May 1969), pp. 2–6.

Lee, James A., "Behavioral Theory vs. Reality," *Harvard Business Review*, Vol. 49, No. 2 (March–April 1971), pp. 20–28.

Migliore, R. Henry, "Improving Worker Productivity Through Communicating Knowledge of Work Results," *Management of Personnel Quarterly*, Vol. 9, No. 2 (Summer 1970), pp. 26–32.

Steinmetz, Lawrence L., "Age: Unrecognized Enigma of Executive Development," *Management of Personnel Quarterly*, Vol. 8, No. 3 (Fall 1969), pp. 2–12.

Sutermeister, Robert A., "Employee Performance and Employee Need Satisfaction—What Comes First?" *California Management Review*, Vol. 13, No. 4 (Summer 1971), pp. 43–47.

Warnimant, Paul F., "What Supervisors and Subordinates Expect of Each Other," *Personnel Journal*, Vol. 50, No. 3 (March 1971), pp. 204–8.

Zima, Joseph P., "Counseling Concepts for Supervisors," *Personnel Journal*, Vol. 50, No. 6 (June 1971), pp. 482–85.

CHAPTER 10

Programs for Retraining and Continuous Training

Continuous training programs are designed to improve the salesman's skills, knowledge, attitudes, and work habits in a never-ending process. Retraining programs, on the other hand, are designed to prepare the salesman to handle new responsibilities or to apply known skills in a new way. Retraining is ideal for an individual salesman because it combines a careful analysis of the man's past training and experience with the new orientation and skills demanded by the new responsibilities. Continuous training is designed to maintain a constant path toward perfection in the same job and is often used with groups, as in the case of a refresher course for experienced salesmen.

Continuous training also occurs on a more informal basis every day the salesman is in contact with his supervisor or manager. It may involve updating the salesman's knowledge through bulletins, sales letters, and audio tapes, as mentioned in Chapter 6, or improving his skills through on-the-job coaching, as described in Chapter 9. It commonly occurs as a part of every sales meeting. Continuous training is a line responsibility rather than a staff function, although a training specialist is often called on to train the trainer and to suggest training needs and methods.

Obviously, continuous training is needed to keep all salesmen up to date on changing product features and company policies, customer or industry changes, and competitive changes, to cite just a few areas. Refresher training is indicated when the salesmen are to be asked to do something which they have not done in a long while. For example, all sales trainees in an organization may learn how to do market research. Years later, if management wants the salesman to do some grass-roots research, a short refresher course would be in order.

Some organizations budget for each salesman to take one-week courses outside the company. Such courses include fundamental, intermediate, and advanced salesmanship (with one or two years' experience between the levels), as well as self-development programs in public speaking, speed reading, and effective listening. Some of the larger companies reimburse salesmen for their tuition after they complete job-related college courses such as psychology.

While continuous training can involve both periodic formal classwork and day-to-day, informal on-the-job coaching, retraining programs are relatively short and oriented to a particular skill. For example, when reorganization of a sales force requires all experienced salesmen to handle a product which is new to them, retraining is important. Retraining might also be necessary if the salesmen were asked to solicit orders from a target segment with which they were not familiar.

But retraining more commonly occurs when an individual salesman has mastered one selling job and is ready for more sophisticated duties and responsibilities. After he has proved he can handle a regular territory, he may want to handle national accounts. This new selling job probably will require different knowledge, new administrative record-keeping skills, and perhaps new selling and research skills. There is no need to have the salesman understudy a senior national-account manager for many years nor simply to transfer him and force him to learn by trial and error. Before he is given new duties and responsibilities, he can be retrained to handle them as the sales manager wants.

RETRAINING TO CHANGE SKILLS
AND ADD NEW SKILLS

Some Common Situations That Require Retraining

In the past, many sales organizations were asked to get orders or to sell the complete line of products without regard to the profit contribution of each item. Today, the use of computers has enabled many companies to allocate production and handling costs to each lot of a product. With various government controls on pricing, more and more concerns are now asking their salesman to sell those items or combinations of items which generate the highest contribution to profit.

For similar reasons, many customers are reevaluating their purchasing procedures to reduce their raw materials or production costs. Naturally, they are also looking for ways to increase their revenue. This kind of value analysis is not new in many industries, but it has become more common. Where it is used, buyers prefer a salesman who is conversant in profit-improvement plans for the customer to the traditional "unique benefit" salesman.

As a result, salesmen are being asked to change their skills and to add new skills. They must acquire a new orientation and learn new methods of selling. Today, for example, they may need a basic understanding of cost accounting, which was not required or even considered five years ago. "Incremental profit contribution," "depreciation," "cost of acquisition," and "cost of life" are just a few of the terms which customers may use in conversations with salesmen. This new quantitative approach to solving a customer's problem—rather than the traditional qualitative approach—may require the salesman to make a financial analysis of the customer's operation to determine where his product will have the greatest leverage on his customer's profit.

Reorganization of a sales force often causes serious retraining problems. For example, experienced, successful salesmen in one division may be asked to sell products formerly handled by another division. The new products and the new customers may require an entirely new approach to selling, and the experienced salesman is suddenly unsure of himself. The realignment of salesmen and some sales managers may also create anxieties and resistance. Customer confusion adds more pressure to the situation.

Planning Programs for Retraining

Before beginning any retraining on account of reorganization, the salesmen should be fully informed as to why the reorganization is necessary and how the sales force and the customers will benefit. It is

also wise under these conditions to ask the people involved for suggestions for implementing the change. When the sales force is encouraged to participate in the development of the new organization,
resistance lessens. Questions, comments, and criticisms can be aired,
and the potentially explosive situation can be defused. As the salesmen
learn more about it, their natural fear of the new situation will
decrease.

Retraining experienced salesmen presents problems different from
those associated with initial sales training. The salesmen know with
the certainty of personal experience what works for them. They are
not apt to give up selling methods which have been successful in the
past for new, untried methods. It is natural to expect their attitudes
to be somewhat skeptical and challenging to most instructors and
managers. They are apt to be ill at ease if the new behavior they must
try is contrary to their lifelong selling habits. These factors rarely
appear in training men new to the profession.

In planning the retraining program, job descriptions can be an
important analytical tool. What did the old job require? What does
the new job require? What are the similarities, and what are the
critical differences? When these factors are identified, the program
can be constructed to begin with the similarities. The experienced
salesmen will be comfortable dealing with known areas, and the brief
review will not offend their intelligence. As a common ground is
established, the program can begin to move into the new areas.

Presenting New Knowledge and Skills

It is important that the salesmen understand in training why their
old way of selling will not be very effective under the new conditions.
Wherever possible, of course, old habits that can be modified to suit
the new situation should be utilized. When this is not possible, the
new method—the critical difference—should be emphasized with clear
theory and practical demonstrations. Each salesman should be given
the time and patient guidance necessary to practice the new behavior.
Practice sessions should be long enough to make each man comfortable in the new role. Some individual tutoring may be required, and
in some situations small subgroups or teams can be organized to help
teach each other through role playing and team critique.

Once the critical differences have been accepted and learned, the retraining program can move much more rapidly. Experienced sales-men are quick to learn new product information, prospecting meth-ods, and the like because they already know how important these factors are in selling. Their questions are apt to be much more perti-nent than those of new trainees, and they will understand new con-cepts much faster. At this stage a degree of camaraderie will often develop, and the sales manager or instructor should encourage this new team spirit. The team will often establish high standards for themselves and will persuade the more hesitant members to join the enthusiastic group. Natural leaders will emerge, and their positive participation in the training program should be eagerly sought.

Reinforcement. Effective retraining does not stop at the end of a seminar. It is one thing to be enthusiastic and self-confident in the protective atmosphere of the classroom and another thing to be so in the office of a tough prospect. The salesman's new behavior is tenta-tive, and his temptation to revert to the old ways is very strong. The experienced salesman needs encouragement and reinforcement perhaps even more than the young trainee. On-the-job observation, praise, and coaching are all appropriate under the new conditions. Any early successes should be made known to the entire team, who will try harder to prove they are as good as the one or two salesmen who caught on quickly. The naturally competitive nature of salesmen will thus encourage the desired change in behavior.

RETRAINING FOR TARGET-ACCOUNT SELLING

While the changes mentioned in the preceding section might be con-sidered radical or extreme, adding new skills, such as target-account selling, is usually an evolutionary process and is more readily accepted by the salesmen. Most salesmen are eager to learn ways to make their day shorter, easier, and more productive. They generally would prefer to sell a hundred items rather than one or two for the same effort. As young salesmen develop self-confidence, they are apt to try to make increasingly larger sales.

Selling to one large account is often an easier way to achieve the same contribution to profit than selling to many small accounts. However, selling to one large account is very complicated and different from selling to a small account. In the first place, the very size of the target account will often attract the best competing salesmen. The potential order may be so large that the account can make considerable demands regarding price, delivery, and service, for example. The third major difference is that no more than a few people make the buying decision in a small account, whereas 20 or 30 people may influence a buying decision in a large account.

When the sales manager or supervisor feels a salesman is ready to try to sell large accounts, he can begin to teach the strategy of key-account or target-account selling. The principles are essentially the same as those for selling small accounts, but the steps must be carried out in much greater detail. The salesman is asked to identify one particular account which he would like to sell and then to study that industry until he can converse fluently about its various aspects. Next he studies the particular target account until he knows what makes it different from other companies in the same industry. Then the salesman is asked to identify all the buying influentials in the company, at least by job title if not by name.

This process normally causes the salesman to think of who will use the product; who will handle and maintain or service the product; who will approve the requisition; who will name the pool of possible suppliers; who will obtain the sales literature; who will weigh the competitive proposals; who may have a say in the final decision; who may veto the entire process; and, finally, who actually places the order. Often groups of people carry out a single function, and they usually have friends and associates who can influence their decisions.

When the salesman has identified many of these buying influentials, he is asked to think of the kind of information in which each influential would be interested. The user, for example, might want to know how easily the product works. The requisitioner or the one who specifies the need might want to know how efficiently it works. The maintenance people might want to know how often the product requires regular service, what tools are required for service, and what spare parts should be available. The people who approve the expenditure might want to know the acquisition cost, the life expectancy, the cost of maintenance, and the final trade-in value. It is likely that each buying influential will require slightly different information to make an intelligent decision.

The salesman is now in a position to decide whom to see on a given sales visit and how to vary his presentation to suit that person's information needs. As he begins to make friends with some of the buying influentials, he will pick up clues and suggestions about the predisposition of other influentials. He will also become aware of a number of informal influentials and should attempt to befriend them too. While he may give a number of very different presentations, he must be completely honest and accurate because many of these people will compare notes. On each visit the salesman sees several buying influentials and plants ideas for future requisitions.

Once the target account makes a purchase, the salesman provides exceptionally good service to ensure that the product is used as intended to provide the customer with maximum benefits. Building friendships after the sale is easier than before because there is no pressure. As things work out as the salesman promised, the various buying influentials learn to accept his suggestions and advice at face value. He will have proved his sincerity. Subsequent orders are then likely to go to this salesman. By working his way through the entire process the salesman learns this more complicated sales strategy and is able to apply it to other key accounts of his choice.

Key-account selling is most often taught to individual salesmen as they mature and seem ready to tackle the big jobs. On occasion, however, it may be appropriately taught to the entire sales force. For example, a large paper manufacturer spent several years developing book papers. When tests showed that the new product was acceptable, the group of salesmen who had been selling magazine papers were selected to handle it. Their initial contacts with buyers and purchasing agents produced few orders and very little encouragement. Every buyer contacted seemed happy with his existing supplier and could not see any advantage in changing.

At this point, the sales manager realized that the men were not contacting the right people because they did not know what to say. He began a program in target-account selling which required one full day of training each month. At the first meeting the salesmen were asked to list the ten best prospects in their territories and the name and title of every person contacted in the past on each of the ten accounts. A number of studies were then presented showing the many different buying influentials concerned with a single purchase of this kind of material.

During the month, the salesmen were given an assignment to

compile a new list of likely contacts for each of their ten accounts. At the second training meeting, a master list was created showing some 40 job positions or titles in each account who could influence the placement of an order. For example, art directors had strong requirements for factors affecting the graphics. Editors were concerned with the bulk of a book. Printers were interested in the strength of the paper and the speed with which it could be run through the press. Then the manager had the salesmen note the kind of information necessary to interest and persuade each of these buying influentials.

The second month's assignment was to begin contacting the many buying influentials and to prepare a report for the third training meeting indicating the kind of reception they received and the degree of success they had. At the third meeting, experiences were exchanged, and most of the salesmen became very enthusiastic as the group offered good suggestions to each man who had a problem.

The third month's assignment was to get as many free trial runs as possible in the ten accounts and again to prepare a report for the next training meeting. At this meeting, several salesmen were able to report not only successful trials but substantial orders from accounts that had never ordered before. The salesmen's enthusiasm was contagious, as each man now had several testimonials from large accounts that reinforced what they had been saying. Within six months, the manufacturing plant could not keep up with the market demands. Clearly, the price, the quality of the product, and many other things helped, but retraining the salesmen was acknowledged to be one of the key factors in the rapid success of this venture.

CONTINUOUS TRAINING TO DEVELOP SKILLS AND IMPROVE PERFORMANCE

Any initial sales training program is limited by time, budget, and trainee experience, so that some topics or skills are given insufficient treatment. The young salesmen are assigned to a territory and go forth—hopefully—full of enthusiasm. Their major concern is to get profitable orders and they rarely think of training again. Some companies require feedback after the new salesman has been out on his own for six months or one year. This feedback helps to evaluate various parts of the initial training program; but even more importantly—and this fact is too often overlooked—it signals what the salesmen now need in the way of current or continuous training.

Another source of information for determining current training needs is the salesmen's call reports. For example, these records may show that men who are generally successful in selling to new accounts have to visit them at least five times before getting their first order. Each visit may involve several different buying influentials and a different sales presentation. When the manager recognizes this kind of pattern, he can check to see how many calls the average salesman makes on a new client before he quits calling. He can see how many different people and job titles were called on and how the presentation was or was not varied to suit the situation. A comparison of these data with the records of the successful salesmen will indicate whether further training is necessary.

Customer letters, either of praise or of complaint, often provide another source of information to assist in analyzing current training needs. For example, a customer may feel that some special service offered by a salesman was so different and helpful that he had to write about it. This salesman may have done something intuitively which made his total product offering unique and irresistible, and it might be appropriate for the entire sales force to learn to do the same thing. On the other hand, a single letter of complaint is something to be discussed in private between the manager and the salesman involved. A number of similar complaints would probably indicate a gross misunderstanding and a need for further training.

Most common, perhaps, is the sales supervisor's observation that the sales force in general is weak in a given area. The men may not be firm in asking for the order, for example. Clearly, a directive from the manager commanding the salesman to be firm in attempting to close a sale will do little good. When a common weakness is identified, by the supervisor or by the salesmen themselves, training is indicated.

In the process of improving performance and perfecting skills, the sales supervisor or manager sets a new standard of performance that is higher than the current norm. For instance, the salesmen might be told that the new standard is to attempt to close a sale three different times during an interview. The appropriate education and training is then conducted, and each salesman is allowed to practice using what he has been taught. Every salesman is expected to meet the new higher standard in the training situation. The sales supervisor then observes each man on his regular sales calls and measures his performance against the established criteria. After the calls, the supervisor provides feedback to the salesmen. If they have done well, the positive feedback is rewarding in and of itself, but it also communicates to the salesmen that management is still strongly interested in this phase of their daily performance. If a salesman has not done well, the critique becomes a learning opportunity, with the coach showing how the salesman can achieve the desired standard.

A still higher standard is then adopted, so that the salesmen once again improve their performance, and this process is repeated in steps that are attainable in the time permitted until the salesmen reach the desired peak. Most of this kind of sales training can be conducted in group sessions, such as regular sales meetings; however, some men will probably need special tutoring in the field to come up to the minimum acceptable standards. With feedback to reinforce the new behavior, it will gradually become habitual at the desired level. At that point a new subject area can be introduced. If possible, the new material should be related to the previous subject so as to communicate to the salesmen that they are expected to continue their high-level performance in the first area and gradually improve in the second area.

A common problem in continuous training is the focus on a single subject or skill to the exclusion of most other material. For a short period of time, perhaps three months, the manager, the coach, and the salesmen are all giving special attention to closing, for example. Then for the next three months they may focus on obtaining new accounts. This period may be followed by three months of coaching in probing and effective listening. If the topics are taught in isolation and the measurement and feedback are confined to the current topic, the salesmen are apt to forget the previous topics quickly.

By relating topics and providing feedback on the salesmen's total performance, some sales organizations have been able to develop two- to five-year continuous training programs. Each year the standard of performance is raised, and the salesmen can easily see their individual growth and achievement. In small groups the salesmen attend one week of centralized formal training. Then, to help them apply what has been taught, every month they receive audio cassettes reinforcing the concept and encouraging the salesmen to continue their efforts and practice. Individually, the salesmen also receive regular feedback from their supervisor on their total performance.

A long-term plan of continuous training requires a great deal of preparation. Its implementation also necessitates the expenditure of a great deal of time and energy on the part of the sales manager, the supervisors, the trainer, and the salesmen themselves. When the plan is carried out with the dedication it requires, the salesmen soon learn that training and self-improvement are an essential part of their job. If this is in fact true, the compensation system should reinforce this point. The salesman who is able steadily to improve his performance on the job is more valuable to the organization in the long run than the lucky salesman in a booming territory who has reached a plateau as an order taker. If the compensation system rewards only actual sales, the salesmen will quickly recognize this fact and give training, at best, merely lip service. Continuous training is hard work and should not be attempted unless the plan includes some kind of recognition and reward for the desired improvement.

CONTINUOUS TRAINING TO UPDATE INFORMATION AND SKILLS

Continuous training programs are essential in most organizations to keep salesmen abreast of what is happening in the market and within their own company and to keep their skills competitive. Equally important, continuous training programs can anticipate changes and prepare salesmen for what will happen in the near future.

Traditional sales managers think of continuous training as a rehash of knowledge—prospecting, preapproach planning, presentation, demonstration, handling objections, closing, and providing customer services. It is no wonder they look upon sales training with distaste and that their poor salesmen are bored to death with it. Continuous sales training should be a developmental process. Modern sales managers are presenting new, exciting material which helps their salesmen not only to sell better today but also to develop skills which will make them better salesmen and better people the rest of their lives.

Many salesmen have never visited the plants which make the products they sell. Very few sales managers, in fact, know what new production equipment or production systems were added or modified in the past year. It might be very important for a salesman to know what changes have taken place at the plant or what changes are anticipated in the near future because such changes can often be translated into customer benefits. What is the plant doing to hold down the prices for his customers? In what way is the new process helping deliveries or extending the life expectancy of the product? What kind of order is now attractive to the plant that has been a costly problem in the past? How does his company's plant compare with competitive plants? These are just a few of the topics in the area of production that a sales manager can explore for new material for at least one annual sales training meeting.

Research and development activities normally fascinate most salesmen. Many organizations spend substantial amounts of money every year to find out in advance that very few new products will succeed. While some projects might be labeled top secret, most R&D activities are routine and to be expected by competitors. The salesmen have a sincere interest, as do their customers, in the things the company is trying to improve, modify, or create. When a competitor tells his customer that something new is about to be introduced, the salesman should have had some forewarning and preparation. He should be able to discuss the R&D problems and critical areas which his account should check before trying the new product. In addition, R&D projects written off as failures in the past can provide the salesman with knowledge about why a certain product or feature cannot be a commercial success. The R&D people can provide a wealth of new information, at least once a year, which will be interesting and useful to salesmen.

In a similar manner, market research people often keep track of such things as population trends, technical obsolescence, foreign competition, foreign market opportunities, and new domestic market segments on the increase. Beyond identifying new profit opportunities, these people often conduct market tests of new products and packaging and new applications of existing products. Once again, many of these ideas may never get beyond the testing stage; however, these facts may be useful to the salesman. Market research people often have the responsibility of monitoring competitive activity in this field, and an early tip from them might very well help a salesman to save an account. Market research specialists have a good feeling for what is changing in their industry, and much of this information can be passed on to the sales force in a series of sales training meetings.

Of all information potentially useful to salesmen perhaps the most neglected is the data collected by people in advertising and promotion. The internal advertising staff and the advertising agency people have a wealth of statistics and creative ideas which can entertain and enlighten most salesmen. Rather than complain about or ignore an advertising campaign, the sales force can be educated about its purpose and methods so that they can contact the targeted market segments and reinforce the message. Advertising is reviewed annually in most companies, and since it can vitally affect the sales organization, not to devote at least one sales meeting every year to this topic seems almost criminal. Sales promotion activities are similar to advertising; however, they are often of short duration and for a specific purpose. Each of these special promotions would justify a sales training meeting.

Another area which may justify a number of sales training meetings is the broad forecasts presented by publications such as *Fortune* magazine, *Sales Management* magazine, *The New York Times*, *Dun's Review* magazine, *Business Week* magazine, and hundreds of trade and association journals. Many of these publications have quarterly reviews and seasonal features which can give salesmen an indication of future trends. They can become conversant with trends in the economy, regional variations, and trends in their own and their customers' industries. This knowledge should help them to identify many new opportunities in the constantly changing marketplace.

The few areas mentioned for possible continuous sales training meetings were selected because they help to update the salesman's current knowledge and, more importantly, they can extend his outlook from the narrow world of his sales problems to a broad and completely customer-oriented marketing approach. When a salesman learns to think in this way, he will be more effective for the rest of his career. Obviously, there are many other areas for continuous sales training, and a creative sales manager will employ many of them.

Training for updating the skills discussed in Chapter 4 is dictated primarily by the needs of the salesmen. These needs can be identified by means of the sales supervisor's observation, a survey of the salesmen, and, most importantly, the felt needs of the customers. In addition, a number of publications may be consulted for new ideas on training, such as *Sales Management, Harvard Business Review, The American Management Associations Reports, The National Industrial Conference Board Reports,* and *The Journal of Marketing.* New and revised approaches to the continuous development of desirable skills are frequently reported in these publications, and they should be reviewed periodically to keep training programs up to date.

GAINING EXPERIENCED SALESMEN'S ACCEPTANCE OF CONTINUOUS TRAINING

While experienced salesmen may be tired of hearing about the basics or fundamentals of salesmanship, they often are the very men who may be neglecting the basics. If they are required to attend a regular sales training meeting, they may contaminate the attitude of the younger salesmen with their cynicism or ridicule. Rather than take this risk, the sales manager might do well to consider two alternatives which have worked well for many sales organizations.

Special Seminars

One alternative is to hold a special seminar. This technique is particularly effective with the most productive men on the sales force. The top 25 percent of the salesmen are asked to attend a special seminar, most often on a quarterly basis. The discussion leader reinforces the high reputation of the salesmen invited and asks their opinions on selected sales problems facing the company. For example, he might present a market change that has been forecast or a new competitive challenge. The experienced salesmen then are free to exchange ideas and techniques and to suggest any number of creative approaches to the problem. Each salesman is a star in his territory, but he also realizes that he is with a peer group at this seminar. To be accepted by this elite group, each salesman wants to make a positive contribution to the discussion. It becomes an honor to be invited to attend this kind of seminar.

When handled with a proper build-up or promotion, such as a

personal letter from the vice-president of sales and a prestigious meeting place, the experienced salesmen enter the training program with very positive attitudes. They learn from each other, and often their suggestions become productive input for training the entire sales force. Experienced salesmen, in effect, teach each other under highly favorable learning conditions.

Using the Salesmen as Trainers

The second and most common alternative to boring the experienced salesman at routine sales training meetings is to assign him the responsibility of teaching a subject. This provides him with an opportunity to exhibit his ability as a salesman, an organizer, a motivator, and a trainer. Many of these abilities are required for promotion into management; hence, the assignment becomes a challenge to the salesman. To avoid appearing ridiculous in front of his peers, the experienced salesman will spend considerable time preparing his lesson. In the process of attempting to persuade other salesmen to use the basic techniques, the experienced salesman persuades himself.

When the salesman becomes the trainer, he often learns more about his subject than the trainees do. His psychological defenses against being trained, against relearning basics, lie dormant, and he readily accepts information which he would otherwise reject. To be prepared to answer questions from the audience, the experienced salesman will take the extra effort necessary to learn what authorities teach on his subject.

Even though the experienced salesman may fully realize what the manager is attempting to do, he also knows he is being given a chance to show off, to be recognized in public, to demonstrate his management abilities, and to win the praise of his peers.

Several experienced salesmen can be assigned to handle one complete sales training program in a similar manner. The manager can exercise some control by outlining the specific topics which he wants covered, but he can leave the division of effort up to the salesmen. The manager, of course, would probably attend the meeting as an observer and technical expert to answer questions which the senior salesmen might not be able to handle. He might also tell the trainers that he planned to get feedback from the trainees or the other salesmen in the class. In this way, many otherwise reluctant experienced salesmen have been won over to the manager's position of enthusiastic endorsement of sales training.

The experienced salesman can also be used as a trainer in the field. He should learn the techniques for demonstrating the desired behavior and observing the trainee recommended in the previous chapter. In addition to gaining the trainee's acceptance of specific criticisms, the senior salesman as a field trainer will strongly influence the trainee to form effective attitudes and work habits.

Without the proper motivation, however, a senior salesman may subconsciously feel that the trainee's presence is a handicap or that the trainee poses a future threat to him. If this happens, the experienced salesman is apt to do a great job in the customer's office but then swear the trainee to secrecy and go to the afternoon movies or a cocktail lounge or engage in some other nonbusiness activity during working hours. The sales manager may never learn of these activities, since the trainee is apt to go along with the conspiracy. The very fact that they successfully get away with such behavior makes the manager look careless and stupid. Unfortunately, such negative training occurs more often than most sales managers realize.

Before the experienced salesman is assigned a trainee, the manager would be wise to provide him with some sort of incentive. The extra time and effort required of the salesman and the additional responsibility imposed on him will not be sufficiently compensated by the opportunity to show off to an interested, if naive, audience. The longer the on-the-job training period, the greater the salesman's rewards will need to be. A reduced quota, a bonus, a letter of recommendation for a promotion, or an override on the junior man's sales, for example, can serve as an inducement for the senior salesman to take the extra time and effort necessary to do a good training job.

Setting Goals and Achieving Maximum Participation

Continuous training is generally most effective when the salesmen know that it is relevant to their current needs. For this reason, the salesmen should be surveyed anonymously on a regular basis regarding their training needs. In a small organization every salesman can be surveyed, and in a large organization a representative sample can be taken to determine many training needs for the entire group.

Problem-solving seminars, as noted above, can also provide ideas for continuous training programs for the entire sales force or for different groups of salesmen.

Group training. Conferences can be held for men on each of several experience levels, for example, or according to levels of sales volume, types of territory, or product assignments. The average needs of the entire sales force may not apply to any one salesman, however, and holding several seminars or conferences can correct for any misleading survey information.

The salesmen themselves are in the best position to know how much they need to improve in various areas. They should participate in setting the goals for which the continuous training is planned. Their participation has the effect of bringing reality into the training process. In addition, the salesmen's prior commitment is conducive to their active involvement in the training sessions.

While technically correct, the label "continuous training" has many negative associations for the salesmen and would not normally be used as a title for any program. "Advertising for 1975," for example, could be the title of a training meeting designed to teach the salesmen how to identify selected market segments and use reprints of current advertisements to reinforce their spoken message.

Any sales training meeting designed to update the salesmen's knowledge can also be useful in obtaining feedback from them regarding their customers' needs. They should be able to provide ideas and suggestions to people in product development, research, advertising, and so forth. When encouraged to do this, they will feel that they can influence what the company is doing and where it may go in the future. This kind of participation in continuous sales training meetings can help boost morale. In the process the salesman's information and skills are updated, and many misunderstandings can be cleared up.

Individual training. The above methods are commonly used in determining the content of group sales training meetings; however, many organizations prefer an individual approach to continuous sales training. Typically, they use periodic performance appraisals to question the salesmen about their personal ambitions and the problems they may have run into. Since training needs vary with the individual, the feedback during a regular performance-appraisal interview can be very timely. The manager can often identify a weakness in performance which the salesman is willing to correct through some specialized training.

Salesmen often have blind spots regarding a particular weakness or will not admit to inferior or ineffective behavior patterns. The sales manager would be wise to exercise some caution in accepting the salesmen's statements about their training needs at face value. Some salesmen will agree to undergo one kind of continuous training simply to divert the manager's attention from their real needs. Thus, although obtaining feedback from the individual salesmen can be an essential way to determine their training needs, other methods should be used in conjunction with it.

The value of determining the individual salesman's training needs lies in the opportunity to establish realistic goals with which he will sincerely agree. When the salesman and the manager are in agreement, the manager can suggest various company-sponsored programs or industry or association seminars. Many courses offered by universities and other public institutions may also be suitable for a particular salesman. In addition, many self-education resources are available to the individual, including programmed-instruction texts, correspondence courses, and audio and video cassettes on a number of special subjects directly related to selling. Clearly, the strength of the individual salesman's commitment to training can have a strong influence on how much improvement will take place. The more he participates in setting his own training goals, the more likely he is to follow the guidance of his sales manager.

Choosing the appropriate alternative. Various external constraints are naturally imposed on any training need of salesmen. The amount of money available is always restricted, as is the amount of time which can be devoted to training. In addition, the amount of travel required by the job may influence the feasibility of any form of training. And the location of a salesman's territory may restrict the training available to him. The value of the various alternatives should be determined before a particular course or program is selected.

An effective sales manager will have personal knowledge of many of these alternatives and will know where to get more information. A few phone calls to other sales managers, to training directors, and to associations will often uncover a wealth of possibilities for training in most areas of the country. Any salesman who seriously wants additional training is well worth the extra effort the sales manager may have to make to guide him properly.

SUMMARY

Every sales organization needs a continuous training program to keep abreast of the many changes taking place every day in the market. Continuous training is designed to update information and to upgrade skills in order to improve the salesmen's performance on their current job.

Retraining programs are indicated when salesmen are asked to perform duties for which they have little or no background or training. Retraining is often required when an organization changes its product line or its target market. It may be required when the market itself demands a more sophisticated approach to selling. Retraining is essential to change salesmen's skills and to teach them entirely new skills.

Developing different skills or adding new skills moves the salesman into unknown areas. Frequently this involves a completely new orientation to the selling situation. Salesmen may need to acquire a knowledge of cost accounting or production engineering, for example, which was not necessary when the salesmen were hired. The techniques and skills required to sell to a very large key account are often different from those used in selling to many small accounts, and target-account sales strategy is thus another area that may necessitate training.

Perfecting what has already been taught—the first goal of continuous training—frequently involves raising performance standards. Education and training are provided to show salesmen how to achieve the higher standard as well as to give them the opportunity to practice the new behavior. Performance is measured objectively, and the salesmen's progress is used as positive feedback to encourage the practice and to reinforce the learning.

Continuous sales training traditionally has been a boring rehash of prospecting, features and benefits, demonstration, and the like. But it can be an exciting and challenging updating of knowledge and skills. Modern sales training draws heavily on people within the company who are specialists in production, product development, advertising, sales promotion, and research. There are many such groups in most organizations, and each one can provide training input which will help the salesman immediately, as well as broaden him as a person for life. Most of these groups recycle their own goals and programs at least annually and can be scheduled on a regular basis to update the salesmen's skills and knowledge.

Experienced salesmen frequently present unique training problems. If they need refresher training to reinforce the fundamentals of selling, they can often be used as trainers. When their role is reversed and they are given the responsibility of teaching, they will often learn more than the audience they address. Certain guidance and controls may be necessary; however, many managers have used this method successfully.

Experienced salesmen who are outstanding producers may need a different kind of training; one proven technique is the seminar for the top 20 or 25 percent of the sales force. The salesmen teach each other as they respond to real company challenges presented by a discussion leader. Each star salesman will try to make a positive contribution to be accepted by his peers. To be invited to the elite seminar becomes an honor sought by other salesmen, and a regular series of such meetings can be scheduled.

Many organizations approach continuous training and retraining programs on the basis of the needs of the entire sales force or several major groups of salesmen. Other concerns approach on-going training according to the individual's unique needs and his personal motivation. There is no conflict of methods; hence, the best of both can be used.

Continuous training occurs either by design or by default in every sales organization. It would seem wise for anyone responsible for sales training to take the time and effort essential to predetermine goals and constructive programs to achieve the best possible results.

SELECTED MATERIALS

Ackerman, Leonard, "Training Programs: Goals, Means, and Evaluation," *Personnel Journal*, Vol. 47, No. 10 (October 1968), pp. 725–28.

Bedrosian, Hrach, "Selecting Supervisors for Training—What Motivates the Boss," *Personnel,* Vol. 48, No. 1 (January–February 1971), pp. 44–47.

Byham, William C., "Assessment Centers for Spotting Future Managers," *Harvard Business Review,* Vol. 48, No. 4 (July–August 1970), pp. 150–65.

Dun & Bradstreet Business Courses. New York: Dun & Bradstreet, Business Education Division.

> *This free 17-page booklet describes eleven correspondence courses from "The Language of Business" through advanced accounting. Very good self-improvement programs for the salesman on the road who is motivated to learn more, the courses generally extend over a six-month period.*

Eby, Frank H., *Sales Analysis: Concepts and Applications.* New York: AMR International, 1971.

> *This work describes steps to establish a sales analysis system and discusses constructing and implementing sales performance measures by product, by territory, and by customer. 8½ x 11″ format (mimeo).*

Gannon, Martin J., and Noon, John P., "Management's Critical Deficiency," *Business Horizons,* Vol. 14, No. 1 (February 1971), pp. 49–56.

Hinrichs, J. R., "Two Approaches to Filling the Management Gap: Management Selection vs. Management Development," *Personnel Journal,* Vol. 49, No. 12 (December 1970), pp. 1015–20.

Jarrell, Donald, and Frigiola, Joseph, "The Role of Training in Supervising Development," *Management of Personnel Quarterly,* Vol. 9, No. 2 (Summer 1970), pp. 11–19.

Silber, Mark B., "Synergy . . . Behavioral Sciences, Organizational Effectiveness and the Training Professional," *Personnel Journal,* Vol. 50, No. 2 (February 1971), pp. 151–55.

Weatherbee, Harvard Y., "The Older Employee—A Neglected Manpower Resource," *Personnel,* Vol. 46, No. 1 (January–February 1969), pp. 31–36.

CHAPTER 11

Career Development
of Experienced Salesmen

BEYOND THE PRESSING NEEDS of day-by-day continuous training, modern sales managers are concerned with the long-term career development of their experienced salesmen. The cost of hiring and training new salesmen is high, but the cost of losing an experienced and productive salesman is exorbitant. Without career development, a sales organization increases the risk that salesmen will either reach a plateau or leave for greener pastures.

Certain career turning points, which are very often under the control of management, directly influence turnover. The first stressful career turning point for a new salesman comes after the first year he works on a quota and puts his training and personal drive to the test in the real world. Equally important is the year in which territory transfers are made. After training and surviving the first territory assignment on quota, the young salesman feels he is ready for a more challenging territory with its higher rewards. This territory transfer then becomes a critical turning point in his career. If he is disappointed, he is apt to quit.

Very often salesmen are brought into a company in groups. While they may be hired one at a time over a period of six months, for example, they are usually grouped for a common training period. Over the years, these salesmen keep in close touch with one another. When the first one or two salesmen receive a promotion, another critical turning point occurs for the rest of their peer group. If the man promoted was generally considered to be inferior by the others, they may easily feel that management is unfair or stupid. Such action can trigger turnover.

The fourth career turning point occurs, and reoccurs, whenever the salesman is asked to move his family to fill a company need in another location. If he accepts the new assignment, he may cause undue stress on his wife, his children, and other relatives. If he refuses the new assignment, he may fear he has ruined his chances for future promotion. This kind of stress often cannot be tolerated, and the salesman leaves the company.

Another career turning point, perhaps less obvious but equally important, occurs when the salesman reaches or exceeds his targeted income goal. This figure is different for every salesman and also depends on the stage of life the man's family has attained. For example, a salesman in his early forties with two grown daughters may realize a substantial increase in his disposable income when they both marry. He may have a relatively stable income, yet suddenly, because of his lifetime habit of living at a certain level, he has more money in his pocket. At this point he will either set new, higher goals than he had in previous years, or he may mentally retire on the job without the courtesy of telling the sales manager. The salesman feels more comfortable on the existing job and the manager may not be aware of this subtle change in the salesman's attitude.

One other critical turning point in a salesman's career is worth noting: the day the man perceives he has gone as far as he can go in his job or with his company. His perception of the promotion situation may or may not be accurate, but it can have a tremendous impact on his attitude and performance. He may give up trying; he may readily accept his fate and become more relaxed; or he may leave the company.

THE SALESMAN'S LEVEL OF ASPIRATION

A salesman's self-image strongly influences what he does throughout his entire life regardless of the training or the opportunities he may be offered. It is impractical to consider changing a salesman's behavior without also contemplating his self-image. For example, if the salesman believes he cannot handle large accounts, he will prove that he can't whenever the occasion arises. If he is convinced he is just an average salesman, he will not recognize or not take advantage of opportunities that would prove him to be otherwise. It he thinks he has poor health, he soon will have. Conversely, if he has a positive self-image, he will try to make something of himself, to live more fully, and to be happy.

Many salesmen are not conscious of their self-image and could not describe it if they were asked. Others, who may speak with firm assurance, often are unconsciously indulging in self-deception or whistling in the dark. A sales manager need not call in a psychiatrist to find out what makes each salesman tick, but he should not avoid the issue.

One simple key to understanding the salesman's self-image is to find out what he wants for himself in life—in other words, what he currently aspires to become in the future. After being given time for serious thought, most salesmen are willing and able to discuss what they want out of life, and out of their job, in the next four or five years. A serious discussion can provide many good clues about the individual and how he sees himself. The manager can guide the discussion away from unrealistic goals, such as the wish to be a millionaire, toward the reality of what the salesman wants to do or be in the near future.

One frame of reference which the sales manager can use to evaluate a salesman's level of aspiration is Chris Argyris' theory of maturity.[1] Argyris notes some of the changes which should take place in the personality of an individual as he develops and matures over the years. An immature salesman is passive and relatively dependent on his supervisor and sales manager. As he learns and becomes more experienced, his activity and independence increase. He becomes more of a self-starter, and he does not need the manager's constant direction. An immature salesman will have only a few behavior patterns or ways of dealing with people and problems. A mature salesman is flexible and can adapt so he is capable of behaving in many ways. The immature salesman will have erratic and shallow interests, jumping from one hobby to another and never really committing himself to

[1] *Interpersonal Competence and Organizational Effectiveness* (Homewood, Ill.: Dorsey Press, 1962). See also Chris Argyris, *Integrating the Individual and the Organization* (New York: John Wiley & Sons, 1964).

any. The mature salesman has deeper and stronger interests in life and will stick to a serious cause in which he believes. The immature salesman has little perspective with respect to time and is normally impatient. The mature salesman's greater perspective of both the past and the future gives him wisdom. The immature salesman has little awareness of himself and often acts impulsively, while the mature salesman is more aware of himself and has greater control over his behavior.

Another frame of reference which the sales manager may find useful in evaluating a salesman's level of aspiration is Abraham H. Maslow's concept of a hierarchy of needs.[2] According to this theory, salesmen may strive to satisfy five levels of needs. Each level must be more or less satisfied before the salesman will turn his attention to the next higher level.

The primary level covers the salesman's basic needs such as food, shelter, and clothing. He needs income regularly to satisfy these needs. The next level is that of safety or security needs. The salesman wants to know he will be able to afford food, shelter, and clothing next month and next year. He wants job security or a feeling that his skills are easily transferable to another job. The third level involves the salesman's social needs to affiliate with other people and to be accepted by them.

Most salesmen have more or less satisfied their needs on these three levels, and many are content there. Either they do not aspire to achieve a higher quality of life or they are not willing to pay the price of seeking more out of life. They will be average producers, at best.

The fourth level in Maslow's theory involves the salesman's need for esteem, both self-esteem and recognition from others. Self-esteem is essential to self-confidence and maturity, which lead to prestige and increase the salesman's desire to exercise power and control over others rather than be directed by them. The salesman at this level feels that he is useful and that he has some effect on his environment. He has the inner motivation to learn new knowledge and skills as well as the drive or determination to influence the progress of his career.

The highest level concerns self-actualization and the need to realize one's potential. This need makes a man practice many hours

[2] *Motivation and Personality* (New York: Harper & Brothers, 1954). See also Abraham H. Maslow, *Eupsychian Management* (Homewood, Ill.: Dorsey Press, 1965).

each day to become a concert pianist, a brain surgeon, a professional athlete, a financier, a captain of industry, or whatever he feels he must be. The man at this level feels he has some control over physical and social factors. He does not wait for things to happen but manipulates his environment to make them happen. He has a compulsion to accomplish a task. He is competent in his field, and he knows it; but the material rewards are of value to him primarily as a measure of his progress as compared with that of other people. He needs concrete feedback about his good work and success. His high degree of independence usually must be checked by an understanding of the need for teamwork in business, although he may already have acquired this understanding.

These theories indicate some of the ways the sales manager can evaluate the individual salesman's self-image and current aspirations. They may be used to determine whether a salesman is ready to accept training and can also give the manager some insight into a salesman's weaknesses. Accordingly, the manager can provide experiences and opportunities to help the salesman develop into a more mature person.

Salesmen do not present a consistent picture of themselves because of the extreme highs and lows in the selling job itself. However, the pattern and range of behavior they show over a period of time will indicate the degree of their maturity. For this reason, experienced sales managers wait until they have observed a salesman's performance and behavior for a number of months before they attempt to evaluate or influence his level of aspiration.

No salesman is necessarily frozen at one stage of development unless he chooses to stay there. Every salesman is capable of growth, and the manager has a responsibility to help the salesman establish realistic personal goals and to encourage him to strive to reach them.

With proper guidance and encouragement, many salesmen can change their way of thinking, their goals in life, and their behavior. In effect, they can change their lives and achieve new heights and long-lasting satisfactions. A salesman may need help in understanding where he is in life and where he can go if he has the courage to try. The manager is in a position to evaluate the salesman's maturity and personal aspirations in life objectively and to assist him. The mature sales manager will not be content to wait for a salesman to take his time to learn, to grow, to get experience. He will manipulate the environment and cause these things to happen.

THE MANAGER'S LEVEL OF EXPECTATION

An often overlooked factor in salesmen's training and development is the vitally important attitude of the manager regarding what he expects from the salesmen. The manager's view of his salesmen will trigger their responses so that the results are as he expected. If, for example, the manager expects that salesmen will not be able to cope with cost accounting, they will have tremendous difficulty trying to learn it and will not be able to use it properly. This psychological phenomenon is true whether or not the manager is conscious of his expectations. People will meet the level of performance expected of them.

In business, traditional sales managers expect the worst from trainees and they get it. Modern sales managers demand a high level of performance, and the young, energetic sales trainees respect that demand and rise to meet it. The sales manager has the option to expect mediocrity or superiority. His attitude is generally quite easily communicated, and it greatly influences the trainees' performance.

Experienced salesmen respond to their manager's attitude in a similar manner. A mature salesman will learn how to use a new sales tool such as the computer if he knows the manager has confidence in him, is willing to train him, and fully expects him to learn. If the senior salesman is not given the training and support he needs, however, he is probably correct in assuming that the manager does not really expect him to learn. Salesmen young and old will meet their manager's level of expectation, and they will do so without reward or punishment.

Unfortunately, the salesman's assumption of the level of performance expected by the manager may not agree with the true level of expectation. For this reason alone, it is essential that the manager define goals, describe jobs, and state manpower specifications very clearly. He must also establish a climate for growth which permits mistakes in the learning process. Given an understanding of the need to learn and a climate in which to become a better salesman, the senior man will be motivated to rise to meet the true expectations of the sales manager. Conversely, if the sales manager assumes that men in their forties or fifties cannot learn new technological methods, they will not learn them.

It is much easier for a mature salesman to emotionally accept objectively written job descriptions and manpower specifications than a seemingly subjective opinion of a sales manager. The salesman in his forties or fifties is under great emotional strain: His body is undergoing chemical changes, his family is maturing, and he may also have financial demands that seem overpowering. Rumors of job changes may be viewed as a threat. Therefore, the more objective and clearly communicated the new expected levels of job performance are, the more apt the senior salesman is to accept the changes and improve himself.

If a job description must be changed to meet new conditions, with the manpower specifications upgraded accordingly, then a realistic timetable should be established for the incumbent salesman to acquire the new knowledge and skills. If a complete reversal in behavior is expected overnight, both the young trainee and the experienced salesman will be overwhelmed. When a partial change is expected, the salesman should be permitted to operate without supervision in those areas which remain constant. But in the areas where change is expected, he should have instruction and close supervision for each phase of the learning process. As the salesman achieves the desired level of performance on the new task, the manager then permits him to operate on his own in that area, with only general supervision. As each phase of the change is completed, the salesman's job is broadened more and more until he can again operate with only general supervision.

It cannot be mentioned too often that older salesmen can learn new techniques and new behavior patterns. Because of their years of experience, wealth of knowledge, and long friendships with many buyers, they can often outproduce the younger salesmen. In many cases, older salesmen get along with older clients much better than younger salesmen do because the older men have a common outlook on life and on business problems.

The traditional sales manager is apt to give up attempting to change the behavior of salesmen who are over 40 years old. The modern sales manager knows that these experienced salesmen can learn when they are properly motivated and given sufficient time, training, and encouragement. When they know he expects them to perform at a new, higher level, they will very likely do so. Thus, the sales manager's positive thinking is critical in the career development of experienced salesmen.

THE ESCALATING ZERO POINT

Most of the needs of salesmen are cyclical; that is, they recur on a regular basis. A man eats, and he soon gets hungry again. He sleeps, and he soon must sleep again. A salesman is praised, and he soon must be praised again. He makes his quota, and he soon must make it again. He feels he needs people; he seeks them out; his need is satisfied; and he needs to be alone. After a while, he again feels he needs people, and the cycle begins anew. Each of these behavior patterns returns periodically to the starting, or zero, point.

The special demands of a business career, particularly a sales career, are different in one very important way: The zero point is not constant. It moves higher and higher each time the cycle is complete, making a spiral pattern. For example, consider a salesman who makes a quota of $250,000 in annual sales. The next year his quota is likely to be raised to $275,000, so that he must work harder or more effectively to reach his goal. Each year the target is raised, so that when he completes his annual cycle, his base point is higher.

Another instance of the escalating zero point occurs when a successful salesman develops a weak territory into a relatively good one. The sales manager divides the territory and puts in a second salesman. Now the first salesman is expected to match or top his sales for the previous year in an area that is only half as large. This is recommended practice for sales managers because it increases the efficiency of the sales effort; however, the manager would be wise to reward the first man in some way for his outstanding efforts. Iny any case, the new zero point is higher and the goal more demanding than previously.

In a similar manner, a salesman making $20,000 a year may earn a $2,000 bonus one year. If he receives a $2,000 bonus the next year, he will feel cheated. He is standing still. His total income is the same. He wants his bonus or his total income to be bigger than it was the previous year. He expects from management something more than he expected last year. Consequently, the standard annual raise—

$1,000 for example—becomes the minimum acceptable to the salesman. Anything less than that amount is considered as punishment or possibly as a warning. The salesman is dissatisfied and may very well develop a negative attitude toward the sales manager and the company.

Salesmen working on a straight-commission basis will often raise their own sales goals and compensation targets each year. This year has to be better than last year, and next year must be better than this year. If the manager does not raise the zero point, the salesman will raise it himself. When his earnings drop off or reach a plateau, he will either divert his excess energy into other, more satisfying activities or he will seek another job. In either situation, he will try to get more satisfaction this year than last, and still more next year.

Clearly, the sales manager who hides his head in the sand of company policy and refuses to recognize the escalating zero point is inviting trouble. Most salesmen will accept an occasional year of little or no increase in pay when their own performance has been off target. However, they expect more and more over a period of years, particularly when many things beyond their control—for example, product improvements, company advertising, pricing, territory assignments, and sales training—can influence their sales record. When salesmen work harder, they expect more compensation, regardless of overall sales results.

Other fringe benefits have a similar escalating zero point. Company-paid insurance, free annual physical examinations, an expense account, a company automobile, and similar benefits are quickly taken for granted. Whatever the company provided last year is expected this year as a minimum: The experienced salesman wants three weeks of vacation this year instead of the usual two weeks. The salesman who has had a number of successful years wants to drive a more expensive car than the kind given to new salesmen. The senior salesman handling large accounts expects more latitude for entertaining his clients than he had last year.

Sales managers can build a program of total compensation which acknowledges the escalating zero point. It can provide for a series of salary steps and a similar series of increasing fringe benefits as sales targets or years of experience, or a combination of the two, are reached. The competitive labor situation in an industry normally determines the starting salary and fringe benefits for a particular job. From there on, the manager can plan a compensation program that takes the escalating zero point into account and, of course, raises the level of desired performance.

Sales managers often do not completely control their salesmen's compensation, and while they may be in agreement with the salesmen's desires, they feel it is beyond their power to establish an effective compensation plan. Since the sales manager is held responsible for the contribution to profit of his sales force, he can argue for the support he requests by explaining to higher management how it will maximize that contribution. If he meekly accepts the constraints imposed on him by higher management, the best he can hope for is good short-term success and rapid promotion out of the job. As often happens when a manager uses a short-term strategy, the man who follows him will inherit serious long-term problems. On the other hand, the sales manager who understands the problem of the escalating zero point and is willing to stand up and fight for what he believes will have a greater and more positive long-term impact on the career development of his experienced salesmen as well as on their total contribution to profit.

The third alternative course of action available to the sales manager is to ignore the problem and do nothing. Such a decision will breed dissatisfaction, low morale, and cynicism among the salesmen. When experienced salesmen reach a plateau and are not motivated to try harder, they commonly reflect the sales manager's attitude. The salesmen are not at fault, and the most ingenious training may not move them one iota. If the manager cannot, or will not, take the naturally escalating zero point into consideration, then the experienced salesmen should not be expected to perform better year after year.

Contrary to the claims of some authorities today, money is the primary factor in early turnover in a sales force. Low compensation causes salesmen to leave a company, and high compensation is the single most powerful magnet that a company can use to attract salesmen from other companies. In its recent study, the Conference Board reported that companies paying starting rates in the top 25 percent of the 230 firms responding retained 89 percent of their new hirees for one year, 83 percent for two years, and 71 percent for three years. In contrast, the 99 firms reporting annual pay averaging less than $7,500 showed only 80 percent retention beyond the first year,

65 percent after two years, and 50 percent by the end of the third year.[3]

Money is very important to the new salesman, and it is relatively important to the experienced salesman. For the career salesman, money in and of itself may be the primary reason for trying hard to succeed and putting up with management directives which he feels are stupid or arbitrary. He may have to send his children to college, support an elderly parent, or meet many other financial demands. Thus, he may need the high monetary reward offered by the selling profession, even though it requires giving lip service to many concepts he may find personally distasteful.

As noted earlier, the mature salesman may seek money for the symbolic, but objective, evidence it provides of his worth as an individual. For example, if a mature salesman earning $75,000 a year already has all the material things he wants in life, he will work harder for another $10,000 only if the extra compensation gives him the recognition of superiority which his ego demands. To a salesman operating on Maslow's highest level, that of self-actualization needs, the amount of compensation he receives for his work is the objective acknowledgement of his progress. He needs this feedback regularly, and it also has an escalating zero point.

MOVEMENT VERSUS MOTIVATION

"Movement" and "motivation" are often used to express the same concept with respect to salesmen, that of activation or inducement to achieve. Fred Herzberg has made a significant contribution to management thinking by making the distinction that motivation comes from feelings within the salesmen, whereas movement is caused by an external stimulus such as a contest or the promise of a raise in salary.[4] This emphasis is pertinent when the sales manager is considering the long-term career development of his salesmen.

[3] *Salesmen's Turnover in Early Employment,* Report No. 545 (New York: Conference Board, 1972).
[4] *Work and the Nature of Man.* Cleveland: World Publishing Company (1966). See also Fred Herzberg, "The New Kid in the Company," *Innovation Magazine* (December 1969).

Movement

There are many sound economic reasons to justify getting salesmen to make more calls and to sell more merchandise and service. Sales managers are frequently besieged with ideas from sales promotion for moving merchandise, offsetting seasonal lows, getting salesmen to push a new product with some extra effort, or achieving some other short-term goal. A new product or model may be a lemon, or the public doesn't seem to want it, and it is jamming up the warehouse. Somehow the company's investment in the poor product must be converted back to usable cash. The very survival of the business may depend on selling this product. Many organizations are very experienced in promotional activities and can document their success.

There are also sound psychological reasons to get salesmen to put forth an extra effort. For example, early in a salesman's career, extra calls that increase his exposure to clients may accelerate his learning.

Sales contests. Experienced sales managers in some of the most successful and respected sales organizations in the world will readily testify that sales contests are effective: Salesmen really try harder, and goals are reached which would not otherwise have been attained. For example, the chance of winning a trip to Europe may move an older salesman to try harder or work longer hours than he would without the extra incentive. European travel may broaden the salesman and make him a more interesting person. Specialists in the field of sales promotion suggest that every salesman be rewarded for his extra effort in a contest, and that the top prizes be large enough to induce even the best producers to try harder than they already are trying. In other words, a well-designed contest offers every salesman a tangible reward for producing any amount above what he would normally produce in the same period.

The problems of establishing fair quotas or handicapping the salesmen, selecting a range of prizes to interest every salesman, and preventing salesmen from holding back orders before the contest and anticipating future orders before the contest ends—as well as controlling the internal competition—all make careful planning necessary. The sales manager need not worry about whether he is using a contest to motivate his salesmen or to get movement. With all the problems and criticisms of sales contests, the best salesmen usually win, and total sales and contribution to profit usually are greater than without the contest.

Motivation

Money, prizes, and fringe benefits are not all that is necessary to get salesmen to do what management wants, however. The sales job must also provide the individual with an opportunity to grow, to become a better person, to contribute to the welfare of others, to belong to an admired group of people, to make measurable achievements, and to earn recognition for his accomplishments. In other words, in order to utilize the human potential more effectively, the sales manager should design the sales job so as to cause his men to grow and develop rather than stagnate and wither. A salesman will be motivated from within when his work is interesting.

The modern sales manager is concerned not simply with maintaining morale by means of attractive salaries and fringe benefits but, more fundamentally, with creating a job environment that satisfies the higher-level needs of the salesman. The most important requisite seems to be to convince the salesman that his talents and skills are being more fully developed and used. He may need to be given increasing authority to operate on his own, to act as a manager in his own right, as he demonstrates his maturity. Clearly, the manager will have to take some risks, but this seems essential if the salesman is to grow.

Two independent forces can operate simultaneously within the salesman to work toward both his own long-term goal of achieving personal satisfaction and the sales manager's goal of long-term contribution to profit. The first force is his need to become mature and independent. The sales manager can encourage this drive through counseling, training, and career guidance. The second is his need to be recognized and accepted by his peers and superiors as a valuable member of the group. The sales manager can encourage this drive by creating peer groups or teams which are judged by their collective efforts and by creating groups of advisers which can influence higher management or participate in making managerial decisions.

As mentioned in Chapter 10, a team of experienced salesmen can be given the assignment of training several new trainees. They are then judged collectively by how soon and how well they develop the neophytes into independent, self-sustaining salesmen. They can also be assigned the responsibility of running a series of sales meetings or a contest or performing any number of management functions.

The manager should provide his men with opportunities to satisfy many of their needs besides the fundamental need for money. When he knows the individual salesmen well enough, he will have many clues as to what each person wants at the stage he has reached in his career. Job enlargement with a number of new duties might be ideal for one salesman. Job enrichment with more freedom to do his existing duties as he sees fit might be ideal for another salesman. Career development must be an on-going, dynamic process because the individual's needs change as he matures.

The sales manager should make territory assignments which will give the individual salesman a realistic chance to make his quota, to achieve, and to earn recognition for his accomplishments. (Recognition may be having his name appear high up on the sales chart or in a company newsletter, or it may be a bonus or raise.) In a similar manner, the manager can assign selected difficult accounts to a salesman because he has shown aptitude in handling that kind of problem or account. In other words, the manager should use his authority to provide opportunities for each salesman to develop throughout his career instead of ignoring this chance and assigning territories and accounts randomly or on the basis of seniority.

Making short-run gains in sales productivity by means of contests and similar sales promotional activities need not conflict with maximizing the salesmen's long-term contribution to profit by motivating them to grow and develop through career planning. Too often, sales managers are encouraged to do either one or the other. It is a fact of business life that reaching short-term goals is essential to the survival of a sales manager. But it is also a fact that the better managers, over many years, develop their salesmen. Sales managers can and should be concerned with both the short-term movement and the long-term motivation of their salesmen.

CAREER PATHS FOR SALESMEN

Some sales managers think of a salesman's career as having three distinct steps: junior salesman, salesman, and senior salesman. Others think of a selling career as having many steps, for example, sales trainee, junior salesman, territory representative, senior salesman, industry salesman, and national-account representative. Many managers create a series of titles through which the salesman may pass in his career while still doing the same basic job. These artificial titles, milestones of age or of years of experience, mean very little to the salesman who is thinking about his career.

To be meaningful, the steps in a career path should involve real changes in responsibilities. Each step would normally have a unique job description clearly differentiating its duties and responsibilities from those of the step below and the next step above it. The manpower specification then would describe the kind of person who could best perform those duties and would include the minimum amount of formal education necessary and the amount preferred (for example, at least two years of college, but graduation from college preferred) and the minimum number of years experience and the preferred level. More important, perhaps, would be the specific training required and preferred. A territory salesman, for example, might need a general business background, but before he could be considered for promotion to a specialty, such as selling to banks only, he would need special knowledge. A formal college course in banking might give him the desired level of specialized knowledge.

Given a series of distinct steps with the duties, responsibilities, and requirements clearly spelled out, the salesman can see what he must do to prepare himself for promotion. He can decide whether or not a goal is realistic for him and whether or not he is willing to spend the necessary time and effort to prepare for it. The importance of careful career guidance by the sales manager cannot be overstressed. It seems foolish to sit back and watch a man prepare for a job in which he will probably fail or be very unhappy. Perhaps more tragic is the emotional impact on the salesman who is demoted or terminated because he was unable to make the grade in the wrong job. The discouragement and loss of pride may stay with the unsuccessful man throughout his life.

Career Paths in Large Sales Organizations

Large sales organizations have many highly responsible and highly paid positions within the sales function. Depending on his background, interests, and ambitions, a salesman could plan to prepare for any one or a combination of the positions. For example, in a national sales organization with many lines of both consumer and technical, industrial products, the job descriptions are all within the direct control of the vice-president of sales:

- Salesman
- Specialty salesman
- Sales engineer
- Specialty sales engineer
- Product specialist
- National-account salesman
- Sales trainer
- Industrial specialist
- Sales analyst
- Sales planner
- Market development specialist
- Distribution development specialist
- Merchandising and promotion specialist
- Sales practices and procedures specialist
- Sales administration and measurement specialist
- Proposals and quotations specialist
- Contract negotiations and sales specialist

These positions are filled by a progression of men from the sales force. Moreover, there can be a group of men in each of the jobs described, headed by a supervisor and a manager.

A large sales organization with a small line of products has the following job descriptions as part of their planned career path:

- Trainee (15 weeks)
- Junior salesman (salary guaranteed for one year)
- Sales representative (commission only)
- Senior sales representative (commission plus override)
- Specialty sales representative (by product)
- Industry sales representative (by customer)
- Government sales representative
- Sales supervisor
- District sales manager
- Regional sales supervisor

- Regional sales managers
  Planning and analysis
  Promotion
- Division sales vice-presidents
  Central training
  Sales forecasting
  Market development
- Merchandising and promotion
- Product development
- Manpower development

Once again, the organization has many jobs at each level. At the division or national level, the staff functions are centralized and controlled, permitting the line managers to concentrate primarily on direct sales. Every manager in this company started as a sales trainee in one of its 300 branches or local sales districts.

From management's point of view, career-path planning is also planning for management development. It ensures that trained people will be available to fill vacancies as they occur and helps to forecast areas where training will be necessary. It also ensures that everyone has a chance to be considered for more responsible jobs and that nobody will get lost in the shuffle. Long-range manpower planning— over a period of thirty years, for example—must always be tentative. The key tools in the scheduling of training, promotions, and transfers are executive inventories and replacement charts of the company organization, showing the years of experience and skill limitations of employees, imminent retirements, promotions due, and so forth.

Career-path planning should provide opportunities for salesmen to obtain both formal, off-the-job training and on-the-job experience before they have the full weight of a new responsibility thrust upon them. For some positions, the salesmen may go through a systematic job rotation, spending several months or years in various parts of a higher job. In other cases it may be more advantageous to have the salesman understudy the incumbent directly for three to six months. In either case, sales management attempts to forecast its needs, select salesmen who have the appropriate capabilities, interests, and desires, and prepare them with training and experience before they are needed. While a perfect record of successful promotions would be impossible, this orderly process has a much better chance of succeeding than the typical sink-or-swim method.

Career Paths in Small Sales Organizations

Career-path planning need not be limited to large sales organizations. A retail automobile dealer with ten salesmen, for example, can prepare a number of job descriptions showing different levels of responsibility and compensation for the young salesman who is looking at his career possibilities. After the initial training stage, the first responsibility might be to sell only new cars. The second stage might be selling new cars and new trucks. A sales trainer and a sales manager could be added to any of these stages. The position of general sales manager might be followed by a limited partnership with responsibilities for sales and service. The possibilities of planning a career path for salesmen are limited only by the creative and analytical skills of the planner. The guiding rule is to have each step distinctly different from every other step in real responsibilities and training or preparation. This provides both an opportunity and a challenge for the experienced salesman to grow and develop throughout his career.

Many a self-made man who owns his business today has come up through the ranks by his own determination and by capitalizing on opportunities. He usually knows the intimate details of most phases of his business because he has learned them from personal experience. He has cut his career path almost alone, without help and guidance from superiors. Today, many salesmen are not aware of their career possibilities; hence, they cannot show their determination. Others have a strong feeling of what they would like to become someday, but they do not know how to prepare themselves for it. Clearly, human resources are wasted if career-path planning is neglected or paths are simply permitted to evolve as pure chance may dictate. Intelligent and empathetic planning by sales managers seems to be essential in planning a career path for salesmen.

BRANCHING CAREER PATHS

Most young adults begin a career with doubts about the job and about themselves. Some enter a profession full of self-confidence and unrealistic enthusiasm. Under these conditions, high turnover is to be expected: While rates vary with different companies, after five years, the sales organization will be fortunate if it retains 50 percent of its new hirees.

The young people who remain with a sales organization beyond the fifth year represent a sizable investment to the company. Many of these salesmen will be reasonably good producers but not necessarily outstanding. Some will show the leadership characteristics which indicate management potential. Others may show interest in areas totally unrelated to sales. Some mature salesmen may be working for an autocratic sales manager and may become frustrated and hostile. For personal reasons, some experienced salesmen may begin to look for career possibilities outside of sales. People low in the sales-management hierarchy may not like their current assignment but may not be willing to take a step backward in their career. For many reasons, experienced salesmen who have had years of better-than-average production may become dissatisfied with their jobs.

Some sales organizations have a policy of periodic promotion or termination. The manager either recommends the salesman for more responsible work or must fire him. Many organizations have an optional retirement point, at age 62, for example, and a compulsory retirement point, usually at age 65. Under such rigid conditions, an experienced salesman with a good record may be forced out of the company if he doesn't want a selling career or if he reaches an arbitrary age limit. Such policies are designed to provide good salesmen with continual opportunities for promotion and to attract other good salesmen or new trainees. Survival of the fittest seems to guarantee a strong sales organization.

More enlightened personnel policies provide branching opportunities which enable a company to keep the good men in whom it has invested so much time, energy, and money. Under the system of branching career paths, good salesmen are shown various ways to achieve satisfaction within the same company. They may be permitted to branch off the line sales organization into a staff function or into another line function. At each new level, they are again offered several alternatives.

Many people in personnel work, up to and including corporate vice-presidents, started their careers in sales. A frequent career path of salesmen passes through the positions of sales trainer, management trainer, management and sales recruiter, and manpower planner to vice-president of personnel. Within the personnel function, there are many opportunities for specialization. Industrial labor relations might interest some people. Motivation and compensation might appeal to others. These illustrations are given simply to indicate the possibilities for branching career paths that some companies offer good salesmen who want to leave their sales organization.

Branching into another line function is perhaps more common. For example, a good salesman who showed strong product knowledge might, if he wished, be transferred into product research and development. From there he might move either toward the research aspect of that function or toward the pilot-production and mass-production aspect. Product research might lead him either to scientific (laboratory) work or to consumer or field research.

Beyond sales but still within the marketing function, one company offers selected men the following branching opportunities in market research: economic studies and analysis, market studies and analysis, sales analysis and forecasting, consumer research, product research, dealer and distributor research, pricing studies, and advertising research. It also offers the following branching opportunities in advertising and sales promotion: advertising, sales promotion, publicity, exhibits, visual media, direct mail, catalogs, house organs, media selection, and media effectiveness.

In a similar way, this large marketing organization offers career branching opportunities in product planning and product application engineering as alternate major groupings.

Organizations handling consumer products, such as packaged food and soap, often draw their assistant brand managers from the sales force. The salesman who has proved he can fight for shelf space in the supermarket and get more displays than his competitors may be offered an inside job to understudy a brand manager for a year or more. Working closely with the manager, the former salesman learns about advertising, sales promotion, pricing, packaging, and public relations as they apply to just one brand or a few brands of products. If he does well, he can be promoted to brand manager, or he can again branch into one of the specialty areas.

Branching career paths are not intended as a way to enable management to hand out promotions indiscriminately or to pamper salesmen who cannot make the grade. They are designed to keep a good man who shows further promise from leaving the company. Often branching out requires several years of formal education, and companies are frequently willing to pay full or partial tuition refunds for courses completed satisfactorily. Each new specialization may require several years of on-the-job training or understudy assignments. Conversely, a new position may require a man to be a generalist with a balanced knowledge of several different specialties; hence, a three- to five-year rotation of assignments may be necessary.

As career paths in sales require careful help and guidance by the line sales manager, branching career paths for salesmen require guidance by someone with knowledge of the opportunities and requirements for many other jobs in the company. If the branching remains within marketing, a manager higher than the sales manager may be willing and able to help. If the branching leads out of marketing altogether, then personnel should be the source of information and guidance. Modifying a career is serious business, and the best advice available should be sought.

SUMMARY

While the many facets of career planning for experienced salesmen cannot be covered in one brief chapter, the importance of this subject cannot be overstated. Career development is an essential part of sales training. If top sales management ignores career planning, it is wasting human and economic resources and inviting the troubles which stem from dissatisfaction and increasing turnover among experienced salesmen.

Career development must be geared to the individual, and sales managers would be wise to begin their appraisal of a salesman by observing his career turning points up to the present. These turning points relate to the salesman's assignments as compared with those of his peers, any changes in the way he earns his compensation, and his family's stage of life and their needs at that stage.

The salesman's self-image and level of aspiration—his perception of where he is in life in relation to where he wants to be—may indicate his degree of maturity. If the manager can get some good clues about these personality factors, he can then encourage and guide the salesman to raise his personal goals realistically. He can advise the salesman about preparing himself so as to attain the future he wants.

Salesmen respond to meet their manager's level of expectation. The manager should consciously set high, but attainable, performance goals rather than accept whatever is given, thereby admitting that he has low expectations. This principle applies to day-to-day sales duties as well as to career development of salesmen. The manager's encouragement and confidence in their ability to improve will help them to do so.

All people have cyclical needs, such as eating or sleeping, which cause their behavior to return to the zero point after the needs are satisfied. Salesmen in particular have additional cyclical needs with escalating zero points: They need to set higher and higher sales goals, to sell an ever larger order, to take home more and more money. As the needs spiral upward, whatever was achieved last year is taken for granted, and something bigger and better is expected this year. This phenomenon is conducive to steadily increasing sales performance as long as the manager provides steadily increasing compensation. Because of the nature of the sales job and the kind of man it attracts, the escalating zero point should be considered in planning for career development.

Many salesmen can be induced to achieve by external phenomena such as the reward of money or the threat of punishment. This kind of inducement, called movement, gets many sales jobs accomplished. When the salesman wants to do a good job because the work itself is personally satisfying, he may be said—according to one narrow definition—to be motivated. Regardless of the semantics, the distinction between movement and motivation is important in the career development of salesmen because it leads a manager to think of ways to provide opportunities for his men to participate, to develop, to achieve, and to gain acceptance and recognition for their accomplishments. These elements of their job are important to all mature salesmen.

In planning a career path for experienced salesmen, a sales manager should be cautious against creating a series of meaningless job titles which indicate little more than increases in age or years of experience. A true career path plans for a series of real changes in job responsibilities. Each level has certain duties which require more training and new on-the-job experiences. In this way salesmen can see the opportunities open to them and what they must do to take advantage of them.

A variation of career-path planning is the concept of branching career paths. A branching career path enables a good, experienced salesman to move out of the sales organization while staying with the same company. Such a change is not necessarily easy because the man may be required to update his education and obtain new experiences on the job. He may have to understudy someone else or accept job assignments in rotation for long periods. However, the combined efforts of the salesman and higher management are rewarded when a good, experienced man is kept with the same company and can contribute in a new way.

The career development of experienced salesmen forces the modern manager to face a number of fundamental issues. Is selling all there is to a sales job? What should a salesman want out of life? Can a salesman grow and develop continuously over a career spanning thirty years or more? Can the job be changed to provide greater long-term personal satisfactions for the salesman? In attempting to answer these questions, the manager will be forced to broaden his concepts and his outlook on his company, as well as his view of his own job and career opportunities.

SELECTED MATERIALS

Dalton, Gene W., and Lawrence, Paul R., *Motivation and Control in Organizations.* Homewood, Ill.: Richard D. Irwin, 1971, 427 pp.

This paperbound book focuses on the establishment of goals, the measurement of performance, and the effect of rewards.

Dowling, William, "Conversation with David McClelland," *Organizational Dynamics* (Summer 1972), pp. 56–72.

Fiedler, Fred E., "How Do You Make Leaders More Effective? New Answers to an Old Puzzle," *Organizational Dynamics* (Autumn 1972).

Gellerman, Saul W., *Motivation and Productivity.* AMA, 1963.

Haas, Frederick C., *Executive Obsolescence.* AMA, 1968.

Hersey, Paul, and Blanchard, Kenneth H., *Management of Organizational Behavior*. Englewood Cliffs, N.J.: Prentice-Hall, 1969.

Herzberg, Fred, "The New Kid in the Company," *Innovation Magazine* (December 1969), p. 26.

————, *Work and the Nature of Man*. Cleveland: World Publishing, 1966.

————, *KITA or What Have You Done for Me Lately*. 16 mm, C, sound. Rockville, Md.: Bureau of National Affairs Films.

Likert, Rensis, *New Patterns of Management*. New York: McGraw-Hill Book Company, 1961.

————, *The Human Organization*. New York: McGraw-Hill Book Company, 1967.

McGregor, Douglas, *The Human Side of Enterprise*. New York: McGraw-Hill Book Company, 1960.

Maslow, Abraham H., *Eupsychian Management*. Homewood, Ill.: Dorsey Press, 1965.

————, *Motivation and Personality*, 2d ed. New York: Harper & Brothers, 1970.

Stroh, Thomas F., *Managing the New Generation in Business*. New York: McGraw-Hill Book Company, 1971.

CHAPTER 12

Evaluating the
Sales Training Program

IF SALES TRAINING has a single, glaring weakness, it is probably in the area of evaluation. Determining the contribution of sales training to selling effectiveness is enormously complex. But sales training is not the only administrative function that has this weakness, and the sales manager need not be embarrassed nor evade the issue. Advertising, for example, is in the same situation, but millions of dollars are requested and received for advertising programs whose effectiveness is only very shakily documented. Top management generally accepts the concepts of advertising and of training and development of personnel. But how much should be budgeted for each function?

Advertising attempts to utilize the DAGMAR principle: Develop Advertising Goals and Measure Advertising Results. Perhaps a similar concept could be used to evaluate the results of sales training.

Unfortunately, sales training programs are often evaluated on the basis of salesmen's success in achieving such goals as the following:

- Increase in sales volume
- Increase in share of the market
- Increase in contribution to profit
- Increase in the number of promotable salesmen
- Decrease in the number of customer complaints
- Decrease in turnover of salesmen
- Decrease in the amount of merchandise returned
- Decrease in sales expenses

Goals such as these are neither appropriate nor realistic for sales training because many factors in addition to training can affect the extent to which they will be achieved. Training is only one part of the total marketing mix, which includes a company's screening, hiring, and compensation policies, its overall marketing program, its competitors' marketing programs, and the many uncontrollable factors in its customers' businesses. These numerous variables make the before-and-after measurements listed above very misleading and often invalid. This is not to say that a good sales training program will not help to achieve the goals, however.

Any correlations between actual sales and the training program for all the salesmen will most likely be questionable. When many factors are changing simultaneously, the effect of a single variable—in this case, sales training—cannot be isolated.

The one factor that can be used to evaluate a sales training program is the observable behavior change and development of the salesmen. Of course, realistic and measurable training objectives must be set. For example, the salesmen may have a deficiency in product knowledge which is contributing to poor sales, merchandise returns, and possibly also low morale. If a sales training program is designed and conducted to correct the deficiency in product knowledge, the salesmen can be tested for that knowledge and the training program can be evaluated on that basis. Training may be very effective even though sales are still poor, merchandise returns are still high, and morale is still low.

A deficiency in a skill such as the ability to draw a client out of his protective shell can also be corrected by a good sales training program. The individual salesman's ability to do and say certain things under realistic field pressures can be objectively measured to evaluate the training program. But success in training does not imply that sales will change for the better. Competition may simultaneously cut its prices or take other action that negates the effect of training on sales. Conversely, training may be poor and wasteful of time, but sales may go up because of some new competitive advantage.

When a deficiency in skills or knowledge is recognized and realistic and measurable objectives are established to correct it, sales training is indicated, and its effect can be isolated. When the deficiency or deviation from the desired behavior is in the area of work habits and attitudes, sales training can help in many cases, but the actions and expectations of the sales manager may be much more influential in changing the behavior of the salesmen.

If the sales training and development function is to be taken seriously by top management and to receive the support it is due, its objectives must be stated as measurable behavior changes. In this way, the results can be documented and reported so as to be meaningful to top management.

EVALUATING THE EDUCATIONAL PROCESS

The educational process in the context of sales training refers to the formal classroom training situation, any outside assignments, related on-the-job training, and subsequent reinforcement of the learning on the job. To evaluate it, one must ask whether it enhanced the salesmen's ability to change their behavior to meet the stated objectives. In other words, did the salesmen learn what the program set out to teach?

For each of the four parts of the total educational process, three measurements may be very useful in evaluation. The most obvious of these three measurements is probably the amount of material learned or the degree of behavior change that occurred.

In the formal classroom situation, it is relatively easy to test a group of salesmen before any training begins. A written test of knowledge or of problem-solving abilities may be given, for example; or a survey may be taken of the salesmen's attitudes. For experienced salesmen, the sales supervisor may prepare a report summarizing his field observations. In the area of skills, the test may involve role-playing a situation in which the use of the particular skills would be natural and appropriate. These initial role-playing situations can be audio- or video-taped for subsequent detailed analysis. By whatever means, a bench mark is established before formal training begins. An objective, quantitative base point is thus established for each salesman, and an average score can be computed for the entire group.

A series of measurements can be obtained in a similar manner before outside assignments are made, before related on-the-job training is given, or before on-the-job reinforcement of the learning occurs. At the conclusion of each phase of the total educational process, a similar test of equal difficulty should be conducted. The scores on this test can then be compared to the pretraining scores. Any differences can be evaluated for both validity and reliability. Individual changes can be measured, and once again, group averages can be compared to see how much the group learned.

The second measurement that may be useful for evaluation is the distribution of learning—that is, who learned how much? The 80–20 principle of marketing can be useful in education. For example, if the top 20 percent of the sales force is writing 80 percent of the orders, then it can be useful to know how much this group learned as compared to the rest of the salesmen. This grouping can be done in deciles (or tenths), quarters, or thirds, depending on the sophistication of the rating system and the importance of the breakdown of results.

Highly productive salesmen may not change their behavior very much between pretraining tests and posttraining tests because they were behaving as desired before the training. These important salesmen may complain that the training program took too much of their time or that it didn't do them any good. In this illustration, such criticism would be justified, although the training program may have been very effective for the rest of the salesmen. The converse is often true: Good salesmen, being highly motivated, learn more than average salesmen and are quick to apply whatever new skill or knowledge they have learned. Knowing which group of salesmen learned how much can make a big difference in evaluating a training program.

The third measurement that may be useful in evaluating the overall educational process is the amount of time necessary for the change in behavior to occur. If most of the change occurred early in the training program, the program may have been scheduled for too long a period. Such a result may also indicate that training was not even necessary, but that setting goals or stating what behavior was desired would have been sufficient to bring about the change. If most of the behavior change occurred toward the end of the training program, the training may not have been long enough, or the objectives may have been too high or unrealistic for the allocated time. Also, the training method may not have been appropriate.

The pace of the learning progress, as noted in Chapter 2, can be plotted as a curve, and the training program can be continued as long as the rise in learning justifies the cost of training. A flattening of the curve normally indicates that additional time spent in training will not justify the minimal changes which may occur. The ideal procedure is to continue training until the cost of training equals the return and then to stop. As long as the benefits are greater than the cost, further training is indicated.

The three measurements (how much was learned, by whom, and how fast) can be made for formal classroom training sessions. They can also be used to evaluate outside assignments, related on-the-job training, and subsequent reinforcement of learning on the job, provided that the reinforcement can be clearly described and objectively measured.

If a three-by-four matrix is then constructed, one can see where in each of the four areas of the total educational process each of the three results was or was not satisfactory. This analysis points to strengths and weaknesses in the process and helps to identify where correction is needed, although it may not indicate what in particular should be changed. The purpose of this analysis is to evaluate the educational process, step by step, to determine whether the salesmen really have learned. If they have not learned, it helps to pinpoint the breakdown or failure in the process. If they have learned, it may point out where the process can be shortened or otherwise improved or upgraded.

The difficulty in applying this training strategy is in setting measurable training objectives which are also acceptable to sales managers. The person responsible for sales training and the sales manager together should establish the training goals. What does the manager think training can do for his salesmen? Are his expectations realistic? How will the manager know when the training goal has been achieved? In other words, before training is begun, objective criteria should be established for evaluating the total educational process. Without this prior understanding and agreement, the trainer and the sales manager are apt to draw entirely different conclusions about the educational process after the training is ended.

When the sales manager is directly involved in training, the problem still exists. Without specific goals and objective criteria, he is apt to begin with vague generalizations and end, off on a tangent, with many doubts about the value of training. Instead, he should think about exactly what he would like to see his salesmen doing differently at the end of the program. This new behavior should then be quantified, and he should force himself to write down specific training goals. These goals become the objective criteria used subsequently to measure and evaluate the educational process.

EVALUATING THE COST-BENEFIT RATIO

One of the most common ways of evaluating a sales training program is to ask the salesmen themselves to rate each subject, each instructor, and the total program. Usually they are asked to compare the program to similar courses offered outside the company. Internal training costs are then compared with the cost to the company of sending its men to an outside seminar of similar quality. In the absence of a better method, this defensive evaluation may be sufficient for higher management.

To rely entirely on feedback from the salesmen or trainees, however, is to endanger the validity of the evaluation. The evaluation questionnaire itself can be worded to favor the program. For example, the question "In general, does this program compare favorably with others outside the company which you have attended?" lacks a qualitative standard. The salesmen probably have attended some good programs and some bad programs. In general, any new program is likely to compare favorably.

The end of a training program is usually a relief to both instructors and trainees and is marked by a friendly, forgive-and-forget attitude. Evaluations made at this point are likely to be favorably biased and to include high praise of one or two of the better features of the program. A few weeks or months later, the salesmen may not be able to recall many of the subjects to which they were exposed, much less to be able to evaluate them.

Evaluating feedback presents another problem. For example, 85 percent of the salesmen may report that the training time was well spent. They felt they really learned many things, and they enjoyed the sessions. This honest feedback may simply reflect their welcome of the relief from hard work, from being alone in the field, or from having to meet a high sales quota for that period. Whenever salesmen are taken out of their territories for a training program, they are apt to feel that they are receiving special treatment, and it is natural that they will be pleased.

The Value of the Behavior Change

The cost-benefit ratio, to be meaningful, should attempt to measure the value of the behavior change achieved. Whatever the training objectives might have been, was the amount of success worth what it cost to achieve it? Suppose, for example, that a group of senior salesmen attended a seminar to learn how to sell large accounts more effectively. After a few months, their call reports would probably show that several of them were applying the new approach in the field. Even if only 25 percent of these older salesmen changed their behavior in this respect, the seminar could be termed very successful. On-the-job coaching, reinforcement, and encouragement might be appropriate as follow-up to increase the benefits of the seminar.

When the lifelong habits of adults can be changed in a training seminar of a few days or one week, the cost-benefit ratio is usually highly favorable. Clearly, the desired behavior change should be of true value to both the salesmen and the company. For young salesmen or trainees, one should expect a 70 percent, or higher, change in behavior for a favorable cost-benefit ratio; this difference reflects pretraining behavior marked by random experimentation, or hit and miss efforts, as opposed to the habitual behavior one expects of senior salesmen.

Two points are worth repeating in these illustrations: The first is that volume of sales in dollars and the other typical measurements noted earlier are not used to evaluate the results of training. The second is that objective criteria are used to measure the amount of behavior change, rather than the subjective opinions of the supervisor or the salesmen themselves. Feedback from the salesmen can be of value when it is used as a supplemental tool, not as the only tool, in evaluating the cost-benefit ratio.

Short-term Costs and
Long-term Accumulated Benefits

A second way to approach the cost-benefit ratio is to write off training costs in the current accounting period while accumulating benefits over a period of several years. For tax purposes, training is an expense item which must be deducted during the current quarter and year. The nature of the desired behavior change may be such that one cannot reasonably expect a complete change in less than a year or two. In this case, the cost of training in the first year may heavily outweigh the benefits derived in that year. This situation can doom a training proposal if higher management is operating on a short-term profit-maximizing strategy.

At times a number of top executives are under great pressure to produce a higher profit during the current year. The company may need to undergo some major changes and to eliminate unproductive activities. When this occurs, the corporate training director can save himself a lot of frustration if he bites the bullet and holds off submitting expensive training programs which will not be funded.

The long-term benefits of training and the short-term cost write-off can be compared to corporate research and development. Just as new products and new methods may take many years to develop, better salesmen and new selling methods may take years to develop. In good times as well as bad, each department and function of an organization requests its share of the budget. Unless the benefits of training are well documented, however, top management is apt to cut the training budget in favor of another function which clearly indicates a better return on investment. Evaluating the sales training program on the basis of short-term costs and long-term accumulated benefits can provide higher management with good objective data. In some cases, that is all that is necessary.

When training people are forced to reduce their activities, they have a good opportunity to do a thorough job of establishing valuable and realistic goals and objective criteria to validate their future programs. In the same way, a sales manager in a branch office may be asked to forego training meetings in favor of a push to achieve more immediate sales goals. Rather than complain and become bitter, the sales manager can use that time to better plan future sales training.

Cost of Withholding Training

A third approach to evaluating the cost-benefit ratio is to determine what would happen if the training did not occur. If certain deficiencies in job performance were not corrected, how much would be lost? If certain deviations from desired sales behavior were recognized and identified but not changed, how would the organization suffer? The savings in training costs may be compared with short-term losses such as sales lost to competition because the salesmen could not compute prices correctly, as well as to long-term problems such as the total number of accounts lost because the salesmen did not know how to obtain new business to offset the attrition of old accounts.

In some cases it may be beneficial to be more specific and determine what would happen if the top producers were not trained, if the average salesmen were not trained, and if the marginal producers were not trained. In the short run, the top salesmen might not be affected at all, but the failure to train average and marginal salesmen might be very costly. In the long run, the absence of training is likely to cause cynicism, lower morale, moonlighting, and higher turnover. Good salesmen who feel they cannot develop further are apt to leave. Average and marginal salesmen may find it difficult to obtain another job, so they stay but are unhappy. Whenever the cost-benefit ratio can be documented objectively with facts, it makes a very persuasive proposal to higher management.

EVALUATING TRAINING METHODS

While the effectiveness and cost of the total educational process are of concern to several echelons of management, the training methods are of more immediate concern to the sales supervisor or sales trainer. Evaluating training methods is equally important, however, because it can materially change the other two.

Difficulties in Evaluation

Some of the major training methods and techniques were discussed in Chapters 6 and 7, and general guidelines were suggested. The evaluation of a training method is highly complex but necessary to improve the sales training program. The difficulties in isolating the effect of a single variable in any method show up in many studies as "no significant difference." Every method seems to involve a group or cluster of variables whose combined effect differs from the sum of the effects of the isolated variables.

In a sales training program with stated measurable objectives, in what ways may the subjects be taught? Typically, several people teach their own specialties, and each instructor uses the method with which he is most comfortable. One instructor may tell a number of jokes in a lecture, while another may ask several serious questions which may embarrass the unprepared trainee. Normally, the more entertaining the lecturer, the higher his students will evaluate him. But entertainment does not necessarily bring about more effective learning. Some of the most demanding and serious instructors, and the key points of what they were teaching, are remembered years afterwards, while the more entertaining trainers may be quickly forgotten.

An instructor who is asked to change his approach from straight lecturing to group discussion, for example, may do a good job with his next group of trainees. Since the audience is different, however, no valid conclusion can be reached about the method. To offset this problem, sometimes a random sample is used in both cases. Unfortunately, two random samples of trainees or salesmen are rarely equal in intelligence, learning ability, motivation, previous experience, and so forth. The problem of comparison remains.

When an instructor who is very effective in one subject area is asked to teach additional, related subjects, he will probably have varying effectiveness. He may be less knowledgeable in other areas, or his teaching method may be less appropriate for other subjects. In other words, it is difficult to separate the teacher from the subject matter for the purpose of measuring the effectiveness of a particular teaching method.

If the same instructors teach the same content for several training groups, varying class size can change the effectiveness of the method. A small group lends itself to much more individual participation and often a deeper penetration of the subject matter. A large group forces the instructor to dominate the learning situation and to highlight or reinforce the important points. In a small group, one or two trainees may tend to dominate a discussion, while they might sit back quietly in a large group.

Two more major variables in attempting to evaluate any training method are the amount of time allocated to one subject as compared to others and the time of day or sequence in which the subjects are presented. It may seem fair to ask several senior salesmen to give two hours each to a sales training seminar and then to assign each man a different subject. One subject, in fact, may be very complicated and critical to the learning objective, and two hours may not be sufficient to permit the instructor to do an effective job. Another subject may be simple and much less critical to the overall program. The salesman assigned to teach this subject is apt to bore the trainees by trying to expand it to fill his allotted time. If the sales trainer changes the amount of time allocated, he still cannot hold the other variables constant; hence, he cannot isolate the impact of time.

The time of day or sequence of subjects and instructors can also modify the effectiveness of the method utilized. Some trainees are slow and lethargic during the first hour of training and may not become involved in methods using participation. Other trainees may have a period of physical and mental inactivity immediately after lunch. Most trainees who have been in a classroom all day will impatiently await the ending bell. Action-oriented training programs often can take advantage of this nervous energy late in the day. Obviously, an effective instructor who follows a poor one will seem outstanding by contrast, and the opposite is also true. Moreover, some difficult concepts may be made easier to understand if a certain sequence of subjects is built into the program. Simply switching the schedule around will not isolate the impact of the time of day or sequence of subjects.

With all of these variables, it may seem impossible to evaluate various training methods. Even if he is successful, the person responsible for sales training always has other constraints imposed on him. Budget restrictions may prohibit the use of video instant replay or of a number of good sales training films. The senior salesmen or other guest instructors may be different for each group of trainees. The total time allotted for formal classroom sessions and related on-the-job instruction may be decided by other managers or by the varying economic demands of unmanned territories.

Controlled Experiments

Fortunately, some ways of evaluating training methods can provide meaningful data. One is the controlled experiment in which a test, or experimental, group is compared with a matched normal, or control, group. A single variable is introduced to the experimental group but not to the control group. Many other variables will change throughout the duration of the experiment, but these other variables will affect both groups in the same way. In a carefully designed experiment, any significant difference in the results for the two groups should be directly related to the single variable being tested.

The experiment can be as simple as having the manager lecture to group A at one o'clock on Tuesdays and to lead a discussion with group B at one o'clock on Wednesdays. If the two groups are alternating their other activities daily, then the isolated variable should be the method—lecture versus discussion—for that particular sales manager. The problem here is to isolate the two groups so that there is no communication between them before the Wednesday group receives different treatment.

The evaluation can be much more sophisticated, particularly if the number of trainees is large. For instance, the split-half technique can be used, in which the control group and the experimental group are each divided in half. With four matched groups, three variables can be tested simultaneously. The key point in experimental testing is to insure that each group of trainees, or test cell, receives the same treatment or experiences as every other group, except for the variable being tested.

Further sophistication can be obtained by identifying the upper third, middle third, and lower third within each test cell. The impact of the variable being tested may be uniform on the entire group or it may be very much greater on one third of the group than on the other two. This type of information may suggest better ways to group the salesmen for future training.

Individual Training Records

Another useful way to evaluate sales training methods is to maintain long-term records that indicate which trainee was exposed to which method for every subject. After a year or two, the training experience of the outstanding salesmen can be compared to the training experience of the lowest producers. Certain hypotheses may suggest themselves at this point. For example, the better group may have had difficult evening assignments covering territory management, while the marginal producers may have seen an entertaining film. Rarely will there be a contrast as vivid as this illustration, but this is the kind of difference to look for.

The intervening variables, such as the district sales supervisors' on-the-job coaching, may destroy the validity of this approach; but it is worth investigating. In some cases, the same supervisor will have different results with a number of trainees. When a number of supervisors are having the same experience, it is possible that something in the initial training enhanced or interfered with later success. When a difference or cluster of differences in training is assumed to be the cause, in-depth interviews with a number of salesmen in each extreme group may or may not support the supposition. At that point, an experimental testing situation can be created to verify the hypotheses and eliminate the training deficiency.

One does not knowingly turn out salesmen with inferior training. Once an experiment has proved one method superior to another, steps can be taken immediately to update the group which had the inferior training. The evaluation process should be used with care to judge critical areas about which strong doubts exist. Change merely for the sake of change can cause complications and confusion in subsequent evaluations.

EVALUATING ALTERNATIVE PROGRAM CONTENTS

A sales trainer may have little or no preference as to the contents of his program, but the subject matter will make an important difference to the trainee. If the trainer is new to his job, he would probably be wise to teach what has been taught in the past or to follow the lead of experienced trainers in other companies. However, once the trainer feels reasonably self-confident in his new role, he has no reason to follow tradition.

Before the training program is constructed, training needs should be identified, and the appropriate subject matter should be selected. Each company will have some subjects to which it wants to give special emphasis and possibly some subjects which are unique to that organization. Each major division or product-line group will probably request some modifications or changes to suit its needs. Even the sales managers of the local branches will normally have some differences of opinion about the value of the various subjects to be included in one training program.

Within the constraints of company politics and finances, the person responsible for the training function is in the best position to evaluate alternative subjects for any given sales training program. Before designing the program, he may find it useful to conduct a time-and-duty analysis. For example, the sales manager of an international organization felt his men needed a better understanding of foreign cultures to improve their communications. The experienced trainer spent several weeks observing and talking to individual salesmen. Each salesman handled only English-speaking distributors in their territories. The men were expected to visit each distributor personally twice each year, but none was able to do so. The time-and-duty analysis revealed that 85 percent of their time was spent in correspondence over mixups in orders and deliveries. A sampling of their own letters pointed to the cause: Even another native speaker of English would have trouble getting through the poor grammar and total lack of organization that characterized their correspondence; someone to whom English was a second language would be certain to misunderstand it.

A sales training program was put together for these experienced salesmen, all of whom were college graduates. The men were asked to describe the foreign culture of their territory and their unique problems in seminars held once a month. Two hours of each meeting were devoted to better letter writing. After the second month, the salesmen themselves asked to have letter writing as the only topic in future meetings. Within one year, each salesman improved to the extent that he had time to make his personal visits, and the mixups in orders and deliveries, while not eliminated, were greatly reduced.

When salesmen are spending a disproportionate amount of time on certain tasks, this may be a signal of a high-leverage area—that is, one in which dramatic results may be achieved in a relatively short time—for which a sales training program may be appropriate. The trainer should tread cautiously before suggesting his program as a solution, however, because the salesmen may be spending their time as they are to avoid doing something else that is expected of them. Or they may be catering to the demands of their manager, and it is he who needs correcting or change, not the salesmen. Training is not always the answer.

In any case, once the manager agrees to the contents of a sales training program, the trainer should not assume that the subject matter cannot be changed. In the illustration above, the international salesmen quickly appreciated the value of the letter-writing portion of the monthly seminar, and the contents of the program were changed to meet that need. The change occurred not at the whim of the salesmen but because the prior time-and-duty analysis pointed to that emphasis. The new contents were difficult and in many cases painfully embarrassing to most of the salesmen, but they filled the manager's need and the salesmen's need.

The manager should establish a training climate that clearly communicates to the men that their needs are paramount within certain preset areas. Once a feeling of mutual trust and respect develops, the salesmen will often admit their weaknesses and ask for help. When the men are motivated to learn a particular subject or skill, it would seem foolish not to change the program contents to meet their needs. This is certainly true if the time-and-duty analysis indicates that their needs are in a high-leverage area.

After each training program, the various parts or subjects can be evaluated to see where and how a similar program might be improved in the future. Objective criteria are usually the most valid in analyzing program contents after the fact. Do the call reports show that the men are using the subjects they were taught? Are they now solving problems which they could not handle effectively before the training? Were some of the subjects simply nice to know but not really useful on the job? Work habits, such as the effective use of time and efficient territory coverage, can be observed and measured in a similar way.

The sales supervisor is often sensitive to changes and the absence of desired changes in a salesman's behavior on the job, and his observations may be used in conjunction with objective measurements. The salesman may have learned what was taught and may be applying it on the job, but that may seem insignificant compared to his true needs as the supervisor observes them. Often the sales supervisor can suggest changes in subject matter to make a future program more appropriate. The more several supervisors agree, the more likely their suggestions will represent real needs rather than isolated exceptions.

After compiling some objective measurements and the subjective opinions of supervisors, the trainer can survey the salesmen for their attitudes, ideas, and opinions. However, if salesmen's attitudes are the major source of criteria for determining course content, the trainer runs the risk of constantly changing the program to better suit the last group rather than the next group.

A final observation about evaluating alternative program contents that applies more to the experienced trainer than to the new man: The trainer should be willing to drop his pet subject from the program when the evidence suggests that it is no longer appropriate. Most trainers have at least one subject which they handle better than any other person. It is natural for them to feel superior about these subjects and to reject any negative feedback. It would seem, however, that an attempt to postpone the inevitable will only accelerate the obsolescence of the trainer himself.

REPORTING EVALUATION STATISTICS

Selecting the Data

The people responsible for the training function would be wise to analyze and interpret the accumulation of quantitative data, including before- and after-training test scores, objective counts, and other measurements, before compiling any reports. Basically, management wants to know if there was any improvement; if so, in what areas; and finally, if the amount was significant in relation to the amount of change which might have occurred without training. If the trainer does not compute some simple ratios but simply reports average scores, he may be in for a rude shock when higher management does so. The change, which he proudly claims to be due to his efforts, may have occurred by pure chance and may be unrelated to the training program.

If the sales training function is to take its rightful share of the limited funds available to the broad marketing effort, at least some simple documentation is mandatory. The person in charge of training need not be a statistician, nor does he have to take a quick refresher course in elementary statistics. If he knows what information and probabilities to ask for, he can give the assignment of mechanically computing the answers to a few young college graduates. In many computer centers, several standard programs are available to compute and relate data such as test scores in a matter of minutes, if not seconds.

One illustration may serve to clarify this point. Assume that a group of twenty experienced salesmen score an average of 50 percent on a test before training, and that the range of scores is from 40 to 60 percent. Assume that after training, the average score moves to 60 percent. This increase could occur by pure chance—that is, without any training—in 50 out of 100 similar classes. Assume, on the other hand, that after training, the new average is 80 percent. This increase might occur by pure chance in only 5 out of 100 similar classes. Stated positively, a movement of the group average from 50 percent before training to 80 percent afterward is due to training within the 95 degree confidence level. Whatever the number of trainees, the deviation of their scores, and the degree of confidence, the computation is simple for a recent student with access to the tables published in almost every elementary statistics textbook.

The statistical formulas necessary for most training situations are readily available to many computer people. The training director can benefit tremendously by developing a procedure for collecting data in an appropriate form to feed to a computer. This could be a simple assignment for a sales trainee with a recent college course in statistics or a new person in the computer center. Once established, the procedure can be followed for many similar problems in the future. The training director need not know statistics to be able to use it to his advantage.

A report consisting of a few simple sentences covering the improvement of salesmen with a high degree of statistical confidence can be very impressive to higher management. By accumulating data on the total educational process, the training methods, and alternative program contents, the training director can design a better program. At the same time, he can develop a well-documented argument to convince top management of the value of sales training at budget hearings when the question of the cost-benefit ratio arises.

Presenting the Results

Statistical treatment of raw data, particularly by a computer, can yield more information than the average person can read and digest. Clearly, one cannot report every detail and expect higher-level managers to spend their own time looking for the important facts. The trainer's problem is to communicate the significant facts honestly and concisely. If the report is to be trusted, the bad as well as the good results should be included, but not the mass of insignificant data which might hide either.

Before preparing a report evaluating the sales training program, the trainer should decide which executives should know the results. The target audience may include several personnel executives, corporate planners, marketing executives, and, of course, sales executives. Once the audience has been identified, their level of understanding can be probed. What kind of information would be most useful to them, and what format would they most easily understand?

The person writing the report is usually strongly tempted to prove how intelligent he is. If a sophisticated statistical analysis has been made, the trainer may want top management to see how the data have been manipulated. However, the impact of the report will be lost if the audience is not interested in the mass of data. Top managers want to know the key issues—what was attempted and what results were obtained. A concise report stating the facts can be written in plain English with a note to the effect that statistical data are available to anyone who desires to go into further details. Busy executives are more apt to read and remember a short factual report than a long and detailed or boastful one.

Often dry statistical data can be made more interesting and meaningful when translated into graphs and charts. A bar graph, for example, comparing scores before and after training, can be understood at a glance. In the same way, improvements in performance over a series of trials can be shown on a chart as a line or curve indicating the salesman's pretraining level, steady improvement, and terminal level. A dotted horizontal line can be used to show the desired performance level and to indicate at what point in time the salesman exceeded that level. By using several colors or kinds of lines, for example, one can compare the current sales training class with previous groups all on one chart. If a new method was employed or new subject matter introduced, an asterisk at that point can be used to call the reader's attention to an explanatory note.

Serious training directors may spend many months preparing a sales training program. They work long and hard to conduct the training and are justly proud of the results. Too often, a quick memorandum is written explaining simply that another sales training class has finished, and that in the opinion of the trainer, it was better than all previous classes. Such a memo makes it difficult for top management to evaluate or strongly support the training budget. Having done all the hard work of training, the manager would be wise to spend a little more time and energy to write a brief report which documents his achievements.

The branch sales manager in the smallest office can operate in a similar manner. If he reports that he spent five hours a week training his salesmen, the statement may be lost or quickly forgotten. On the other hand, if he establishes training goals, measures individual progress, and reports the results in one or two pages, including a graph or chart, his report will be noticed and remembered by superiors in the home office. In these two illustrations, the time spent in training and the results achieved may be identical. However, the branch manager who spends an extra hour or two preparing a meaningful but concise report will gain the favorable attention of higher management.

SUMMARY

Sales training rarely, if ever, occurs in isolation. The intelligence and desire of the trainees have a strong impact on the training function. The compensation policy of the company further affects how much and how quickly the salesmen learn. The sales supervisors and managers responsible for on-the-job coaching and supervision also have a strong bearing on the effectiveness of sales training. Career planning and the way in which the men are motivated and encouraged also ultimately enhance or inhibit their later learning.

Even as only a part of the marketing mix, sales training can make a significant contribution to long-term profits. The growth and development of each man on the sales force is probably as important as the development of new products and the growth of plant facilities. The director of the sales training function need not be embarrassed by nor apologize for any inability to relate dollars invested in training to short-term profit. Many other corporate functions that often spend a hundred times the training budget have little or no documentation to support their efforts.

Nevertheless, the training function is likely to go unrecognized and unfunded if it is not evaluated and the results are not reported to those who matter in an organization. Clearly, evaluation involves setting realistic and measurable training objectives. It usually requires a pretraining measurement or bench mark, a series of progressive evaluations, and a measurement after the training.

A judgment about sales training based on only one phase of the entire process would be inaccurate. The essential skills and knowledge for successful selling can be taught in the training center or classroom. But formal classroom training is only one step in the educational process. Skills are developed by daily practice until they become habitual; hence on-the-job coaching with feedback to the salesmen is an important part of the learning. Furthermore, the way something is taught—the methods and techniques—depend on the subject matter, the facilities available, time and money constraints, and the instructor's competence. These interrelationships must be understood before one can attempt to evaluate the total training process.

Evaluations can be made of the progress of individual salesmen, the appropriateness of the subject matter, or the effectiveness of the training methods. Knowledge and skills may be objectively tested in the classroom by means of written tests and role playing, and in the field by means of on-the-job observation. The measurements of the individual aspects of training may be compiled separately or combined in an evaluation of the entire training process.

Periodic evaluation of this type serves two important purposes: First, it continually indicates ways in which sales training and development can be improved to the benefit of the salesmen, the trainers, and the company. And second, it provides sales managers with a documented argument to support their budget requests. To this end, people in charge of the sales training function should take the time to analyze the evaluation data and present the significant results to higher management clearly, honestly, and briefly.

The sales training profession has an abundance of qualified men and is attracting many other good people. Competition is increasing, and those already in the profession must continually upgrade their skills. The resulting steady increase in the quality of sales training will, in time, provide the documentation needed for this function to command the respect and support it so well deserves.

SELECTED MATERIALS

Chance, William A., *Statistical Methods for Decision Making.* Homewood, Ill.: Richard D. Irwin, 1969.

The basic textbook in introductory business statistics at the undergraduate level discusses techniques for decision making under conditions of uncertainty. The computer appendix frees the student of much "busy work" and emphasizes the value of the computer in statistical analysis.

Davis, Harold J., and Tompkins, Ellsworth, *How to Organize an Effective Team Teaching Program.* Englewood Cliffs, N.J.: Prentice-Hall, 1966.

This book defines team teaching and describes its use in schools. Particularly pertinent are the discussions on evaluating the results of team teaching.

Miller, Robert B., "Analysis and Specification of Behavior for Training," in *Training Research and Education.* Robert Glaser, Ed. Pittsburgh: University of Pittsburgh Press, 1962.

This is a good discussion of task analysis and selecting effective media.

Payne, David A., *The Specification and Measurement of Learning Outcomes.* Waltham, Mass.: Blaisdell, 1968.

This book describes the nature of measurement and its relationship to objectives and discusses the planning, constructing, and evaluating of measuring instruments as well as the reporting of results.

Popham, W. James, *Educational Criterion Measures.* Inglewood, Calif.: Southwest Regional Laboratory for Educational Research and Development, 1968.

This self-instruction program teaches procedures for constructing tests that measure behavioral objectives.

Short Cut Statistics for Teacher-Made Tests. Princeton, N.J.: Educational Testing Service, 1964.

This free pamphlet describes how to compute some simple statistics that can be useful in evaluating tests.

Tuckman, Bruce W., *Conducting Educational Research,* New York: Harcourt Brace Jovanovich, 1972.

Each step in the research process is covered, including data analysis by computer, report writing, and the preparation of graphs and tables.

Index